SANTA MARIA PUBLIC LIBRARY

D0049561

More praise for A RENEGADE'S GUIDE TO GOD

"I grew up pursuing religion, and it left me lifeless and hopeless. It takes a renegade like David Foster to challenge our misconceptions about Christianity and consider a life of freedom and fulfillment. I choose the nonreligious life. It's what God intended for me. (And it's a lot more fun.)"

—Tony Morgan, pastor, author, and executive director of WiredChurches.com

"A RENEGADE'S GUIDE TO GOD is for those who are tired of religion and long for something deeper, something real. Foster calls the reader to break free from moralism and legalism in the church into the freedom and wonder of a relationship with Jesus."

—Donna VanLiere, *New York Times* bestselling author, The Christmas Hope series

"Dave Foster is irreverent *and* a passionate follower of Jesus. He has had it with church as usual. He will no longer tolerate allowing the captivating Story of Jesus to be relegated to the dusty file of 'religion.' Grabbing metaphors from Barna to Bono, Foster lights up the pages with the captivating cadence, street wisdom, and inspiration I've come to expect when I hear him speak."

—Jim Henderson, front man for Off the Map

continued . . .

"It's as if this book was written to free me personally from the tyranny of expectations and past baggage. I can't help but believe that you will feel the same way once you've read it."

—Bil Cornelius, lead pastor of Bay Area Fellowship,
Corpus Christi, Texas

"David Foster has done it again and just at the right moment! The old structures are crumbling; yet authentic, adventurous, and advancing faith lives! Bravo, Dave, for an in-the-face challenge to be a redeemed renegade!"

—Dr. Ron M. Phillips, senior pastor, Abba's House

"I found in these pages a refreshing and impassioned call to follow the Jesus of the Bible. Not a 21st century, sissified Jesus—but the One Who calls us to a life of authenticity and adventure."

—Tim Stevens, co-author of the Simply Strategic series
and executive pastor, Granger Community Church

A RENEGADE'S GUIDE TO GOD

FINDING LIFE OUTSIDE CONVENTIONAL CHRISTIANITY

DAVID FOSTER

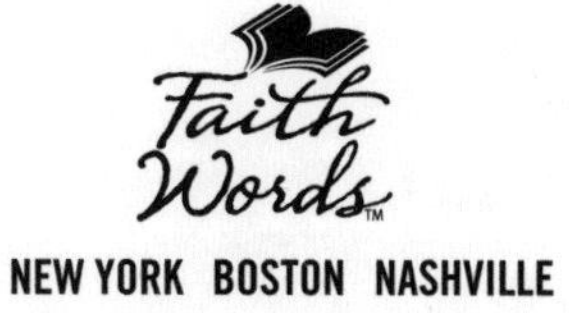

NEW YORK BOSTON NASHVILLE

FaithWords
Hachette Book Group USA
1271 Avenue of the Americas
New York, NY 10020

Visit our Web site at www.faithwords.com.

Printed in the United States of America

First Edition: November 2006
10 9 8 7 6 5 4 3 2 1

Library of Congress Cataloging-in-Publication Data

Foster, David
A renegade's guide to God : finding life outside conventional christianity / David Foster.
p. cm.
ISBN-13: 978-0-446-57964-3
ISBN-10: 0-446-57964-5
1. Christian life. I. Title.
BV4501.3.F68 2006
248.4—dc22 2006006560

DEDICATED TO AMERICA'S PASTORS AND CHURCH LEADERS

I dedicate this book to the most underpaid, underappreciated, under-celebrated group in this country—America's pastors.

You are our visionaries, missionaries, and leaders. You are the benchmark by which authentic Christianity is measured. You are our renegades for God, keeping dead religion from squeezing Jesus out of our churches and eventually our lives.

When we go astray, you welcome us back. When we slander your name, you refuse to attack. When we take without giving, you keep giving your best. When we listen without responding, you still lift us up.

When we take you for granted, you still come to our aid. When we treat you with contempt, you turn the other cheek. And when we treat you as a hireling, you refuse to complain.

When we trade churches faster than we trade cars, you remain to keep the church fires burning. As God's first responders, you hold back the rush of evil that longs to ruin us. And though we're stupid sheep who refuse to thank you, never forget—you are God's anointed among us and you've never needed our approval anyway.

You are a special class of warrior the likes of which we are not worthy. On your broad shoulders rests the future of the American church. You are our heroes and champions of hope. Forgive us for our sins against you for they are many. May there come a day in this land when we, the church of Jesus, rise up with one voice and call you blessed.

CONTENTS

ACKNOWLEDGMENTS

This book represents what I've learned on my spiritual journey to date. And since no one gets far on this journey alone, I'd like to acknowledge the epic impact of my five spiritual guides.

My first important guide was my college professor, Dr. Leroy Forlines. His compassion, thoughtfulness, and tenacious search for the truth helped me fall in love, not only with the Bible, but with theology and how the truth of Scriptures fits together in a thoughtful, intellectual, yet compelling way.

My second compelling guide was Dr. R. C. Sproul. When I heard Dr. Sproul speak about the holiness of God, and the priceless nature of Christ, he made me feel like he'd just stepped out of God's presence into mine, in order to guide me up higher. For the beauty of his love of Jesus, I will forever be grateful.

The third guide along this journey is Rick White, Pastor of Peoples Church in Franklin, Tennessee. He is one of the few fellow pastors in my life who believed in me, inspired me, and encouraged me to pursue my dream of starting a church for renegades. He is the person God used to bring me to Nashville, Tennessee, and he defines what it means to be a true friend.

My fourth guide along the way is Rolf Zettersten, my publisher. Rolf was willing to believe in me and take a chance not only on whether I could write a legible sentence, but that I might have something compelling to say. It's his faith in me that has kept me writing, long after the discouragements of writing would cause me to quit. Rolf revived in me a dream I had all but given up on.

David Foster

My fifth, and most important guide, is my wife Paula. She has made the J-life incarnational and personal in her everyday life. The theological certainties and mysteries that I assert throughout this book have been displayed beautifully in the elegance of her godly life.

INTRODUCTION: CONFESSIONS OF A CLOSET RENEGADE

I believe a very large majority of churchgoers are merely unthinking, slumbering worshipers of an unknown God.

—*Charles H. Spurgeon*

You can safely assume you've created God in your own image when it turns out that God hates all the same people you do.

—*Anne Lamott*

"I'm not into the *God thing* and I hated being drug to church as a kid, so don't even start trying to shove your *religion* down my throat," said the young Brooks Brothers clad CEO in an uncomfortably loud voice. His sudden outburst was in response to my answer to the question he'd just asked me. We were standing in line together at Chicago's O'Hare airport waiting to board a flight to LA. To pass the time, I asked what he did for a living and of course he in turn asked me my line of work. It's a question I always dread hearing and try to avoid answering at all costs. But for the shock value alone, the renegade inside me wanted to blurt out, "My name is Dave and I'm a professional Christian who handles holy things for a living." But of course, I didn't. I'm too chicken and too civilized.

Tell anyone, anywhere you're a "preacher" and they treat you like you have leprosy. So to avoid the "big freeze," I told him I was an author and a life coach. That usually satisfies most people, but no such luck with this guy. My cryptic response just piqued his interest. "What kind of books do you write and what does a *life coach* do?" he asked. I answered his questions in the broadest, most generic way possible. But this thirty-one-year-old, self-made millionaire didn't get that way by being slow on the uptake. He put two and two together and declared, "I know what you are, you're a preacher, aren't you?" My heart sank. I was busted.

My first response was to just lie. I thought, "I'm never going to see this guy again." But there is a fine line between avoiding confrontation and being just plain embarrassed by what you do. Outright lying would mean I'm secretly ashamed of my life's calling. So, since I'm not, I said, "Yes, I'm a pastor." I thought using the word "pastor" might make me sound a bit more humane. With my next breath I said, "What I really am is a Renegade for God." That caught him a bit off guard. His boyish grin reappeared across his face. If he was interested before, now he was downright intrigued.

"How can you be a preacher and a renegade at the same time?" he asked.

I looked at him. "To explain what I mean, I need to ask you a couple of questions."

"Shoot."

"Do you have an inner yearning to live a free, untamed, bold, adventurous life? One that is exciting, fulfilling and fun?"

He said, "Sure I do."

I continued. "Do you resist being told what to do and how to think? Do you resent being defined by what you do? And do you gag when people try to force their religion down your throat?"

He said, "I sure do and that is why I can't stand all these self-righteous, goody-goody, gotta-go-to-church people." The man then spewed out his own story of abuse and boredom with church and all the goofy stuff he'd seen on TV posing as Christianity. It is a story I've heard a thousand times and it is the reason I felt compelled to write this book.

I'm fed up with boring speakers using the Bible as a brickbat with which to beat you and me into submission. We have tolerated *their* gross mishandling of the gospel long enough. It is way past time we canceled their contract and sent them back to wherever it is these weird religious know-it-alls come from.

Before I became a speaker for God, I was a full-bore, angry, get the hell out of my way, allergic-to-all-things-religious rebel. I was raised in a typical county seat church in the south whose mission centered on fear, guilt, and manipulation. Like most guys my age, I viewed the whole church thing with a jaundiced eye. Church was little more than an obligatory nod to God every seven days. It was a cheap form of fire insurance against burning forever in the fiery flames of a devil's hell. So I went to church, lied about reading my Bible, made a "decision" for Jesus, endured boring sermons, and got with the program like all the other good little religious robots. After all, acquiescing to the church-thing one hour a week seemed like a small price to pay for an eternity of bliss and happiness in heaven, especially since death seems pretty much unavoidable.

The religious side of me was easy to manage, but the little rebel inside kept getting me in trouble, especially when I dared ask questions. Everything my pastor said was infallible and, man, did he have a lot to say! He was an expert on everything from the apostle Paul, to politics, to the proper time to plant my garden. According to him, all God required of me was to walk down to the front of the church and sign a "decision" card. This qualified me for a one-time dip in the church's new wading pool and I'd be good to go to heaven. It all seemed as fine as wine to me except the weekly sermonizing. The rebel side of me resisted being "preached at." I've always loathed being talked down to. I wasn't interested in being named, shamed, or tamed. I wanted to have fun, go fast, party hard, run with my friends and make a lot of money. All of this, I was told, was bad for my little robot brain to think about and would certainly incur the wrath of God—eventually.

This little "ticket-to-ride" arrangement was blown to "heaven in a hand-basket," so to speak, the night I was abducted by Jesus in an out-of-church conversion experience. I was a seventeen-year-old college freshman the night the ever-living, wild-loving, revolutionary Jesus entered my room, my heart, and my life. The command I heard that night was "follow Me." It wasn't "decide for Me" or "accept Me" as a part of your world and life view. He dared me to move to Him. I said "yes" and nothing has been the same since. I'm still not quite sure what happened, but I am so glad it did.

That night, my religious understanding morphed into a mysterious, radical, relationship with the real Jesus. It was like walking out of a stale, stuffy, self-absorbed existence into a bright, brand new world of freedom, fun, and great adventure. That night rebellious Dave died and I became an R4G (Renegade for God). I was reborn with purpose, direction, and the sheer joy of being alive.

Great anticipation for the future replaced my rage and rebellious swagger. Almost instantly I knew things would never be the same. I felt freer and more alive than I ever thought possible. I traded my cold, dead, rule-based religion for an untamed, unpredictable relationship with the ultimate renegade of all time—Jesus The Christ.

For all the Sundays I was drug to church and force-fed religion, it was a Friday night in a one-bedroom apartment in Bowling Green, Kentucky, where God broke in and took over. That night I became a missionary in a worldwide revolutionary movement, aimed at the radical renovation of the human heart. The reality of that night is still as real to me as the keyboard I'm typing on right this minute.

RENEGADES COME FORTH

God is too good and life is too short to allow rigid, self-righteous, do-gooders with a religious agenda keep you from Him. So if you're done worrying about what "they" say or do, then join the club. If you're weary of the morality police and their cellophane sainthood, then lean in and let's talk. If you're repelled by the pointless, prosaic preaching of self-appointed prophets with a Messiah complex, then you, my friend, might just be a closet renegade and today could be your coming-out party.

I'm calling for the creation of a renegade nation where love is the ethic and freedom is the goal. Declare your independence from lazy legalism, feeble faith, and domesticated religion. If you suspect that deep down inside you lives a vibrant, vital, virtuous soul ready to rid itself of shame-bound religion, then you're a renegade ready to step forth free and fully engaged in the art of the J-life. You can love God passionately and with deep conviction without becoming an arrogant, self-righteous, know-it-all.

I have been a professional Christian for my entire adult life. I make my living talking for God to people. This, I believe, is a noble calling. But something happens along the way to people like me. We start out honestly wanting to help people. We begin by speaking to God, then for God, but somewhere along the way we start speaking "as a god." It is this group I refer to when I say "they." Somewhere along the line we forget we're only "newspaper boys" for God. We don't publish the paper or create its content. We deliver it and get out of the way—period. And as I learned delivering the *Courier Journal* as a kid, you don't throw it on the roof over people's heads. You don't throw it in the dirt under their feet. My job is to place the unabridged and undiluted good news right in front of the door within easy reach.

It's way past time to blow the lid off the whole myth of "they." I have bitten my tongue and held my peace long enough. It's time to charge out of the closet and into the sunlight to dethrone the lies. My charge is to set you free, not make you more dependent on me. I am always only a messenger and never, never, never the message. I am not an adversary, an artist, or an academic speaking ex cathedra. I am always and at all times an advocate standing in the middle between God and people, helping the two get together.

God created you with the heart of a lion, not a mouse. He desires you so much He became a man and died on a cross for the privilege of loving you. He doesn't seek and won't accept brainless, heartless, robotic compliance. His joy of being alive and free bridges the great divide between you and Him. He doesn't aim to shame or tame you. He specializes in setting renegades free to live the freed-up, joy-filled life He had in mind when He created you.

An R4G dares to question the conventional wisdom and spiritual infallibility of the religious elite. "They" fear your freedom and at the same time display little confidence in the gospel's power to renovate the human heart, renew the mind, and redirect the renegade spirit within toward the epic, ethical purposes of God. "They" want only mindless, spineless adherents who spout out an endless stream of "praise the Lords" as you pack their pews and fill their offering plates.

A GUIDEBOOK NOT A RULEBOOK

This is a guidebook, not a rulebook and there is a big difference. R4G's run from rules. The following pages are filled with firsthand discoveries. I did not come to them in seminary (though I spent ten years in formal academic training trying to fit in), nor did I read them in a book. I've learned them over a lifetime of living in the real world. My conclusions will place me at odds with some of my peers, but the stakes are just too high for me to be silent any longer. I am through doing things "their" way while waiting for change. I have decided to *be* the change I want to see in this world. So this is a guidebook of discoveries I've made about authentic Christ-centered spirituality. It is one renegade telling other renegades where he has found bread that's satisfying, free, and abundant!

I am a renegade for God, which means I am an unashamed follower of Jesus Christ. He died that I might live forever free. He has called me to set the captives free and serve those whom "they" have classified as unworthy, unwanted, or uncivilized.

This guidebook will expose a few of the most common myths, which distort the message of authentic Christ-centered spirituality. It will free you from the half-truths and hollow promises propagated by the religious elite. It will be my glad privilege throughout the pages of this guidebook to reinforce the truth: "God loves you as you are, not as you ought to be." He wants more for you than you've ever dared hope for yourself. He asks only for your whole heart and He will accept nothing less. My goal is to lift you up, not weigh you down. My reward will come when you fall fully and freely into the wild, devastating embrace of renegade Jesus; the one who loves you without regret, reserve, limitation, boundary, or breaking point. Life is too short to waste it wallowing in guilt and shame and it is too precious to spend it gagging on the gospel of good works or religious compliance.

WHAT "THEY" DON'T WANT YOU TO KNOW

One of my favorite songs of recent days is simply titled "They" by the artist Jem. It is a beautiful, lilting melody which gives expression to the questions which haunt me. The lyrics ask, "who are they, where are they, and how can they possibly know all this?" I too want to know who "they" are and why "they" are so bent out of shape. You've heard of the dreaded "they" group, haven't you? For our purposes, it is enough to identify "they" as the massive amalgamation of religious elitism who speak and act as though they have a direct phone line into the throne room of God. They speak in high-sounding hyperbole and are fluent in all forms of cryptic Christianese. They act as though God left the planet and threw them the keys to the kingdom on His way out. And they are more than willing to use them to lock anyone out who dares challenge their god-like authority.

This book covers the core issues that can make knowing and loving God in the real world a reality. Each chapter addresses the most common and chronic lies and illusions "they" pass off as Christianity. Everywhere I go people say, "I dig Jesus, but I'm not into organized religion." I try to assure them it's not all that organized. I must admit "they" have been so effective in their mission of misery you might be a bit taken back by what you read at first. But trust me, the renegade side of you will want to know more—much more.

For example, would you be surprised to hear God and religion are like oil and water—they won't mix? Religion is man's pursuit of God while Christ-centered Christianity is the story of God's pursuit of you. Would you be shocked to learn God isn't interested in your moral makeover? And even though way too many sermons demand you be more like Moses, Joseph, David, Joshua, Peter, James, John, Paul, or even Jesus, God isn't interested in you being a better version of the old you. Are you aware Jesus never asked anyone to "accept" Him or make a "decision" for Him? He dared demand that people reorient their lives around Him. That's what He meant when He called people to take up the cross and follow Him. And Jesus never taught that Christians would be known by their arrogant, self-righteous, know-it-all swagger and rhetoric, but solely by their unconditional love and acceptance. Jesus bids you and me to travel the non-religious road to real.

Contrary to what "they" teach, trying to be good enough for God is futile. According to Jesus, there is nothing you can do to fix yourself. Why would God come down out of heaven and dwell among us if there were any other way to save us? When did we exchange blockbuster events like virgin births and empty tombs for boring, long-winded sermons bloated with religious trivia?

Calling people to be more like their favorite biblical character falls far short of God's goal—the radical renovation of your heart. Jesus didn't die for a denomination or a certain school of theological thinking. He died for the privilege of loving you as you are, where you are. Obviously, we have a lot to discuss, my renegade friend, and I can't wait to get started.

THE PRICE OF AN R4G LIFE

As appealing as it is to live renegade real, let me warn you there is a price to pay. Not everybody is going to like your newfound freedom and fire. The "people-pleaser" in you must be silenced because you're surely going to hack some people off—big time. You might even be forced to find a new crowd to hang with. It's even possible you will be forced to change churches or maybe (hold onto your hat, Hanna!) find one for the first time. Family members may not understand it (mine didn't), friends may not go along with it (mine wouldn't), but there is a renegade nation forming out there and you need to be a part of it.

As an R4G, get intentional about your one and only life. Don't be afraid to express the outrageous joy of your newfound freedom in Christ. Dare to be rowdy, to run, jump, skip, make some noise. You are not here to fit in, but to stand out, play hard, dream big, and struggle mightily. Right here, right now is your time to roar. God, who makes no mistakes, made you the way you are for a reason. And it wasn't to let me or anyone else stuff your soul into a tiny "god box," nor stifle your spirit by allowing you to settle for a safe life built on the illusion that God is absent and we are on our own.

To an R4G, life yields its best gifts, its most noble rewards. The only questions which remain are:

What will you do with what you discover on this adventure?

What wrongs will you right on your quest?

What hurts will you heal?

What loads will you lift?

What dreams will you pursue to the summit of glorious victories?

What adversities will you overcome?

What discoveries will you make?

What demons will you defy and what defeats will you risk in the quest to be fully and creatively alive?

Who will you rescue?

Who will you oppose?

Will your life be a cautionary tale or an adventure of daring deeds done and bold actions taken?

Will you be renegade real, or a religious robot?

Hear me when I say that Satan hates your freedom. To him, your joy is like the screeching of a googolplex of fingernails dragging across a cosmic chalkboard. He will not let you go without a fight, but fight you must, because your future hangs in the balance. I invite you out of the closet and into the sunlight and sweet glow of God's radical grace. Dare to be what you were made to be—a renegade for God.

By the time we parted ways in LA, my new "allergic to all things religious" friend promised he would give God another go. In a moment of rare honesty he confessed much of what he had achieved seemed hollow and unfulfilling. He bemoaned the fact that he felt stuck on the treadmill of more, chasing after God knows what. He was tired of trying to be good enough for God. Like me, he longed to be different; not just better. I prayed for him then and I pray for him still. I wonder, is this splendid young man on the renegade road to real? Is he today living the life for which he was created? I hope he is and I pray you will be too. Welcome to the revolution that Renegade Jesus birthed over two millennia ago!!

A RENEGADE'S GUIDE TO GOD

1

YOU MIGHT BE A RENEGADE IF . . .

FOUR REAL REASONS RENEGADES ARE ALLERGIC TO ALL THINGS RELIGIOUS

Paradoxically, what propels people toward atheism is above all a sense of revulsion against the excesses and failures of organized religion.

—Alister McGrath

Steve was my big brother and though he was shorter than me, I still looked up to him. I wanted, no I craved, his approval. I would do almost anything to make him think I was cool, so talking to him about my newfound faith was about the most uncool thing I could think of doing.

Religion was a touchy subject for us both. We swore once we got old enough we would never darken the door of a church again. But, I had just experienced a radical conversion. Today, we might call it a "total spiritual makeover." Without intending to, I became an all out, full-bore follower of Jesus. All I wanted was a chance to break the news to him gently, face to face, in my own words. Knowing his aversion to all things religious, it was going to take a careful, sensible explanation to convince him I had not gone "religious weirdo" on him. I wanted him to see "it's still" me, only it was a different me.

We decided to meet at Gary Force Ford in Bowling Green, Kentucky—the town where he lived and where I was going to college. We both liked cars and since the new Mustangs were out, it seemed like a perfect place to spill the beans. As we walked to the new car lot, I looked for a way to begin the conversation. I started by talking about religion, something we both disliked. As carefully as I could, I told him the Jesus we heard about had become real to me. I poured out my heart about how Jesus changed my entire outlook on life. Because of this experience, I felt more alive and excited about my future. Every day was different than the one before. I faced each day full of energy. I sensed my life mattered. I assured him this wasn't a religious phase and I wasn't going to turn into the kind of "goody-goody" guy we'd always made fun of. As I shared my faith as sanely as I possibly could, I could see the disapproval moving across his face like dark clouds advancing a storm. The tension thickened. He'd stopped listening and started waiting for me to breathe. And when I did, he leaned in and with fire in his eyes said, "Why in the hell would you want to waste your life being a G___ D____ preacher?" My heart sank. Man, I'd messed up big time. If I had known this would be our last conversation on the subject, I'd have lingered longer. But I was mortified.

This was not the response I prayed for. But instead of being angry or hurt, all I could think about was, "You know, he's got a point. Why would I want to spend my one and only life talking about a dead guy who lived 2,000 years ago?" Without thinking through what I was about to say, and as he climbed into his flaming red GTO to leave, I blurted out, "You gotta waste your life doing something. It might as well be about something big." What I blurted out as a seventeen-year-old nobody from Barren County, has stuck with me from that day to this. Little did I know I'd stumbled onto something that would become the prevailing principle of my life. I believed then as I do today: Jesus is the key to everything about the life worth living.

THE RENEGADE SPIRIT

Everyone I've ever known is looking for a way to fit in and stand out all at the same time. Reputation and persona are important. No one sets out on a bland, boring, meaningless march to the mediocre middle. That's why we dress cool and drive cars with image. We want to be the person people want to be with and like. I saw a great example of this in a recent TV ad for the new Hummer 2. It opens with a bunch of kids racing homemade go-carts. The commercial has a rugged retro feel to it, harkening back to a simpler place and time. The kids are hunched over the steering wheels of their slick formula-one racers high-tailing it down the hill. But there's the one lone-wolf kid who defies convention in his homemade, rough-hewn Hummer go-cart screaming straight down the hill, oblivious to the winding, gradual course set out for the normal people.

He loves knowing that his is the most unique machine in the race. This kid has guts. He's cutting his own way through the great outdoors, blazing his own trail, and to everyone's utter chagrin he glides across the finish line in first place and wins the race—all to the accompaniment of the Who's "Happy Jack": a song about a boy who dares go his own way. After he wins the race you hear playing in the background, "But they couldn't stop Jack with the waters lapping and they couldn't prevent Jack from feeling happy."

Each time I watch it, it stirs something deep inside me. What are the Hummer people trying to tell us? A Hummer 2 isn't for the average person with prosaic aspirations. It's a machine with personality, crafted solely to inspire the soul of those who love kicking back against the encroaching boundaries of convention. Hummer people revel in the rockier road less traveled. They pride themselves on having a bigger and better machine and they are very pleased to outsmart all the others. They're unafraid of unrutted roads or unfamiliar territory. They live for it.

God created you with a stalwart spirit. It's the part of you that longs to live a free, fun, fulfilling life, brimming over with purpose, place, and meaning. And of all the fears we face and for all the demons who snipe at our souls, they can all be reduced to one common, core obsession. The number one fear of every man and woman I have counseled, coached, or conversed with is *the fear of living a wasted life*. And it's this constant craving to live a free, fun, fulfilling life which best identifies the renegade spirit.

Let's get this straight right here, right now; R4G's aren't rednecks. They weren't born with a proclivity to whine or wring their hands. They can't be identified by an outward appearance. They can't be pigeonholed as conservative, liberal, democrat, republican, or independent. They may or may not ride motorcycles. They might or might not have tattoos. They are as apt to wear Brooks

Brothers' suits as Bermuda shorts or a Tommy Bahama shirt. They work in high-rise office buildings and on construction sites. They are teachers, lawyers, salesmen, statesmen, artists, painters, blue-collar workers, and ditch-diggers. They come from all races, creeds, and colors. They spill over into every social stratum. Many are highly educated while others are not. Their faith is neither cosmetic nor cultural. Hot-wired into their motivations is the drive to live life to the max. But they're not stressed out, over-reaching, success hounds.

Let's dispel another myth—Renegades are not rebels. They're not angry anti-socials. The sacred Scriptures say, "A rebel doesn't care about the facts. All he wants to do is yell" (Prov. 18:2, LB). Rebels are angry people. They use anger as a mask to cover up their hurt and disappointment. Rebels look for someone to blame, something to hit, and something to run from or over. Renegades aren't angry people. They are simply people who will not settle for less than the free, fun, fulfilling life for which they somehow know they were meant.

From the cradle to the grave, life comes at you hard and fast. Easy is not an option. If you are a bum, life is hard. If you're a businessman, life is hard. If you're a mother, life is hard. But it's never easy we're after. As a matter of fact, renegades avoid easy because we bore easily. It's not *easy* we crave, but *worth it.* To be who God created you to be and to do what God has called you to do is never easy, but it is what we won't live without, if we can help it.

Renegade real is an inner quest for authenticity, not a particular temperament or style. Renegades know they were created to be unique, distinctive people. As a matter of fact, the renegade spirit can be understood with these three words—energy, individuality, and significance. It's a desire, a passion to be an individual who lives a significant life. Like the hippies of the sixties, we want our chance at revolution. We look around us at the pain and we dare to do more than wring our hands and say our prayers. We want to get our hands dirty in the act of making this a better world because we lived.

A renegade is a live wire, someone who gets up with a positive outlook every day. They savor the moments by understanding that every breath is a miracle, every sandwich is like manna, and every person met is a priority. It doesn't mean they don't get down, it doesn't mean they don't go through hard times of hurt and pain, but they are resilient and resourceful. Give them enough time and opportunity and they'll find a way to make life great. They choose to live—not to lose. They are winners, not whiners. They are truth-seekers, not agenda pushers.

Renegades are mavericks. We don't necessarily mean to be, but we have a low B.S. quotient. As such, we resist second-hand faith and hand-me-down rules. Orphaned obligations feel as distant and plastic as disco. Second-hand faith, second-hand experiences, second-hand rules chafe at the soul and the spirit of the renegade on the road to real.

At the core of the renegade spirit is an insatiable curiosity. They want to know why things are the way they are. We ask lots of questions. That's why for us, rule-based religion is a stodgy, staid, and provincial way to live. Renegades surmise if God can be known, it should be through a relationship, not through a set of rules, which do not relate to real life in the real world.

If there is one all-inclusive characteristic, which captures the spirit of the Renegade, it's the desire to be real. We want to be aligned with people who are real. We want to invest our lives in issues that matter, endure, and will prevail in the end when everything else melts away.

Renegades are spirited, positive, energetic people. We love life and want to experience everything it has to offer. We want a big life that matters and makes a difference. We're not looking for neat and tidy. We want our lives to count, *now and forever.* We want to live everyday unafraid, unashamed, untamed, and unleashed. And as a renegade myself, I join all my mates in the renegade nation as we dare to imagine and create a better world.

Renegades are also curious; they want to know "why?" And this curiosity starts early. If you doubt that, spend an afternoon walking in the park with a four-year-old. He will ask you a thousand questions without taking a breath, about everything he sees, touches, or smells. He will ask, "How do bees fly?" or "Why do humming birds hum?" or "How can brown seeds buried in black dirt produce a green watermelon with a red center?" If you dare to offer answers, he will counter with, "Why?" Why do we always have more questions than answers? It's because life is best lived as a quest—an adventure through uncharted territory, fraught with great peril, yet loaded with great reward. Renegades know that "why" questions, when asked openly and honestly, lead to truth, then to the reality, then to God, the one whose life and love makes us real. The goal we all have.

ALLERGIC TO ALL THINGS RELIGIOUS

OK, here is where the Renegade Spirit is most misunderstood. While renegades run from religion, they're not necessarily running from God. For us, religion is like a refrigerator filled with three-month-old moldy pizza. It may fill your stomach, but it's probably going to make you sick. To a renegade, religion is about man-made do's and don'ts. Religion is finger-pointing preachers screaming, "Turn or burn and die and fry while we go to the sky." It's about someone's mythical opinion about how we can get the franchise on God. And we all know opinions are like noses; everybody's got one.

In an interview with a long-time friend, international superstar Bono, of the hit band U2 and professed Christian, made this astute observation, "Religion can be the enemy of God. It's often what happens when God, like Elvis, has left the building. A list of instructions where there was once conviction; dogma where once people just did it; a congregation led by a man where once they were led by the Holy Spirit. Discipline replacing discipleship."[1]

Renegades run from religion because they resist being named, revolt at being shamed, and rebel against being tamed. Stephen Brown said, "If we are only out to be nice, mild-mannered folk, we should either change our name or change our calling." We crave a bigger, better, bolder life than religion allows. My gut tells me I was meant for more than just being a nice guy and maybe that's why men are so noticeably absent from church. I don't want to be Pee-wee Herman or the Terminator, but I do want to be a man of love and honor. In his insightful book, *Why Men Hate Going to Church*, David Murrow observes:

> *Although males have not completely abandoned the church, tough, earthy, working guys rarely come to church. High achievers, alpha males, risk takers, and visionaries are in short supply. Fun-lovers and adventurers are also under-represented*

> *in church. These rough-and-tumble men don't fit in. Today's churchgoing man is humble, tidy, dutiful, and above all, nice. What a contrast to the men of the Bible! Think of Moses and Elijah, David and Daniel, Peter and Paul. They were lions not lambs—take charge men who risked everything in the service of God. They fought valiantly and spilled blood. They spoke their minds and stepped on the toes of religious people.*[2]

I crave the free, fun, fulfilling life my gut tells me I am destined to live. Like a stallion kicking against his cramped stall, renegades smother under the smallness of rule-based religion. It doesn't take a spiritual giant to see God is bigger than the Baptist, Presbyterian, Catholic, or "__________" (fill in the blank) box. Surely He didn't create you and me, the crowning jewel of His creativity, to live little, safe, self-absorbed, cookie-cutter, humdrum lives.

Renegades are allergic to religious know-it-alls passing themselves off as God's anointed. This is a huge issue with me, because I grew up listening to preachers who were not real or nice once you got to know them. Real will be a core character quality of anyone who dares speak for God. When the messenger is disingenuous, we discount the message. Renegades are not contentious, but we retain the right to decide for ourselves. Renegades are mission-driven, movement-oriented, get-it-done activists. That's why we are attracted to Jesus; the one who draws His circle of friendship large enough to include "whosoever will" may come. Christianity is a big tent with lots of room for characters, comrades, and cohorts.

There are four very real reasons why renegades run from religion. They are: the fear of being shamed, tamed, lumped, and limited.

Renegades shy away from being shamed. They know something is terribly wrong with the world. They feel the effects of sin and brokenness, they agree that what's wrong with everyone else is what's wrong with me, but when we say we sin we're not saying we're worthless or unlovable. Religion makes little or no distinction between guilt and shame. And that is one of its many fundamental flaws. Real guilt, the kind which drives you into the waiting arms of a merciful, forgiving, grace-infusing God, is a good thing. But shame only drives us away from God, deeper and deeper into our own depravity and despair. Shaming is not just wrong—I believe it's one of the reasons why we see so much violence plastered across the nightly news. If you beat into my head I'm bad, then don't be shocked when I am.

Renegades buck at being tamed. They see religion as the denial of desire and ambition. And that sucks because desire and ambition are the two commodities we have in abundance. The Renegade's active mind thinks, wonders, dreams, and imagines better days and bigger things. We're not interested in sitting in rows of church pews like little clones looking at the back of other cloned heads in a robotic Sunday morning nod to God. We won't be "told" what to do or "commanded" how to behave. For us, compliance and conformity are the ultimate sellouts. We want to give our entire heart, mind and soul to something bigger than ourselves. Renegades know we need to do things better, but we live to do better things.

They don't want a small, simple, or safe 9 to 5 life. They want a big, bold, exciting, life; one more like an adventure, a quest, or a roller-coaster ride with God at the helm with better days and great victories ahead. We want to go way beyond good into great. We yawn at safe. We yearn for dangerous! We have William Wallace's confession, in the movie *Braveheart*, "All men die, but not all men really live!" tattooed across the front of our brains.

Renegades loathe being lumped together in a homogenized herd. In this way they're like cats, they can't be herded but they can be led. They don't join monolithic groups of people who may or may not represent their own heart commitments. In other words, renegades don't like labels. They don't like one denomination or group lording over everyone else. They don't like being divided by what really seems to be trivial matters. They like large groups of interesting, diverse people. They like movements aimed at achieving greatness motivated by larger-than-life ideas, not petty arguments over outdated allegiances.

Renegades also fear being limited. They won't listen to long-winded, red-faced preachers telling them what they can or cannot do. Their wild heart tells them a well-lived life can't be built on a negative foundation or a long list of religious clichés. Sermons on the evils of smoking, drinking, movie-going, the clothes we shouldn't wear, or the theme parks we should boycott seem insulting.

THE RENEGADE CRY

The renegade's heart cries to live free, have fun, and change the world. Freedom is what we want and from Jesus freedom is exactly what we get.

Renegades long to be free from rote religious rules and regulations. The idea of rules is not the hang-up here, but their meaning must be rooted in love. Wherever love is the ethic and gratitude is the motivation, you can expect Renegades to gather. Jesus frees us from the pain of the past and the regrets we have over the things we should've but didn't do. As the Scriptures say, "You, my brothers, were called to be free. But do not use your freedom to indulge the sinful nature; rather, serve one another in love" (Gal. 5:13).

I almost want to apologize on this one, because fun is so trivialized in the minds of religious people. But fun is exactly what we crave and without it our lives dry up, our relationships crack up, and our jobs become jails. Southwest Airlines has adopted as its recruiting slogan, "Feel free to actually enjoy what you do." Fun lubricates the friction of the mundane and routine. The renegade wants to have fun because he believes loving God and living in His wonderful world is a privilege, not a right. When God looks at me, He smiles. Dare I do less when I look back?

No one I went to church with as a kid would mistake it for a fun time. I'm not advocating a frenetic, frivolous, self-serving emotionalism here. I'll never forget the Tuesday morning I was called to report to the seminary president's office. He came to hear me speak the Sunday before and man did he intimidate me sitting there looking presidential. I thought, "He was so impressed, he wants me to speak at chapel?" I was ushered into his office. Sitting behind his over-sized mahogany desk, leaning back in his high backed, overstuffed red leather chair, he said, "I heard you speak this weekend and your sermon was nice." "Nice" is not the word I was hoping for. He said, "Son, you have a big choice to make. You have a gift to be funny, but humor has no place in the pulpit. You can either be a comedian or a preacher, not both. You're dismissed." I was stunned, embarrassed, and mortified. I left his office feeling emasculated, fighting back tears. I continued to respect him for the godly man I knew him to be, but from that day on I was deaf to his influence. Why? Because, though I couldn't argue with him, my gut told me he was wrong—dead wrong.

Laughter is as necessary as air. It is a gift from God and when the Bible says a cheerful heart is like medicine, it is right on. What I'm calling fun, the kind which shakes the soul awake, the Bible calls joy. Joy is the reality of Jesus experienced and expressed here in the real world. Life is difficult and it's not always fun, but if you're not having any fun at all then you've been hoodwinked. Because living, loving, and serving Renegade Jesus is fun. And how could it be anything less? If Jesus is who He claimed to be, then there's no way you can be somber, sad, and serious all the time. In Christ, we're wanted, loved, and free. God's love paid a debt He did not owe—that's plenty enough reason to shout—Yea God! After all, the largest book in the Bible is a songbook. You can't sing all of those songs as a dirge. Sometimes they're an anthem and a march. David was a musician before he got into politics. On one occasion, he was filled with so much fun and he danced so hard down the middle of Main Street his clothes fell off (see 2 Sam. 6:20–22). Religious people frowned on it then and if you dare dance today, they'll frown on you. But not to worry; God's got rhythm and He definitely invented soul.

In 2005, for the first time since records have been kept, people participating in sports and exercise programs decreased while attendance at all sporting events rose. We are losing our drive, because we're losing the belief that one life can change the world. That's one of the battle cries of the Renegade life. We are not consumers; we are world-changers. We wake up every day with the conviction that how we live today does make all the difference.

The J-life is a life of action. We are so hungry for it we deify athletes and actors who portray it. We watch *extreme* sports to live vicariously through those who refuse to be couch potatoes or pew-warming wannabe's. R4G's are tired of being over-stimulated and under-involved; over-stressed and under-stretched. We won't settle for being over-weight and under-challenged.

As a Renegade for God, I refuse to sit on the sideline watching things happen. I want Jesus to place me on the crest of God's new wave. I won't be here long so I dedicate my life to fulfilling God's divine design for me. As Jesus lives and loves through me, I will meet needs, right wrongs and run to the eye of the storms. "It ought to be possible to live a Christian life without being a Christian," laments Roy Hattersley, a columnist for the *U.K. Guardian*. An outspoken atheist, Hattersley came to this conclusion after watching the Salvation Army lead several other faith-based organizations in the relief effort after Hurricane Katrina.

"Notable by their absence," he writes, were "teams from rationalist societies, free thinkers' clubs, and atheists' associations—the sort of people who scoff at religion's intellectual absurdity." Hattersley concluded Christians "are the people most likely to take the risks and make the sacrifices involved in helping others."

"The only possible conclusion," says Hattersley, "is that faith comes with a packet of moral imperatives that, while they do not condition the attitude of all believers, influence enough of them to make [Christians] morally superior to atheists like me."[3]

Wow, what a statement! And what is the moral superiority the R4G displays most proudly? It is the ability to rally to action when compassion thrusts us to the frontline as first-responders.

Using Jeff Foxworthy's famous tagline, "You might be a redneck if . . ." as a starting point, let me just say, as we travel along this road to finding life outside conventional Christianity, you might be an R4G (Renegade for God) if you want to live an expanding life; where you're totally free to become all that God's love, God's gifts, and your willingness to work hard and prevail, can make of you. If you want to have fun, smile a lot, lighten up, and live the joy-filled life Jesus promised, you might be an R4G. If you want to seize your divine moment to fulfill your destiny; if you believe God made you for this moment in time, you might be an R4G.

Jesus came to love you and give you life. He did not die to make you religious, but to give you a new heart. Because nothing changes until your heart changes, and the heart never changes by itself, we need help. Jesus' death and resurrection is God's promise fulfilled. "I will give you a new heart and put a new spirit in you; I will remove from you your heart of stone and give you a heart of flesh" (Ezek. 36:26). And this new freed-up, joy-filled heart of flesh doesn't tame, shame, limit, or lump easily. Instead, it sets the R4G in us free to be an agent of change with a message of hope for a world in pain.

As R4G's we will dedicate ourselves to living a Christ-centered, grace-empowered, mission-driven life. We will jam-pack our lives with other happy people who ache to be wave-makers in the dangerous, uncivilized Renegade Nation. Our corporate mission is the fueling and funding of a global revolution aimed at the radical reclamation of the human heart. We are driven by a relentless, passionate pursuit of the divine scandal—namely—every life matters to God.

THE R4G CRY

Late in his life John Steinbeck, winner of the Nobel Prize, decided to travel across the country. He wanted to explore the human condition and chronicle his discoveries. His friends warned him it was too late in his life for such a quest. Of their objections he wrote, "I had seen so many begin to pack their lives in cotton wool, smother their impulses, hood their passions and gradually retire from their manhood into a kind of spiritual and physical semi-invalidism. In this, they were even encouraged by their wives and relatives, and it's such a sweet trap."

Steinbeck knew the potential problems of driving thousands of miles alone in a truck with only his dog. But as he said, he was not about to surrender fierceness for a small gain in yardage. His adventures are recorded in *Travels with Charley: In Search of America.* Much of it portrays the sad, cellophane age we live in, so safe and sterile, and the profound consequences of such lifelessness. He noted, "It was all plastic too—the table linen, the butter dish, the sugar and crackers were wrapped in cellophane, the jelly in a small plastic coffin sealed with cellophane. It was early evening and I was the only customer. Even the waitress wore a sponge apron. She wasn't happy, but then she wasn't unhappy. She wasn't anything."

Steinbeck observed how insulated our society has become and how mediocrity overtakes us little by little, day by day. Before leaving, a well-known political reporter said, "If anywhere in your travels you come on a man with guts, mark the place. I want to go see him. I haven't seen anything but cowardice and expediency. This used to be a nation of giants."

God is looking for men and women to be giants in the land of the dying. Imagine the unlikely, against-all-odds miracles Jesus performed through the first little band of feeble followers. They were the definition of ordinary. They had no money, no connections, and no master plan. Jesus didn't write a manual or give them detailed instructions. He simply sent them out to tell what they'd seen and to give away what He gave them—new life. In the Book of Acts, Jesus welcomed those who gathered in the upper room to the revolution. It would start in Jerusalem and spread like a love virus to Judea, and then like a world-wide tsunami, the J-life slowly covers the known world. Jesus made them different and that difference is still making all the difference.

In 1997, Apple came out with an ad campaign called "Think Different." The commercials were short clips of influential figures in the twentieth century. They included Albert Einstein, Mohandas Gandhi, Alfred Hitchcock, Pablo Picasso, and several others. In the background was Richard Dreyfuss reading the following:

> *Here's to the crazy ones. The misfits, the rebels, the troublemakers, the round pegs in the square holes, the ones who see things differently. They're not fond of rules and they have no respect for the status quo. You can quote them, disagree with them, glorify or vilify them. About the only thing you can't do is ignore them. Because they change things, they push the human race forward. And while some may see them as the crazy ones, we see genius, because the people who are crazy enough to think they can change the world, are the ones who do.*
>
> —Apple Computer, Inc. commercial "Think Different"

The renegade's cry will guide us along this non-religious road to real. I will, by the power of Jesus Christ, live free—free from the bondage of past shame, past guilt, and free from past prejudices and put-downs. I will have fun every day understanding that the joy of the Lord is my strength as I walk in the real world power of the resurrected Christ. Death has been defeated because the love of Jesus paid the bill. As an R4G, I am a citizen of the Renegade

Nation. Together, we will do the one thing religion can never do—love like Jesus loved, live like Jesus lived, and leave the revolution intact. We won't tolerate anyone wanting to hijack our sacred honor for their religious agenda. We are joined to the revolution Jesus set in motion two thousand years ago—the radical renovation of the human heart.

Welcome to the journey to life outside conventional Christianity, where men and women learn how to live big, bold, bodacious lives. On this road, we do not cower in corners, or spend our lives apologizing for our freedoms, our joys, or our ambitions. Welcome into the sunlight of our Savior Jesus Christ. He loved us back to life, placed a servant's heart in us, and a hero's path before us. Our fight is against anyone who tries to water down Jesus or His radical message; love conquers all. We boldly proclaim "we are more than conquerors through Him who loved us [and gave Himself for us]" (Rom. 8:37).

As we walk this non-religious road to real together, we will praise God for our freedom, as well as our future. We're going to see God show up at all our stops along the way, as we discover the majesty and the mystery which is Jesus. You'll experience for yourself the power of the human heart, set free to dream, to dare, to move, to risk everything for love. His aliveness, His realness, and His mission is still shaking the world. After 2,000 years, Jesus is still cool, as He should be, of course. As Jesus people, our challenge is to live out His aliveness in front of a dying world.

2

JESUS IS COOL, BUT CHRISTIANS CREEP ME OUT

WHICH JESUS DO YOU KNOW; CIVILIZED JESUS OR RENEGADE JESUS?

I like your Christ, I do not like your Christians. Your Christians are so unlike your Christ.

—*Mohandas Gandhi*

After speaking to a large group of North Carolina State students about the J-life (the life Jesus gives), a freshman came up to me afterward and said, "Hey, the Jesus you talked about tonight sounds cool, but Christians kinda like, creep me out, you know." I said, "Yes, I'm afraid I do." With his candid comment, this eighteen-year-old from Four Oaks, North Carolina, framed the current state of American Christianity.

More and more people consider Jesus cool and His teachings

current, while there is an ever-widening credibility gap between the words Christ, Christian, and Christianity. When you compare who Jesus was and what He said with how Christians come across these days, there's little family resemblance. Everyday, here in the real world, people advocate policies and prejudices in the name of Jesus which betray the very truths He taught. Most of the emails I receive from Christians contain unkind and un-Christian cuts and put-downs about other Christians. We boast of our love for Jesus, but can barely stand each other's company.

Jesus' "cool" status is even more remarkable when you consider in our post-modern culture we have a collective case of ADD. We use slogans like, "it's a thirty-day world" or "fifteen minutes of fame" to describe the fickle and transient nature of our media-driven society. We bore easily so we're always looking for the next new big thing. And yet, even after 2000 years of history where nations, kings, and religious leaders have appeared and vanished into obscurity, Jesus' life and message prevails. He lived well and loved mightily. He was and is the original religious Renegade who promised freedom and still delivers today.

So heroic was His life we mark the division of time by His entrance into the world. His enduring influence after more than 2,000 years since He walked on this planet is nothing short of astounding. Just think, Socrates taught for forty years, Plato for about fifty, and Aristotle for another forty. In contrast, Jesus' public ministry lasted for a little more than three years. Yet when you compare the influence of Christ's 1,000+ day ministry, it infinitely exceeds the impact of over 130 years of the combined teaching of three of the greatest philosophers of all time.

Jesus was born in a backwoods village. His mother was a peasant teenage virgin who came up pregnant under questionable circumstances. He worked in obscurity in His father's carpenter shop until He was thirty, after which He became an itinerant preacher. He never owned a home, never wrote a book, and never organized an army. He avoided big cities, except for Jerusalem during the last days of His life. He walked everywhere He went and traveled less than two hundred miles from the obscure village in which He was born. When He did go public, He chose a rag-tag group of twelve unlettered, underachieving men, some of whom were of questionable character. He was famous for His constant head-butting with the religious ruling elite of His day. He was a renegade (someone who rejects conventional wisdom) of the first-order. When it came to making all the wrong people mad, He excelled. His message was like oil and water when compared to the religious norms of His day. But to the common man He was seen as "every man's" champion while at the same time He was feared and hated by the religious elite.

When the winds of public opinion turned ill against Him, the cheering crowds dispersed and His friends stepped into the shadows. When questioned, Peter, the leader of the disciples and one of His inner-circle, denied even knowing Him. Without just cause, Jesus was handed over to the avarice and caprice of His enemies. He went through the mockery of an illegal trial. He was publicly beaten and humiliated. He was forced to carry His cross outside the city to the top of a garbage dump. There, they nailed Him to a cross, gouged it into the ground, and sat down to watch Him die. As Saint Augustine said:

Man's Maker was made man, that He, Ruler of the stars, might nurse at His mother's breasts; that the Bread might be hungry, the Fountain thirst, the Light sleep, the Way be tired from the journey; that the Truth might be accused by false witnesses, the Judge of the living and the dead be judged by a mortal judge, Justice be sentenced by the unjust, the Teacher be beaten with whips, the Vine be crowned with thorns, the Foundation be suspended on wood.[1]

As He suffered unspeakable agony, His executioners gambled for the only piece of property He owned on earth—His robe. When He was dead, He was laid in a borrowed grave through the pity of a friend. Not quite the résumé you'd expect for a religious leader. Oh, by the way, did I mention He rose from the dead? Now, that's way too cool and it makes all the difference.

Over twenty centuries have passed since He walked the earth and yet no single person has affected this tiny blue marble as powerfully and dramatically as Jesus, this one who claimed to be the Savior of the world. As John wrote, "His life is the light that shines through the darkness—and the darkness can never extinguish it" (John 1:5, LB). Quite a prophecy of the enduring legacy that is Jesus (the name refers to His work) the Christ (the name refers to His authority or office).

Jesus painted no pictures; yet some of the finest paintings of Raphael, Michelangelo, and Leonardo da Vinci were created by the inspiration they received from thinking about Him. He wrote no poetry yet Dante, Milton, and thousands of the world's greatest poets were inspired, again, by Him. He composed no music nor sang a song, yet Haydn, Handel, Beethoven, Bach, and Mendelssohn reached the apex of their professions and perfection while writing hymns, symphonies, and oratorios dedicated to His glory. Every sphere of human achievement has been enriched and inspired by this simple, humble carpenter from an obscure place called Nazareth. Even after all these years where fads, philosophies, governments, and revolutionary regimes have risen only to recede like the tides, Jesus prevails. The realities of virgin births, sinless lives, and empty tombs have a way of sticking around. Jesus is still today the only credible, durable reason for the hope we have.

A CREDIBILITY GAP

There exists in our culture a strange duality dogging Christianity. On the one hand, most people are of the opinion that Jesus is pretty cool. He lived simply. He taught that love is better than hate and people are more important than things. But on the other hand, Christians come off as being a subculture of smug, self-righteous, know-it-alls who exude an attitude of arrogance and moral superiority. How can this be possible? Maybe it's because we've tamed Jesus and made Him more like a sacred Santa, than a death-defying, hell-storming, life-giving lover who shattered conventional religious wisdom by hanging around people thought to be undesireable.

While Jesus is admired across the board, Christians and Christianity come off feeling creepy and artificial. For example, Mel Gibson can make a movie about the sacrificial death of Jesus and millions attend and are reminded, or learn for the first time, of the sacrifice He made for love of us. And yet fewer and fewer people attend fewer and fewer churches (an average of eight churches close every week in America).[2] While Christianity is burgeoning around the world, in America it is shrinking, at least in terms of weekly church attendance.

Say these words to yourself: Christ, Christian, and Christianity. Christ is a cool word. Christian gets a little nebulous, but the term Christianity is just downright murky when it comes to its true meaning. Why? It's primarily because those of us who say we love Jesus speak and act in ways which can't be reconciled. I've even read surveys of Christians who say they do not accept the divinity of Jesus or the reality of His bodily resurrection. We talk the talk, but we do not walk the walk. We claim to know God but our lives bear little to no resemblance.

On a bitter cold day in downtown Chicago, a small boy stood shivering on a steel grate in the sidewalk. His clothes were threadbare and tattered. A woman, appropriately dressed for the weather, stopped and engaged the youngster in a conversation. He was indeed a child of the street. The compassionate stranger took him to a clothing store and outfitted him from head to foot, including cap, scarf, and gloves. The lad was overwhelmed by her kindness. He couldn't stop thanking her and as they said their good-byes and walked in opposite directions, the elated boy turned back and shouted, "Are you God's mother?" The gentle woman answered, "Oh no! I'm just a child of God." He smiled and whispered to himself, "I knew you two had to be related."[3]

The greatest apologetic we have is a changed life. It's simple. If you love Jesus, you'll do what He did and love whom He loved. And when it comes to tooting your own horn, you won't. As Solomon said, "Let another praise you and not your own mouth" (Prov. 27:2).

Christians today tend to give off an air of self-righteousness and moral superiority. This isn't just my narrow, cynical view; it's an objective observation. This is often seen in the blanket statements Christian power brokers make in public. A few years back, James Dobson, founder of Focus on the Family, called for all Christians to remove their kids from public schools.[4] Because people tend to "lump" all Christians together, I had to make it clear Dobson was speaking for himself, not for me. I'm glad we live in a land where we can say what we like, but these kinds of blanket moral condemnations only cloud the issue and create resentment. I saw an example of this recently when I was in Colorado Springs, home of Focus on the Family, and saw a guy in a restaurant with a T-shirt which read, "Focus on your own d_ _ _ family." Maybe it's just me, but neither side strikes me as the one I want to land on.

I spend too much time trying to undo the damage these un-Jesus-like pronouncements do. I know every time a big, influential Christian ministry comes out in opposition to deep, dark evil like Disney, they raise money, but they also raise the defenses of people who look at us from the outside in and wonder where Jesus is in all the hoopla. They want to know why, wherever there's controversy, Christians seem to be right in the middle of it, laying claim to the high moral ground. Then comes the revelation of some scandal—moral, sexual, or otherwise—and the moral ground gained is given back, plus some. Instead of proclaiming the beautiful righteousness of Jesus, we're prone to promote our own morality and expose our hypocrisy, time and time again.

Christianity has not cornered the market on morality. The people who practice it have, at times, not been able to prove "Christianity" as a world-view that has much of a moral advantage at all. The problem with saints is we're also still sinners.

The other bogus "Christian" claim afoot in the land is the confusion around what we know. When I say, "I know God," I am saying I have a personal, real knowledge of God as a person. I am not claiming to know everything there is to know about God nor am I saying absolute knowledge of God is even possible. Just because we say we know God does not mean we know what He knows nor do we know much about what we know we know. We are "know-enough's" not "know-it-alls." As Paul said, "we can see and understand only a little about God now" (1 Cor. 13:12, LB). As a matter of fact, if we had God and the universe all figured out, we would be gods ourselves, wouldn't we? The assurance of what we do know (see 1 John 5:13) gives us confidence to trust God for what we don't. We know enough to want to know so much more. As the Scriptures warn, "without faith it is impossible to please God, because anyone who comes to him must believe that he exists and that he rewards those who earnestly seek him" (Heb. 11:6).

Though I do claim to have gone through a powerful conversion experience, I do not claim to understand much about the relationship. Now I know this admission makes some people nervous, but not me. I don't claim to know a lot about my wife Paula, but that doesn't diminish my love for her. It only intensifies it. She is still a wonderful mystery to me. Saying I have a love-relationship with Jesus is saying I understand enough but not everything about the relationship I'm in. As a matter of fact, as a renegade for God, I am constantly growing and changing in my understanding of exactly who Jesus the Christ is. I live in a culture which constantly wants to redefine Jesus and put Him in a box, but I serve a Savior who is wild and wonderful and who will not be tamed.

SWEET JESUS IN A BOX

The Jesus of the Scriptures and history bears little resemblance to the Jesus of religious culture. Because Jesus was a revolutionary, plain and simple, civilized Christianity tries to clean Him up to make Him more presentable. What we've ended up with is Sweet Jesus in a box, the sole sustainer and satisfier of my every wish and whim. My job is to rip the lid off your God box and let wild-loving, ever-living Jesus loose on our sad and painful world bringing hope and healing through His grace and love. Jesus is dangerous outside the box and that's why civilized religion wants His voice muted and muffled.

Ask people, "Who is Jesus?" and most will say, "Jesus was a nice, sweet, simple, calm guy who went about doing good. He taught us to share and play nice and not to always want what we don't have." Yet Jesus Himself said anyone who doesn't love Him more than his or her own father and mother is not worthy of Him (see Matt. 10:37). If, as a parent, you love your son or daughter more than Jesus, you are not, I repeat, *not* a Christian. How insane and unsafe is that? How dare Jesus put Himself above even your own family, of course unless He is family? How is that sweet? Man, that's radical, that's renegade, and that's most definitely revolutionary. And unless He had the right to make that claim He is not good. He said, "He who is not with me is against me" (Matt. 12:30). That's not the claim of a sweet Jesus, that's the price demanded by a revolutionary.

Christianity attempts to civilize Jesus by relegating Him to a Sunday morning sermon in a boxy little church building. It is amazing to me that millions and millions of people will attend churches each weekend, month after month, with little or no appreciable effect in their lives. Consider this: more people will attend church on one weekend in America than all amateur, professional, and collegiate sports through the entire year put together.[5] And yet those same people, who affirm their allegiance to Jesus on Sunday, are the very same people who will warn you not to take this whole religion thing too far. It's okay to worship and praise Jesus on Sunday, but to take Him to work, to the classroom, or the most intimate places of our life Monday through Saturday seems to be a really odd idea to people. I've actually had leaders in the church say, "Now Dave, you can take the Jesus thing too far." Too far? How in God's name can we ever take our loving, living redeemer of all life too far? I say we haven't even begun taking Him seriously enough.

This may burst your bubble, but here it is; Jesus wasn't sweet and He isn't safe. He isn't the least bit impressed with your big plans or your political agenda. He can't be fit into anyone's religious or moralistic box, neither can He be bought off or ignored for long. When He spoke, demons screamed, the lame walked, and the dead got up out of their graves. After forty days in the wilderness, He stood toe-to-toe with the devil; defeating him at his own game. He turned mere water into vintage wine and healed the blind with muddy spit. He was crucified, not in a cathedral between two candles or in a church's choir loft, but while nailed to two pieces of lumber lashed together to form a device called a cross. Though he was innocent, He died among thieves, on the town's garbage heap, a smoky, smelly putrid place where vulgar men gambled and virtuous men trembled.

From the cross, He defeated death and then descended into hell for three days to set the captives free. He is not a republican or a democrat. He is not white and His native tongue is not English. He is a jealous lover and He does not abide lukewarm love, and He will not tolerate divided loyalty.

Today in America, it costs you nothing to be a "Christian," but for the first believers, it cost them everything. Why were they willing to lay down their lives unless they were convinced Jesus was the Messiah? They committed their hearts, their lives to Jesus and as a result, they jump-started a redemptive revolution. Of Paul and Silas it was said, they "have turned the rest of the world upside down" (Acts 17:7, LB). Voluntarily, they sold their possessions and pooled their money in order to move the Jesus revolution outward and onward (see Acts 2:44–45).

Jesus called people to leave their homes, their families, and their careers to follow Him (see Luke 18:29–30). This seems a bit radical unless of course He is God and does hold life and death in His hands. Of course, if He's just a sweet, flannel graph Jesus or a story we tell the kids so they'll have morals, then all of this is strange and wrong. As C. S. Lewis suggested:

> *A man who was merely a man and said the sort of things Jesus said would not be a great moral teacher. He would either be a lunatic—on a level with the man who says he is a poached egg—or else he would be the Devil of hell. You must make your choice. Either this man was, and is, the Son of God: or else a madman or something worse. You can shut him up for a fool, you can spit at him and kill him as a demon; or you can fall at his feet and call him Lord and God. But let us not come with any patronizing nonsense about his being a great human teacher. He has not left that open to us. He did not intend to.*[6]

Jesus is either Lord, Lunatic, or Liar. If He was a lunatic, we should pity Him. If He was a liar, we should expose Him, sell our churches, and give the proceeds to the poor. But if He is the Lord of Glory, we should do as Moses was told to do, take off our shoes, for the ground on which we stand is holy ground.

Domesticate Jesus and He disappears. In His place a religious artifact, which makes no demands, inspires no sacrifice, forgives no sin, nor saves any soul is erected. Cultural Christianity's Jesus is no more the real Jesus than the velvet Elvis you buy in a gas station parking lot is the king of rock and roll. It may make you feel fuzzy for awhile, but it won't change your life, free your soul, calm your fears, or save the world from utter and complete self-annihilation.

RENEGADE JESUS

One of the dictionary definitions of the word "renegade" is: "someone who pushes back against conventional wisdom." That would make Jesus the original R4G (renegade for God). He pushed back against conventional wisdom so hard it got Him killed. And the crazy cool thing about it is that's exactly what He wanted it to do. He upset the proverbial apple cart everywhere He went. He stirred up the status quo. He poked big, gaping holes in the popular notions about God. He was viewed as a troublemaker and the leader of a rag-tag revolution. He was anti-religion and pro-people.

The first church I served as an eighteen-year-old and while still in college was in a little wide spot in the road, called Fordsville, Kentucky. On my first Sunday, about twenty-five brave people showed up. The only reason they would have considered a novice like me was because this once thriving church had fallen on hard times and was forced to close because no real pastor-type wanted it. From the moment I arrived, I was smothered with stories about the glory days when the church was packed with people. Every Sunday there was standing room only in the good ole days. "Why, there were so many people they were lined up all around the walls," they'd say. On big days people stood outside in the open windows to hear the fiery preacher hold forth mightily. I knew it would take more than me to return them to their former glory.

The first time I walked into the sanctuary I saw something I had never seen before. Hanging prominently behind the pulpit was a huge picture of a longhaired, scruffy, hippie-looking, pale white guy who I assumed was their version of Jesus. I'd seen pictures of Jesus before, but not one depicting Jesus with fair skin, long, flowing blond hair, with blue eyes. (I'm thinking, wasn't Jesus Jewish?) I asked one of the deacons about the picture. He explained they had hung it up there a couple of years before because they were worried people were forgetting what Jesus looked like. They took the verse, "But I, when I am lifted up from the earth, will draw all men to myself" (John 12:32), literally. They truly believed a physical picture of a Jesus of their own making, hanging high in front of the church would be like a lucky charm, which might save their dead-as-a-doornail church. Though it was the first, it's not the last time I've seen people try to create Jesus in their own image.

Contrary to popular opinion, Jesus is not a nice, civilized, white, blonde, blue-eyed savior. He is not the author or sustainer of my suburban dreams. But that's the subtle, subliminal message being sent by white, middle-class Christians. We want to tame Jesus, for fear of what He might do. You see, if Jesus lives down at the church then all you've got to do is go to the church and visit

Him once every seven days. Then you can check off your obligatory religious act for the week. But what happens to the revolutionary spirit if we act as though Jesus loves hanging out with nice, wealthy suburbanites?

As I travel across the country speaking, I have a habit of checking out the Christian radio stations. More and more I'm hearing the tagline, "Safe for the entire family" or "your positive alternative." Is this what we have reduced Jesus to? Safe? Jesus was anything but safe. He was a revolutionary. He came to shake things up and set religion on its ear. Yes, He was compassionate and tender when the situation called for it, but He was also confronting and demanding. Would a safe, sane, sweet Jesus say:

> *Do you think I have come to give peace to the earth? No! Rather, strife and division! From now on families will be split apart, three in favor of Me, and two against—or perhaps the other way around. A father will decide one way about me; his son, the other; mother and daughter will disagree; and the decision of an honored mother-in-law will be spurned by her daughter-in-law.*
>
> —Luke 12:51–53, LB

> *Anyone who does not take up his cross and follow me is not worthy of me.*
>
> —Matt. 10:38

That's kind of rude, isn't it, unless it's true? It is as though we've tried to cast Jesus in the least offensive light possible. But can a non-offensive, undemanding Jesus "save completely all those who come to God through Him" (Heb. 7:25, LB)? This kind of bold, gritty, confrontational rhetoric cast Jesus as a revolutionary. How dare we recast His message as something safe and sanitized?

Jesus made Himself the issue and the dividing line. Life with God is not about going to church once a week. Christianity is not about politics, morality, education, or lifestyle choices. Christianity is Jesus. He is the founder and reigning Lord. Everything real about Christianity is Jesus, and everything fake is religion. Jesus is our unity. He is our power, our purpose, and our plan. If you want to draw a dead line, Jesus would be on the life side of it. Religion would be on the dead side. And when we divide, it should be over Jesus, not the color of carpet, style of music, or the purchase of pink polyester robes.

John said, "He who has the Son has life; he who does not have the Son of God does not have life" (1 John 5:12). Jesus taught you're either with Him or you're against Him. Real life is the J-life—period. You're free to jump and wave your hands in the air or not. Praise music is fine, songs by the Dave Crowder Band, Hillsong, Vineyard Praise, Martin Luther, Wesley, Fannie Crosby, the Baptist Hymnal, or U2. It's your call; as long as it's about Jesus our great God and King, we're good to go. Jesus is the deciding factor. Why? He alone wields authority over life and death.

Renegade Jesus left no room for ambiguity when He said, "I tell you the truth, I am the gate for the sheep. All who ever came before me were thieves and robbers, but the sheep did not listen to them. I am the gate; whoever enters through me will be saved. He will come in and go out and find pasture" (John 10:7–11). These are words that demand a decision from you: "Yes" or "No." Jesus' invitation is simple; all-or-nothing, me or them, my way or no way.

I, along with my brothers and sisters in the Renegade Nation, would fight for your right to reject Jesus. If you understand what's at stake and you walk away because of Jesus, so be it. But we will not let you morph the Lord into a religious relic or an irrelevant footnote to history. Decide for or against Jesus as He is, but don't you dare dismiss Him because we at times act like a bunch of dweebs. As an R4G, I am, at best, only a poor reflection of which He is the real deal.

Jesus is like air to the lungs and water to a desert dweller. He is not a religious artifact. He's not dead. He is alive. He is engaged and engaging. He is here now, changing lives all over this world this very moment. When He walked on earth He changed everything for everyday, for all time. What started then continues today. It can't be stopped though many have tried. Jesus is the rock of redemption and His church will prevail. He is here in this moment with you, doing what He always does, calling you to a higher place, calling you to break free from convention and to stop *going* to church and start *being* the church everywhere you go. Let's be "Jesus people" again. Let's be men and women whose hearts are captured, redeemed, renewed, enlivened, ignited, set free! Let's return to the revolution to be the change we want to see in the world! Here and now, decide, let go, leap, be free, and live the J-life!

A couple of years ago I was invited to speak at one of the seminaries I attended. It was an honor I had not expected but took very seriously. Because I'd been viewed by some as a bit of a renegade (surprise, surprise) when I was there, I wanted to be careful to show respect and appreciation. I wrote out a complete manuscript of my talk. The day I showed up, the president and faculty were nice and polite. The students seemed to respond OK, but after chapel, our good-byes were, to say the least, a bit cool. I've never heard one word from them again except when they want money. A year later I was back in Memphis speaking at a gathering of college singles. After my talk, a guy came up to me and said, "I was there the day you spoke at seminary." He continued, "Would you like to know why you'll never be invited back?" I said, "Sure." He said, "Number one, you didn't wear a suit and tie. And, number two, you didn't carry or read from an actual leather-bound Bible. You read from a manuscript. You were the subject of classroom gossip for a whole week." I thought, if my not wearing a tie or not reading from a leather-bound Bible rises to the level of something worth being discussed, they've got a lot more problems than me. How would Jesus have treated a suit-less, tie-less, leather-less guy like me? Stone him?

Renegade Jesus turned human relations upside down. The down and outs, notorious sinners, the sick and the poor brought out the compassionate, patient side of Jesus. In contrast, He loved exposing the hypocrisy of the self-righteous every chance He got. How would you like to be on the receiving end of this scathing rebuke: "Woe to you, teachers of the law and Pharisees, you hypocrites! You travel over land and sea to win a single convert, and when he becomes one, you make him twice as much a son of hell as you are" (Matt. 23:15).

Jesus wasn't rude. He was real. No doubt this would be viewed as divisive and harsh by today's standards, but Jesus didn't seem to care about appearances or convention. By the way, the word "woe" is equivalent to the English word "cursed." Jesus cursed these people because humanity hung in the balance. He was controversial.

He preached a forceful, full-throttle, follow me, faith message everywhere He went. So stirring were His sermons that Matthew observed, "The crowds were amazed at Jesus' sermons, for he taught as one who had great authority, . . ." (Matt. 7:28–29, LB). You might not like what He said, but you could never accuse Him of stuttering.

Is this the Jesus you know? Is this the Jesus who is worthy of your absolute allegiance? Is this the Jesus you are willing to hinge all your future hopes on? This is really radical stuff when you stop to think about it! Jesus' message was crazy, unless of course it was true. He by-passed the elite and spoke straight to pain and emptiness everyday people felt every day. Here's how Jesus described the revolution, "The kingdom of heaven has been forcefully advancing, and forceful men lay hold of it" (Matt. 11:12). Forcefully advancing! Those were Jesus' words 2,000 years ago. Have they proven true? Are they still the truth today? Depends on where you live.

Historians postulate it took from the beginning of the church to the year 1900 for followers of Jesus to make up 2.5 percent of the world population. In the seventy years beyond that, it more than doubled. By 1970, the number of committed believers in the world expanded to over 6 percent. From 1970 to 1992 the number doubled again. So right now, in the world it's something like 12 or 13 percent. These are followers of Jesus Christ, people who say, "I am born again." Here's what's really interesting. Seventy percent of this growth happened in the last fifteen years. The tragedy is 70 percent of that growth is happening outside the United States.

In America today, over 85 percent of the churches are stagnant or dying. And while the appearance is there is an abundance of churches, the truth is most are nearly empty buildings with an average attendance of fewer than seventy-five. Every week more churches close their doors. Even in Nashville, where I live, churches are being turned into storage buildings, office complexes, and strip joints. Some of our downtown churches are more famous for the architecture than the person and purpose they were built to glorify.

America is becoming the land of empty church buildings and hollow religion. Of 450,000 Protestant churches, we lost fifty thousand churches in the '90s. I heard a denominational leader say recently roughly 5,000 ministers are leaving the ministry every month.[7] These are obscene and sobering numbers and all the more reason why renegades should run the revolution.

TO GOD OR NOT TO GOD?

A famous quote from William Shakespeare's *Hamlet* inquired, "To be, or not to be: that is the question." This was his way of contemplating his real-life son's death. You must ask and answer a similar question—"To God or not to God?" Because religion is so confusing, it is tempting to throw up your hands and dismiss the idea of certainty and just hope for the best. But a relationship with the living, breathing, loving, intimate God, is not only a good thing, it is the best of things.

C. S. Lewis said, "man even at his highest sanctity and intelligence has no direct 'knowledge about' the ultimate Being—only analogies. We cannot see light, though by light we can see things. Statements about God are extrapolations from the knowledge of other things which the divine illumination enables us to know."[8]

To understand Jesus and who He was, you have to first of all understand some fundamental things about His claim to divinity. He did not claim to be God inhabiting a body. He did not claim to be a man with god-like qualities. He claimed to be 100 percent God and at the same time 100 percent man. That has direct and serious implications for how relevant Jesus is in your real life right here and now.

As God, Jesus is the creator. In Genesis 1 we're told, "In the beginning God created the heavens and the earth" (Gen. 1:1). Jesus was there as creator, before and above all things (Col. 1:16–18). Our capacity to create, imagine, dream, and aspire are His gifts to us. His creative energy in us is why we renegades feel this urge to move, to advance, to aspire, and to make this world a better place.

As God, Jesus is ultimate reality. He is truth. He spoke the truth because He is all the truth there is. As God, Jesus is a lover, the ultimate lover. John said in one of his letters that God is love and whoever lives in love, lives in God and God lives in him (see 1 John 4:16). When Jesus claimed to be God, He claimed to be the ultimate personification and demonstration of love. When Jesus claimed divinity, He also claimed to be the ultimate giver. The first verse I learned as a child still holds together today. "For God so loved the world that He gave His only son, that whoever believes in him shall not perish but have eternal life" (John 3:16).

Jesus is God. As creator He is ultimate reality. His love defines love and His life gives life. He was born. He lived. He preached and was arrested for it. He was tried and crucified for the claims He made. He died a horrible death, while dead He went to Hell for three days, then rose from the dead, appeared to people, ascended into heaven, runs the world, is preparing a place, and is coming again in the eastern sky. He was alive, is alive, and will always be alive. Everything related to Him comes alive and stays alive to experience eternal life.

HIS FIVE A.L.I.V.E.'S

Jesus is life. He was alive in the truest and fullest sense, and is still alive, giving life to all who ask. The key to understanding what is still cool is in what He claimed, "I am the way and the truth and the life" (John 14:6). The allure of His aliveness is at the heart of His enduring popularity. To get a handle on this big, epic idea, it helps me to use the word "alive" as an acrostic. His five A.L.I.V.E.'s are; His Authenticity, His Love, His Integration, His Vision, and His Engagement with His creation.

AUTHENTICITY

At the core of what we all want to be is real or authentic. The highest compliment you can give another person is to say, "He/She is the real deal." Collectors pay obscene amounts of money for sports memorabilia because it's authentic. Why? Because real is rare. It can't be faked or conjured up.

This incident helps illustrate the kind of authenticity Jesus has. The founder and CEO of a multi-national multi-billion dollar company entered a crowded conference room late. Anxious to get on with the meeting, he plopped into the chair nearest the door. One of his young assistants, eager to make a good impression, stood up and said, "No, no, you're supposed to sit over here at the head of the table." "Young man," replied the CEO, "wherever I sit is the head of the table." This captures the idea of Jesus' authenticity perfectly. Wherever He is, that's the place you want to be. Jesus said, "I am the Alpha and the Omega, the Beginning and the End. To him who is thirsty I will give to drink without cost from the spring of the water of life" (Rev. 21:6).

Jesus was a completely self-centered and perfect person. For Him, self-centeredness is a virtue, not a vice. He existed before He was born and said so: "I tell you the truth before Abraham was born, I am" (John 8:58). It's not that Jesus just *claimed* to predate Abraham; He actually did and does. Lots of people claim to have lived before this life, but Jesus claimed to live before all life. He also claimed to live on into the future (see Rev. 2:6).

Jesus was real. He was no poser. He didn't pretend. He didn't have to. Many products are designed to imitate the real thing. There is plastic decking which looks like real wood. Vinyl flooring has the appearance of ceramic tile. You can purchase fake fur, phony jewelry, and expensive hairpieces. The purpose behind all of these items is fairly obvious.

There are imposters among us. Phony preachers try to pass themselves off as prophets of God. Religion can be misconstrued as spiritual achievement. Bumper stickers with fish on them are considered evangelism. Cool music often covers up a cold heart. Moralistic or political ranting and raving is passed off as prophetic preaching. Christian clichés crowd out biblical truth. A perky, positive personality can be mistaken for a Spirit-filled life. In contrast, Jesus makes us authentic versions of ourselves.

For decades, Coke has flooded the airwaves with commercials aimed at getting our attention, then our allegiance. Through the years, the one mantra they keep coming back to is, "Coke is the real thing." Why, because there is so little in life that is real, enduring, and authentic. Jesus is the real deal. You could say Jesus was an original and you would be right. Unlike anyone before or since, Jesus was authentic. His words carried enormous weight because He Himself is the word (see John 1).

LOVING

Jesus was uniquely loving. He blew away the old paradigm of love and replaced it with a new one. Jesus said, "Greater love has no one than this, that he lay down his LIFE for his friends" (John 15:13, emphasis mine). According to Jesus, love is a verb. It's not an emotion or a pit you fall into. Love acts on behalf of the one it loves. Love is giving and sacrificial. What makes it a scandal is that Jesus talks about a new, unique, wild, and irrational way that I am loved by God. Jesus came to love me in a way I could never have deserved or even hoped for.

Jesus revealed He came to earth to love us back to life, then to God. This is a cardinal point to the Christian faith. My attempts at loving God produce nothing more than religious fever. Jesus' radical message was that God came to love me. Loving me back to life meant Jesus would lay down His innocent life to redeem my guilty one. This is crazy enough, but what really rips the wheels off the bus is what Jesus claimed: "No one takes it from me, but I lay it down of my own accord. I have authority to lay it down and authority to take it up again" (John 10:18). He loved because He could. He came to earth because He wanted to. He died for the privilege of loving us; the innocent dying to let the guilty go. This is a crazy notion! Jesus' love was uncivilized.

Because of Jesus' love, we now know what we could never have known on our own; we are loved, in the words of the old Protestant hymn, "Just as I am." This love is a dazzling and dangerous love. It produces real transformation wherever it's unleashed. More than sixty years ago, H. Richard Niebuhr indicted American Christianity by saying we worship, "A God without wrath [who] brought men without sin into a kingdom without judgment through the ministrations of a Christ without a cross." Jesus, the just one, dying on the cruel cross for the unjust ones is unacceptable to many world religions. In Islam, for example, Jesus does not die on the cross because such a fate is considered unfitting for a prophet of Allah. By Hindus and Buddhists, Jesus is often regarded as a spiritual master, but the story of His suffering and death are considered unbecoming of an enlightened sage. Like the Buddha, the truly liberated transcend suffering and death. But Jesus submits to it—willingly, motivated by love alone. The just dying for the unjust.

In the book, *Bono,* the lead singer of U2 said, "Grace defies reason and logic. Love interrupts, if you like, the consequences of your actions, which in my case is very good news indeed, because I've done a lot of stupid stuff. It doesn't excuse my mistakes, but I'm holding out for grace. I'm holding out that Jesus took my sins onto the cross, because I know who I am, and I hope I don't have to depend on my own religiosity."[9]

INTEGRATED

Jesus was perfectly integrated. He was fully fit together. Since Adam, the earth never supported the weight of a man who was everything He should and could be until Jesus. He never knew a day when He was in conflict between what He should have been and what He was. Unlike the rest of us, He lived without sin. His life was friction-less. By friction I mean no opposition ever existed between what Jesus said and what He did. What He believed always showed up in His behavior. There was never a day when Jesus wasn't fully what He ought to have been. Everything the Father wanted, He wanted too and was willing to pay the ultimate price.

There was no breakage in His life whatsoever. He was consistent in both His words and His actions. He was perfect in His person, purpose, and priority. He said, "My nourishment comes from doing the will of God who sent me, and from finishing his work" (John 4:34, LB). Even Peter, the big burley, loudmouthed fisherman, who no doubt watched every move Jesus made and hung on every word He uttered privately and publicly, said, "He committed no sin, and no deceit was found in his mouth" (1 Pet. 2:22).

Never since have we seen a man who was totally everything, at all times, and without exception everything He should have been. He always did what He should have done, in the way it should have been done, and for the right reasons. Not one scintilla of misalignment was there even during times of scalding temptation. His words and work, His methods and motives, His message and His motivation, all were perfect. No law in the land could find a flaw in Him. And even when people were paid to lie and accuse Him unjustly, Pilate (no friend to faith or Jesus) had to say, "I find no fault in Him."

VISION

Jesus had a kingdom vision. He was a revolutionary who saw the world as it was and how it should be. After all, He was the architect. He drew the plans. He knew where the deviations were from the original and He came to be what Isaiah promised, "the prince of peace." The world into which Jesus was born was brutal, violent, and warlike (not unlike our world today). Corruption was pandemic and life was cheap. Oppression of the common man was commonplace. Poverty made lives miserable. He was born in a time of Roman domination and heavy taxation. It was a time of unrest and rebellion in Israel, for the Jews never wore well the harness of a foreign master. It was a time of political intrigue where kingdoms were made and lost in the span of a few years. Inflation was rampant, crime was viral, and hope was futile. Survival wasn't just day-to-day, it was hour-to-hour.

Though Jesus conducted His life and ministry in relative obscurity, it became clear He had a unique vision of the future. He envisioned the value of a single human life, in dominant culture where human life was a ubiquitous commodity. Everywhere He went, He touched people at the point of their deepest need. He focused on the individual. He spoke to growing crowds, but more times than not, He dealt with individuals, either healing them or giving them a word of love and direction while others looked on in amazement. Jesus envisioned a kingdom where love was lord, and every life was precious to God. People mattered to Jesus; therefore they must matter most to us.

He envisioned a new kind of community He called the Church, and He promised this revolutionary community would assail the very gates of hell, or as some translate, death itself would not prevail against it.

Today the Church, Jesus Christ's unique vision, has spread all over the entire world with billions of adherents even two thousand years after His life. Jesus often envisioned the future with amazing accuracy. The New Testament tells us in the future there will be wars and rumors of war, there will be natural catastrophes, nation will rise up against nation, governments will continue to rise then fade away. And yet Jesus' vision for the church (the Renegade Nation) remains.

He envisioned His kingdom covering the earth. Not a kingdom of thrones, with boundaries on a map guarded by guns and diplomatic treaties, but a kingdom bringing people together heart, mind, and soul. He envisioned a place called heaven where real life would begin after this life was over.

He promised eternal life. He guaranteed His own aliveness would one day make all death and dying a distant memory. It would be a perfect place of peace and harmony where God the Father would walk among us. He envisioned an existence so far beyond our imaginations that human descriptions of heaven do it no justice. Streets of gold, and walls of jasper simply exhaust the meaning of mere words to describe their reality. Jesus envisioned real people, giving real hope to real people facing life and death in the real world.

ENGAGING

Consider the ramification of this statement, "We love because he first loved us" (1 John 4:19). All of the love we see expressed today is a result of this wild, crazy, cool love of the totally alive person—Jesus. Though He had every right to be, Jesus was not touchy, condescending, or standoffish. He loved people. He engaged people in conversations about common everyday subjects. He welcomed interaction even with people who were considered pariahs. He enjoyed being with people—common people, ordinary people. His disciples are proof positive He was not enamored with the upper class or those who had positional power. When Jesus called His disciples, He said, "Come and follow Me and I will make you fishers of men" (Matt. 4:19). Not only did He engage with people, He wanted His followers to understand that people were the priority of their ministries too.

At the end of His life, before He ascended back to heaven, Jesus gathered His disciples together and gave them what we call "The Great Commission," to go into all the world and preach the Good News to all creation. Jesus was far more than a teacher. He was a revolutionary. Something of the same idea as Robert Frost conveyed when he said, "I'm not a teacher, but an awakener." Jesus was the One who awakened the world to a new day and greater reality. He gave the only enduring rumor of hope, which exists to this very day.

Think of the audacity to believe that Jesus is God come down to human level to engage us at the point of our need. Think of it, the ultimate insider of all eternity, the Lord of Lords, Himself, came down into our brokenness, to empty Himself and then extend the life of God through a baby and then a young boy, and a carpenter, an itinerant preacher, and then one brutally beaten and crucified—all for the love of you and me.

He died not to fix us, but to bring us back to life, to allow His aliveness to animate our spirits. His aliveness, His realness, and His mission left an impression on this tiny globe, which continues shaping as you read these words, now over two thousand years.

3

I DON'T WANT TO BE BETTER, I WANT TO BE DIFFERENT

YOU CAN STOP TRYING TO BE GOOD ENOUGH FOR GOD

The closest to perfection a person ever comes
is filling out a job application.

—*Unknown*

I'm not Mother Teresa, but I'm not
Charles Manson either.

—*Boxer Mike Tyson*

Tennessee voters were finally going to get to decide for or against a State Lottery. Our bordering states already had one. We were losing precious tax revenue as people drove over the state line to do their shopping and buy their lottery tickets. The argument seemed simple enough, but of course it wasn't. Is it ever?

Not everyone thought the lottery was a good idea. As you might guess, the most vocal opponents were the various religious groups across the state. Denominational groups lined up alongside other anti-lottery groups. TV and print ads as well as billboards dotted the landscape warning of the impending and certain demise of our state if gambling got a foothold. Here we went again, the churches spending what precious little influence we had left in the public square betting on the wrong horse.

Lined up behind the "church sponsored" push to defeat the lottery were some pretty impressive names. Because the church I founded is one of the largest in town (and maybe because I am considered a renegade) they sent one of their biggest guns to see me. He was a well-known and much-celebrated Christian businessman. He was well connected in our state, so I was a little flattered and quite intimidated when we finally sat down face to face in my office.

Our meeting started out friendly enough. He complimented me on the success of planting and growing a mega church. He told me of the good reputation I garnered in the community. He reminded me that with influence comes the responsibility to use it wisely. I totally agreed, but I knew he was buttering me up for what was coming next.

He voiced his concern that I had not publicly come out on either side of the current controversy. He rattled off an impressive list of real reasons why the lottery would be bad for Tennessee, and honestly, I found myself agreeing with most everything he said. He then asked if I would give him and his associates all or part of our four weekend services in order to inform people of the evils of the lottery and enlist their support in opposing it. I dreaded what came next, but a line had been crossed and the Renegade in me had to respond. I politely and gently explained this was not the right fight for us. He argued the church must hold the moral high ground and fight for the right against the precipitous encroachment of gambling. He followed up by showing me an impressive list of churches and church leaders who were already actively opposing this evil. I'd be lying if I said I wasn't thoroughly intimidated, but by now I was mostly mad and getting madder.

Running out of ways to be nice, I got down to the core issue. I said, "OK, I will give you the entire weekend to make your case if you can guarantee me every person you convert to an anti-lottery stance will get into heaven because of it." He said, "I can't make that kind of promise." I said, "Then why would you, a Jesus guy, want to turn the gospel of God's grace into a message of moralism?" He said, "I guess the rumors are true about you." I said, "Depends on what they are." He said, "You'll do anything to gather a crowd and get a hearing." To which I said, "Absolutely!" With that, the meeting was over. I lost a friend, but I struck a blow against "Christ-ianity," the religious elites' effort to substitute God's radical grace for mere moralism. Good works should never be confused with the good news. One makes the other unnecessary. Rather than trusting the gospel to work in the real world, moralists are out working hard for the gospel. They are trying to do for God what He can alone do for us. The Bible says, "All over the world this gospel is bearing fruit and growing, just as it has been doing among you since the day you heard it and understood God's grace in all its truth" (Col. 1:6). This describes what we would call today—viral marketing.

THE RISE OF "IANITY"

My good buddy Vinnie said to me, "Dave, I love the 'Christ-thing' but it's the 'ianity' that keeps getting in the way." Amen and I agree, but this is what religion does so well. It makes me the cause and cure of the world's current calamity while reducing Christ to a distant, disapproving, disappointed bystander. When this happens, we end up talking about such high-sounding concepts as "biblical world-view" and "Christian values" and a lot of other catch phrases, which muddy up the real issue. How did the pure essence of Jesus get so twisted and tainted? Does *just* Jesus bore us or scare us to death?

Historians estimate Christians numbered about 1,000 by AD 40. This number grew to over six million by AD 300. From there, what began as an obscure Jewish sect exploded into a worldwide movement. Ultimately, it proved stronger than the state, who, unable to stamp it out with persecution, drew it in close and made the church its ally.

Kenneth Scott Latourette said, "Never in so short a time has any . . . set of ideas, religious political, or economic, without the aid of physical force or of social or culture prestige, achieved so commanding a position in such an important culture."[1]

Christianity spread, primarily as a "network phenomenon" through family and friendship webs. The early apostles weren't anchored, but traveled widely and became links between forming communities. Local, part-time amateurs ran individual congregations. Add to this the fact that Constantine was proclaimed Emperor of Britain in 306. Within the next six years he gained control of Gaul and Spain.

Constantine turned his attention to his rival Maxentius. As he led his army south for battle, Constantine saw a vision of the cross superimposed on the sun and above the words *In hoc signo vince*—"Conquer in this sign." He crossed the Alps and marched on Rome. After a decisive battle against overwhelming odds at Milvian Bridge (where his troops marked their own shields with the sign of the cross), Constantine issued the "Edict of Milan" putting an end to the persecution of Christians and providing Christianity with full legal recognition.

Christianity was granted favored status, which meant massive amounts of state funding previously channeled to the pagan temples were now funneled into the church. Awash with public money, humble structures gave way to magnificent public buildings. Constantine built the Church of St. Peter in Rome modeled on the basilica form used for imperial throne halls. The See of Rome received extensive land endowments and an imperial residence for the Bishop and his growing staff.

Church leaders, once recruited from the ranks of the faithful and sustained by voluntary offerings, suddenly became men of power, status, and wealth. They went from God's service to civil service with the stroke of a pen. The result was a stampede into the "ministry" by the sons of the aristocracy eager for privilege and exemption from taxation.

Constantine took an active role in crafting the church of his liking. He presided over church councils and involved himself in theological disputes. The Church honored its part of the arrangement by praising Constantine as the model Christian emperor, the "friend of God" who "frames his earthly government according to the pattern of the divine original" (Eusebius). No mention is made of the fact this model Christian emperor had murdered his father-in-law, wife, and son.

Why would sun-worshipping Constantine be interested in an alliance with Christians? According to the historian Tertullian, Christianity was gaining such widespread influence that "the subversive sect" could easily take over the empire by force if it continued its burgeoning growth. Whatever his true motives were, Constantine co-opted Christianity for his own political purposes. Its ideology fitted neatly into the aims of his state. A marriage of convenience with the bride of Christ and the state, as history proves, is an unholy union which has served only one side well.

Christianity grew dramatically as a state religion. But most of these new converts were nominal Christians at best. The church's rolls were artificially inflated and its ranks bloated with forced conversions. As historian Rodney Stark said, "From a popular mass movement, supported by member donations and run by amateurs and poorly paid clergy, under Constantine Christianity was transformed into an elite organization, lavishly funded by the state and bestowing wealth and power on the clergy. Thereupon church offices became highly sought by well-connected men, whose appointments greatly reduced the average Christian leader's level of dedication."[2]

With this shift, the nature of the Christian "mission" changed. Love, sacrifice, and a persuasiveness of a changed life were replaced by coercion, legal decree, and threats as techniques of conversion. Dissent was not tolerated; therefore the renegade spirit was quailed. The Church now wielded the sword of the state, as it identified itself with Graeco-Roman civilization. By AD 500, the vast majority within the empire reluctantly called themselves Christian, not for love, but by fear.

The new leadership of the Church had no interest in taking the Gospel to the "barbarians" beyond the empire. The revolution of radical Jesus morphed into a civilized Christian network for the purposes of command and control. The responsibility for missions was now limited to the dedicated few within the monastic movement. The dominant method was to reproduce the model of Constantine's conversion through the baptism of kings and the imposition of the Christian faith by force. There are stories of conquered armies converted to Christians by marching through rivers symbolizing baptism. This man-made model of mission lasted for over a thousand years. It's got to go and we must return to the revolution. But one of our greatest threats is not hedonism, but moralism.

THE MENACE OF MORALISM

Understanding the historical realities of the rise of Christianity wouldn't be complete without understanding the power of the renegade spirit that, by the providence of God, rises to call the church back to her only Lord and lover—Jesus. Tragic stories of compromise and capitulation are offset by the heroic renegades who dared call Christianity back to her roots. Names like Augustine, Calvin, Knox, Luther, Swingli, Whitefield, Wesley, Torrey, and Graham remind us that God will not abandon the gospel to the scourge of religious moralism. He has always had and will continue to raise up mighty R4G's who love Jesus and the Gospel of God's hope more than power, popularity, or privilege.

I believe we are today at another epic moment where moralistic, man-centered, rule-based religion must be unmasked. As noble and high-sounding as moralists can be, they must not be allowed to turn the sacrifice of Jesus into a sad story of good intention gone too far. If there exists the slightest possibility that morality can fix what's wrong with us, then Jesus is an utter joke.

The dictionary defines a moralist as one concerned with regulating the morals of others. True goodness cannot be legislated. The hunger of holiness gushes up like a hunger or thirst from within. Therefore a new heart, not a longer list of "do's" and "don'ts," is what we need. Short of radical heart surgery, we remain bound, bored, and broken while sitting inside church buildings week after week, year after year. Christian Moralism is rotting the church in America from the inside out. Why? It's sterile and self-defeating.

Spike Lee, the gifted movie director, released his critically acclaimed film in 1989 titled *Do the Right Thing*. It sounds good, doesn't it? Do the right thing and life will turn out all right for you. The problem with the idea of Christian do-gooders is two-fold. First, who decides what is right for whom? Not all Christians agreed on the lottery question. There are so many right things to do. How can you do all the right things or enough of the right things? God only gave us Ten Commandments and all we can agree on is that we know people who are breaking more of them than us.

This brings up the second problem: how good is good enough for God? And if you do enough of the right things for a long enough period of time, what do you get for it? The Scriptures seem clear on this point: "a man is not justified by observing the law, but by faith in Jesus . . ." (Gal. 2:16). Doing good is a good thing, but it is not enough because you can never do enough.

Let's say you always drive your car on the right side of the road. You always obey the posted speed limits. You buckle your seat belt and you keep your car in perfect working order. For twenty-five years, you've had an impeccable driving record. You've even received awards for your exemplary driving skills. But, one night and only for a split-second, you fall asleep at the wheel. Across the median you go, head-on into a car full of kids on their way to their senior prom. Push pause on this scene and ask yourself this question: "In the next second, people will die because of my momentary lapse. Does my twenty-five-year perfect driving record exempt me and the kids in the other car?" The answer of course is no! And this truth is the awful lie of moralism. Perfection is an awful prison, which shackles the soul and chains the spirit in shame and despair.

Let's say you get married. You took your time to find "Mr. Right," you courted honorably. You both went to pre-marital counseling and abstained from sex until your wedding night. You do all the do-right-things for years, but one day your spouse walks out on you without so much as a reason, a warning, or a good-bye. Don't you deserve better? But there is nothing you can do to change things. What if you work hard for thirty years, building up the company for which you work, can you be guaranteed you will never be laid off and turned out to pasture? Jesus was clear when He warned that doing the right thing could actually get you in more trouble than doing the wrong thing; look where it got Him.

In His famous Sermon on the Mount, Jesus said, "For I tell you that unless your righteousness surpasses that of the Pharisees and the teachers of the law, you will certainly not enter the kingdom of heaven" (Matt. 5:20). With this, Jesus set the moral goodness bar out of reach for us all. He didn't condemn the Pharisees for their good deeds, but He did destroy any hopes that being good could make you right with God or cure what's gone wrong inside. Jesus taught being bad is not our problem; so being good can't be the cure.

The scandal of religion is that it promises what it can't deliver; "good people" go to heaven and "bad people" go to hell. Sounds simple enough, right? But who are the good people and who are the bad people? It was so much easier when they wore black and white hats.

In the minds of many people, the church has become a hotel for the holy. It is what I call the church of "Mr. & Mrs. Do-Right." Good people go to church to get better at being good. No need for thinking or meditating, for all of life's dilemmas will be solved by the end of a thirty-minute sermon. According to "them" there is no need to ponder the big questions because they are your moral conscience. You don't have to bother with researching both sides of a political issue; they'll tell you who to vote for. In religion, the ordained decide what's virtuous and what's not. Your opinion is handed to you—signed, sealed, and delivered in weekly worship. How quaint.

Morally, we Christians are failing big time. A recent survey revealed Christian kids were more likely to download music illegally from the Internet than non-Christian kids. Christian couples are just as likely to divorce as non-Christian. A well-known movie mogul said Hollywood couldn't afford to make movies with violence, vulgarity, and nudity if Christians didn't attend.

Does this surprise you? It shouldn't because accepting the role of "moralist" places the church on the wrong playing field. The role of moral watchdog places the church in competition with TV for the attention of the American public. And the church is losing.

Oprah, Dr. Phil, Geraldo, and others define what is normal and what is not for millions of Americans. These shows are interesting, fast-paced, and provocative. They even have short breaks, called commercials, so you can go to the bathroom or to the kitchen for a snack. Why should anyone rise early, on one of their rare days off, to attend a dull church service, with dragging music, and listen to a boring sermon on how we ought to "be good" and "play nice"? The church of "Mr. & Mrs. Do-Right" is being out-classed, because it is out of its league.

Since Jesus is our Lord, virgin births and resurrections are our specialty. Religion offers padded pews and potluck dinners; Jesus offers the cross and an empty tomb. Religion says, "you better be good or God will get you." Jesus says, "come be made different." With religion, you do the dying at the end. With Jesus, you die up front and get it out of the way. His message is not "obey" but "trust." His awesome, awe-inspiring aliveness is available for the taking. You can't earn it, barter for it, or buy your way in. The J-life can't be inherited from your parents or put on and taken off like a cheap Sunday suit. It's like a tattoo on your heart; the ink is permanent and the mark is forever.

Let TV talk-shows debate the hottest moral topic, but let the renegade nation be a place where Jesus is lifted up. Let the civilized church traffic in denominational minutia. Let us be a Christ-centered, people-loving, mission-driven, and world-changing church without wires or walls. Let the church of Jesus be an open, welcoming community of faith, rather than a closed, judgmental, legalistic composite of "do-gooders." Let those who have been made different by Jesus inspire greatness by our love in action. Let the church be the stream out of which flow the thinkers, dreamers, and builders who move into the mainstream committed to classic ideals like truth, beauty, love, and honor. Let the church's truth be Jesus, her ethic His love, and her morality gratitude.

GOD CAN'T BE

The real menace of moralism is that it perpetuates an unreality about life and God. This lie says, if you were a better person, God could and would be better to you. If you were more like Moses, David, Peter, James, and John, then a limitless supply of material blessing would flow from heaven to you. Material things or lack thereof become the barometer of God's blessings. Yet the Scriptures are clear. "Watch out! Be on your guard against all kinds of greed; a man's life does not consist in the abundance of his possessions" (Luke 12:15).

Good works are fine things, but remember they can't appease God. The Scriptures warn, "It is a fearful thing to fall into the hands of the living God" (Heb. 10:31). Sooner or later you're going to stand face to face with a perfect God. At any moment death could usher you into the presence of God. That's reality, but must you live in constant dread of that day? Must you be afraid you've not done enough to appease God's anger? The religious answer is *absolutely*; that's why you'd better be a faithful churchattendee or at least a member. The Jesus answer is, *not another day do you need to doubt you're standing with God.*

The reality is you are living in a moral and spiritual deficit every moment of every day of your life. It's like using a credit card for which you've never received a monthly bill. After a while you assume this must be a magic card because you just keep charging stuff with it and no bill ever comes due. But one day you open up your mailbox and there you see it—the dreaded credit card billing statement. You lay it aside for a day or so, dreading the reckoning that's due. You open it. You stare at the amount owed and wonder, *how in the world could I have charged this much?* Then it dawns on you. *I can never pay this off.*

Truth—you owe God a debt you can never begin to pay off with your good works. You owe God and the account is coming due and He can't be appeased. So if goodness is the payment for entrance into heaven, you're screwed—end of story. So have a great time for at least what's left of your life.

Good works are wonderful things, but remember they won't make God indebted to you. God can't be obligated to love you. To act as though He has need of anything from us is blasphemous. Moralism is the man-centered myth, which shrinks God to the point where He actually owes you. Imagine the creator a beggar of His own creation. This doctrine of obligation makes good intentions the deciding factor in all moral and spiritual realities. I get to choose how God will be. I get to choose whether or not I will answer for my life and what the circumstance and consequences of my accounting will be. I've been good . . . God owes me.

To be honest, religion does sound logical, doesn't it? If you're good, God is good back. If you're not, He's not. Simple, safe, and easy to understand and even easier to manipulate. You get what you deserve. I must admit it sounds pretty fair to me. But life isn't fair. God isn't fair. Love is not fair. Jesus dying my death, paying my debt, and bearing my sin isn't fair, but it is love. And it is the lack of this love for which our world is dying. We crave to be loved as we are, not as we ought to be.

The obvious problem here is that you can't obligate love! You can feed it, give it away, enjoy it, grow it, show it, or refuse it, but you cannot demand it. As the Scriptures clearly teach, "I will have compassion on whom I have compassion." It does not, therefore, depend on man's desire or effort, but on God's mercy (Rom. 9:15–16). That's scandalous, isn't it? How dare God choose whom He will and will not love! His love leaves you with nothing to contribute and maybe that's the real rub. We want to earn our own way so we create a pay-as-you-go religion, but God will have none of it.

As a kid I remember hearing my friends say, "What your mother doesn't know won't hurt her." I think grown-ups adopt this same kind of infantile philosophy when it comes to God. We think, if I ignore God, or act as though He doesn't exist, He can't see me. If I act small and keep my nose clean, maybe I can just slip on by. If I put on a big smile and a happy face, God won't look deep into my heart and unmask my pain, my sin, or my loneliness. And if ignoring God won't work, maybe I can postpone the appointment to another time when I've got my act together.

Here's the Gospel truth, there will never be a day better than today to turn and face God. Today's the day of salvation. Religion is spelled "someday" while the Gospel is spelled "today." As an act of faith you can reach out and exchange all your sin and shame for His aliveness, love, grace, and future. What does He demand in exchange for His pardon? He wants your garbage! Not your pitiful promises to "do better" or "never do it again." Confess. Come clean. Admit your utter helplessness when measured by His holiness. Do this and you will never need to cower in a corner or walk in darkness. Become an R4G and live the joy-filled, freed up life. Remember, religion is spelled "try." The J-life is spelled "trust."

Religion is what you do for God, while the J-life is what God has done for you. You can't earn it by trying to be a better version of the old you.

DEFINING "CHRISTIAN"

Words have a way of morphing and losing their meaning over time. This is certainly true of the word "Christian." When someone says, "I'm a Christian," you can't automatically assume you know where they're coming from. For some people, Christian is a way of hyphenating things to make them safe for consumption. As a result, we have entire niche markets for Christian-music, Christian-art, and Christian-novels. For others, "Christian" is a political statement. Maybe the best way to clarify what it is, is to contrast it with what it is *not.*

When I say I'm a Christian, I'm not advancing an ancient European religious system. I'm not into rule-based religion drenched in dry doctrinal distinctions, which have no relation to reality. Religion is small and restrictive. It divides people. It draws the circle small, to shut the wrong kind of people out. Christianity draws the circle large to include as many as possible. Jesus said, "Whosoever will let him come drink freely from the water of life" (Rev. 22:17). John Greenleaf Whittier said, "From the death of the old, the new proceeds and the life of truth from the death of creeds." When I say I'm a Christian. I'm not advocating allegiance to a set of assumptive traditions. As the Scriptures command, "Test everything. Hold on to the good" (1 Thess. 5:21).

Something can be labeled Christian and not be true. And yet so many people assume if it has "Christian" on the label it's safe without filtering through the test of truth. Christianity is a noun, not an adjective. It is all and always about the real Jesus the Christ. Jesus, not some idea about Him or some delineated theory from His teachings, is the way to truth and life. Jesus is a real living person who can be experienced in this "now" moment in this "here" place.

When I say I'm a Christian I'm affirming all truth is God's truth. Paul boldly proclaimed:

> *. . . I have been sent to bring faith to those God has chosen and to teach them to know God's truth—the kind of truth that changes lives—so that they can have eternal life, which God promised them before the world began—AND HE CANNOT LIE.*
>
> —Titus 1:1–2, LB, emphasis mine

He taught Titus, one of his young protégés, to teach them only God's truth—the truth that changes lives and brings eternal life.

Christians love truth because all truth is God's truth. So we never need fear the truth wherever we find it or wherever it leads us. Truth never has to be feared or denied, just confronted and embraced. As an R4G, you never shut yourself off from truth no matter from where or from whom it comes. The ancient philosopher Confucius is credited with saying, "Thus absolute truth is indestructible. Being indestructible, it is eternal. Being eternal, it is self-existent. Being self-existent, it is infinite. Being infinite, it is vast and deep. Being vast and deep, it is transcendental and intelligent." Truth is a real person—Jesus.

When I say I'm a Christian, I'm confessing I worship Jesus, the

God-man who lived in history, but was not bound by it. His birth fulfilled prophecy and in His life He defeated demons, and at His death He satisfied the righteous demands of God's law. He lived and died and rose to live again. He was not murdered, but willingly laid down His life and then had the power to take it up again. When I cry out from the darkness of my frustration and futility, "What a wretched man I am! Who will rescue me from this body of death?" (Rom. 7:24), Jesus answered, "I will." and He did. He set me free and led me back to the Father. It is Jesus who promises me all things will be made right and I will be safe. He assures me of the Father's love and welcomes me to the bounty of my Father's table. In Him, I am adopted into God's forever family. Because of Him, I dare call God—Daddy.

THE MAJESTY OF REAL

Herman Melville made an impact on the world with his novel *Moby Dick.* His great-great grandnephew is making an impact today with music. Richard Melville Hall, known as Moby, has seen great success in the music world. His 1999 album, *Play,* went platinum; his single, *Go,* was named one of the "200 Essential Rock Recordings" by *Rolling Stone* magazine. MTV described Moby as "infamous for his devout, radical Christian beliefs, as well as his environmental and vegan activism." In an interview with Darren Philip, Moby describes the universal need for God:

> *One of my favorite quotes is, "Those who are sick are in need of a doctor." And the sad thing is we're all sick. It's part and parcel of the human condition, and it's especially part and*

parcel of living in the United States in the 21st century. We're all sick. We're all deeply unhappy, disconnected, unwell people. We need each other, and we need God. And if God made the universe and if God made us and if God made the world, it just makes sense to invite God into our lives and ask him, "You made me—what should I be doing?"[3]

Moby makes the point that we are all on a search for life as God intended. Everyone is somewhere on the road to real; either going to it or away from it. Jesus is real while moralism is an enemy of real. Jesus is the author of real and its champion. If good morals get me to God, Jesus was a joke and we should outlaw "Amazing Grace" and install lie detectors on every seat in every church in the land.

If moralism is spelled "d-o" then real Christianity is spelled "d-o-n-e." That's why Jesus is at the heart of all things Christian and that's why the J-life (the life Jesus gives) is what we pursue. Jesus is the final word on God's opinion of you and me. We've rebelled and walked away from Him and there is a great chasm between us. Because God is love and love always wins, Jesus came to bridge the gap. On the cross, He paid our debt and earned the right to love us.

In Christianity, God does the pursuing. Now that's a radical idea. Yet Jesus said, "The Son of Man came to seek and to save what was lost." Just think of it, the God of heaven has come down in pursuit of you. I remember when I was a kid playing "Hide and Go Seek." I'd find the very best hiding place, one where I just knew no one could find me. And yet, somehow, they always seemed to know where I was. My hiding place was under the kitchen table. What was I thinking, as a kid, to believe that I would be invisible under there giggling and laughing but exposed to the world. Huddled between the legs of a kitchen table is a lousy place to hide. Everyone but me could see me.

Oftentimes we're like that with God. We think we're hiding, but He knows exactly where we are. And why do we hide? Why do we fear the God who loves us and pursues us in Jesus? It's because we've bought—hook, line, and sinker—the whole theology behind religion. And that is, "God is watching." And God is watching to catch you doing something so He can thump you on the head. After all, that's what a touchy God looking down from heaven likes the best, punishing sinners, right?

In Christianity, God does the dying. It's amazing to think over 400 years before Jesus was born, Isaiah the prophet could say with such accuracy,

> *He was despised and rejected—a man of sorrows, acquainted with bitterest grief. We turned our backs on him and looked the other way when he went by. He was despised, and we did not care. Yet it was our weaknesses he carried; it was our sorrows that weighed him down. He was wounded and crushed for our sins. He was beaten that we might have peace. He was whipped, and we were healed!*
>
> —Isaiah 53:3–5, NLT

Imagine God suffering willingly. Why would He do such a thing? We suffer against our will, but Jesus willingly came and bore our sorrows. We go out of our way to run from discomfort, yet God bore our pain and punishment willingly. Oswald Chambers said, "Jesus Christ did not come to teach men to be holy, he came to make men holy. His teaching has no meaning for us unless we enter into his life by means of his death. The cross is the great central point." We enter into life by means of His death. Jesus, the loved dying for the unloved, the sinless dying for the sin-stained, the ultimate insider dying for the outsiders. He is our entrance, our equalizer, the place where brokenness becomes beauty, pain becomes pleasure, and religion becomes relationship.

One day soon you will stand before God and give an accounting for your life (see Heb. 9:27). Religion says it will go easier for you if you rehabilitate yourself. So from a religious point of view, Christianity is a sin management program. Sinning less is a good thing, but it's not the answer; your sins are not your problem. Our trouble is not the sins we commit. Our defect is we are able to sin at all. We don't sin because we have to, we do it because we like it. We want to sin; it feels good for a while. Even when our sin is killing us, we go back to it over and over again. We're broken and fractured in our soul. We are sin prone, not God prone. Sin has cut a deep swatch into our hearts and our personalities. Therefore, this is why it has a place in our everyday lives. This dreaded spiritual disease affects us all. It doesn't matter where you were born or the conditions under which you were born. You are a sinner both by birth and by choice.

I often wonder where sin resides within each one of us. In our therapeutic society, we're told it results from the denial of equal rights and opportunities. Academics preach that education is the key to our societies' redemption. Psychoanalysis say sin is a religious invention used to describe behavior resulting from familial, economic, or societal breakdowns. But we know it goes much, much deeper than that. Every night, news programs show high-profile cases in which men and women of privilege and power are exposed for committing deep, dark, heinous crimes. No one is immune to the sorrow and suffering that sin rains down on us everyday.

Maybe sin resides somewhere in our genes, deep within our DNA, but we know for sure sin is birthed first in the heart, entertained in the mind, fueled by toxic emotions, and executed in the split second of evil opportunity. And no matter where sin may come from, we all suffer because of it. Sin is destructive, corrosive, and everyone pays for it. Even nature shudders under the weight of sin's cosmic corruption.

Into this benighted, beleaguered world, Jesus came to pierce the darkness. The majesty of Christianity is that God dared come down to pursue us sinners and die for the privilege of taking on Himself our guilt and shame. His death and resurrection provided my atonement with God. Jesus was the promised Lamb of God who bore my shame in His own body (see John 1:29). He was punished so I could go free. What a Savior! What a life! The cross is gross and ghastly but for us R4G's it is our statue of liberty. Down from its isolation and shame reaches the blood-splattered, flesh-shredded, nail-pierced outstretched arms of Jesus. There He is forsaken, suspended between heaven and earth with me on His mind. What a scandal, what a story, what a savior!

In Christianity, God does the pursuing, dying, and the rescuing. One of U2's recent songs is titled, "Stuck in a Moment You Can't Get Out Of." This seems to be an apt description of life in America and the rest of the world these days.

As I write this book, we are now many years beyond the horrible deeds of 9-11. And yet somehow we're stuck and it's hard to move beyond it. Since then, we're at war in Afghanistan and Iraq and people are dying. People wonder if the tsunamis, hurricanes, and earthquakes are signs of the end of the world, as we know it. September 11, 2001 tells us we're not safe anywhere, anytime. Government can't protect us and war is not the answer.

We're looking for someone to save us; a white knight who will ride upon his trusty steed and make everything right again. With all its might and resources, government has failed to save us. Our military, our educators, our scientists, our inventors, our physicians, and our poets are powerless to bring lasting peace. Who will resurrect this dying world? We're looking for solutions and saviors and we have only one—Jesus. He is our advocate interceding for us, for our nation, for our world. The Perfect One is pleading for mercy here on earth. He will never disappoint, never abandon, never leave. His hand is not short, but extends to the far reaches of our need, plowing deep into the pain of our worst tragedies.

It's Jesus who has done the suffering, the searching, the dying, the resurrecting, and the rescuing. He said, "Come unto me all you who labor and I will give you rest." He saves me from my awful thoughts, my anger, and the emptiness of my soul. He adopts me and you into His family as His son. He gives to us a sense of value and significance. I am a trinity of sinner, saint, and son.

WHOEVER TAKES THE SON GETS IT ALL

There once was a fabulously wealthy man who loved his son above all things. To stay close to his son, they began to build an art collection together. Every spare minute, they were out at auctions and sales acquiring rare works of art: everything from Picasso to

Raphael. By the time the Vietnam conflict broke out, they had built one of the rarest, most valuable collections in the world. A letter came one day informing the son he had been drafted. The father offered to pull some strings, but the son felt compelled to serve his country as his father and grandfather did before him.

The son went off to war, but he wrote his dad everyday. One day the letters stopped. The father's worst fears were realized when he received a telegram from the war department informing him his son had been killed while attempting to rescue another soldier. About six months later, there was a knock at the door. A young soldier with a large package under his arm said, "Sir, you don't know me, but I am the man your son saved on that faithful day he died deep in the jungles of Viet Nam. He had already saved many lives that day, and as he was carrying me off the battlefield, he was shot through the heart and died instantly.

"Your son was my friend and we spent many a lonely night 'in country' talking about you and your love for art." The young soldier held out his package and said, "I know this isn't much and I'm not much of an artist, but I wanted you to have this painting I've done of your son as I last remember him." The father tore open the package and fought back the tears as he gazed at a portrait of his one and only son. He said, "You have captured the essence of my son's smile in this painting and I will cherish it above all others." The father hung the portrait over his mantel. When visitors came to his home, he always drew attention to the portrait of his son before he showed them any of the other masterpieces.

When the father died, the news went out that the entire collection was being offered at an exclusive private auction. Collectors and art experts from around the world gathered for the chance of purchasing one of them. The first painting on the auction block was the soldier's modest rendering of the son. The auctioneer pounded his gavel and asked someone to start the bidding. The sophisticated crowd scoffed and demanded the Van Goghs and the Rembrandts be brought forth. The auctioneer persisted. "Who will start the bidding? $200? $100?" The crowd continued to turn up their noses, waiting to see the more serious paintings. Still the auctioneer solicited, "The son! The son! Who'll take the son?" Finally a squeaky voice from the back said, "I'll bid $10 for the son." The bidder was none other than the young soldier the son had died saving. He said, "I didn't come to buy anything and all I have is $10 to my name, but I bid it all." The auctioneer continued seeking a higher bid, but the angry crowd began to chant, "Sell it to him and let's get on with the auction." The auctioneer pounded the gavel and sold the painting for the bid of $10. An eager buyer from the second row bellowed, "Finally, on with the auction." And just then the auctioneer said, "The auction is now officially closed." The hostile crowd demanded to know how after coming all this way could the auction possibly be over? The president of the auctioning company came to the microphone and said, "When I was called to conduct this auction, I was told of a stipulation in the will I could not divulge until now. According to the wishes of the deceased only the painting of the son was to be sold today and whoever takes the son gets it all. So today, for $10 this young man has bought one the world's most priceless art collections and the entire estate in which it is housed—auction closed." And with the swing of the gavel, the crowd sat in stunned silence staring at the young soldier.

The moral of the story is simple. You can stop trying to be good enough for God. If you take the son, you'll get everything else the Father has to offer. It's this simple and yet this sublime: "whoever has God's Son has life; whoever does not have his Son, does not have life. I have written this to you who believe in the Son of God so that you may know you have eternal life" (1 John 5:12–13, LB).

4

WHAT'S SO COOL ABOUT BEING CHRISTIAN?

THE THREE PURSUITS AND SEVEN SURE SIGNS OF THE J-LIFE

The Christian ideal has not been tried and found wanting. It has been found different and left untried.

—*G. K. Chesterton*

The Christian way is horse sense. It is sanity. And anyone who thinks otherwise is a damned fool, and I am not swearing when I say that.

—*Charles Edward Pugh*

Jena was a good kid, raised in a good Christian home. She started going to church at six weeks old. From the nursery, she grew up into a faithful member of the youth group, and one of its top leaders. Jena made a profession of faith, was baptized, and joined the church. She was even a counselor at summer camp for four years. Jena did all the right things and affirmed all the right doctrines. She was the poster child for how a child could turn out if taken to church and kept far away from worldly temptations.

But what Jena's parents and church didn't prepare her for was the real world. Eventually all young girls and boys leave the safety and refuge of the church-world and enter the big, bad real world. For Jena, her crisis of faith came when she opted to go off to a big state university instead of the small local Bible college most of her church friends chose.

For the first time in her life, Jena hung around the cool kids on campus. And for the first time, she ran with kids her age who didn't buy into her naïve small town religion. Everything she thought she believed, they questioned. She had never met educated, sophisticated adult authority figures who not only challenged her beliefs, but poked fun at her naivety. Questions about the reliability and relevance of her faith came from well-read intellectuals and classmates alike. Jena was in a crisis of faith.

Before long, she was reeling from the questions people with a bias toward unbelief kept throwing her way. It wasn't that the questions didn't have answers; Jena just wasn't prepared "to give an answer to everyone who asks you to give the reason for the hope you have" (1 Pet. 3:15). She never had to in her safe church circle.

Even in her new collegiate world, jammed with new friends, new experiences, and new questions, Jena's faith still survived. You don't wipe away a lifetime of good intentions and great memories in a single semester. So what happened one Sunday morning while she was getting ready for church didn't seem like a big a deal at the time. As usual, Jena's roommate was sleeping in. Jena had tried witnessing to her by telling her how important going to church was. But Nancy wasn't raised in church, so going to church while attending one of the South's top party schools wasn't going to happen.

As Jena was leaving for church one Sunday morning, Nancy popped her head out from under the covers. Wiping sleep out of her eyes she said, "Hey, Jen." Jena stopped, and with her hand on the doorknob, turned and said, "What?" In a sleepy, half-awake, hung-over voice, Nancy asked, "Jena, what's so great about being a Christian that makes you want to go to church this early every Sunday?" Though Nancy's question was benign, to Jena it cut like a knife. It was as though a door in her soul had cracked open and a foul-smelling stench had been released. It made her mad and then it made her afraid.

Jena felt a cloud descend over her. She leaned back into the room and said, "Nancy, just go back to sleep, I'm late for church." And she did, but something had awakened in Jena, which wouldn't be bedded back down. It was the question, "What's so great about being a Christian?" The part about going to church wasn't hard. Going to church was what good people do. It's a place where nice people go. Church is where she met all her friends. Church is a good place, a safe place, a moral place.

It was the first part, "What's so great about being a Christian?" for which she didn't have a clear answer. She could say, "It makes me happier." But Nancy was happy partying every night. She could say, "I don't sin anymore." No one would believe that. Try as she might, the question wouldn't go away and she couldn't come up with a good answer. From that day on, Jena stopped bugging Nancy to go to church. Jena was in over her head and she knew it. For Jena, the old assumptions and answers weren't working.

But like the good girl she was, Jena hunkered down and weathered the storm of doubts she was dipped in everyday. Her only hope was to hold out until she could get home and be around the safe people who believed like her.

By the time she got home for Christmas break, her parents noticed the change. They dismissed it to her being away from home so long. Once they got Jena back home into the old routine she would be herself again. But Jena had changed. The questions she had about her faith hung like a log chain around her heart. Doubt, like a cancer, gnawed at the core of who she thought she was. If she seemed distant, it was because her home felt distant and strangely small and parochial. While driving to lunch at the country club after church, Jena's mom broke the silence. "What's wrong, honey? You seemed a little out of it today at service," she said. That was all the opening Jena needed to release what was simmering inside.

Jena looked at her mom and dad with all the sympathy a grateful child can muster just before she's about to break her parents' heart and said, "Mom, Dad, I'm not sure I believe like you guys do anymore." From the front seat her dad retorted, "What do you mean, young lady? Has all this college business gone to your head?" Jena said, "Dad, Mom, this Christian thing may work for you but it doesn't work out there in the real world. All my life I have accepted everything you've told me and everything my church has taught me. But now I'm in a world where it's not so easy to just accept this stuff because it's the way I was raised. I need real answers and real reasons why it's better to be a Christian than not. Did you know Christians have done some horrible things in the name of their religion? As a matter of fact, religion may be the worst thing ever forced on the world. Did you know that? My suite-mate, Nancy, asked me what was so great about being a Christian and I couldn't give her an answer. I feel lost and confused."

In the front seat, Jena's parents sat in stunned silence. What happened to the good little Christian girl they sent away to college just three months before? How could a lifetime of trying to protect her and keep her safe be undone in just a few months away at college? Where had they failed? What were they going to do and what would their friends think once they hear the news? How could they face their church again?

This story and ones just like it are repeated thousands of times every year. Young high school graduates leave home and enter the real world without real reasons why they call themselves Christian. Accepting Jesus as your Savior just because it's all you've ever known won't wash in the real world where religion runs off like cheap makeup in a rainstorm. A relationship with Jesus isn't a matter of agreeing with what we've been told. Jesus is truth experienced in a relationship, which can't be handed down second-hand. It takes first-hand faith for the mind to be renewed and the heart to be reborn. Jesus is too big to be reduced to padded pews and potluck dinners. Crosses, crucifixions, and empty tombs are the signs of a revolution, not kid stories to offset the violence on TV.

Nancy was right to ask Jena the question, "What's so cool about being a Christian?" And Jena was smart enough to know if she couldn't give an answer by now something was wrong. Jena had a religion without real reasons or a conversion experience to go with it. As a result, her religion was more like a ball and chain than roots and wings. The one single reality which makes being Christian cool is that at conversion Jesus' resurrected aliveness is born in us resulting in a new heart, a new life, and a new freedom. The Bible promises, "If anyone is in Christ, he is a new creation; the old has gone, the new has come" (2 Cor. 5:17).

I'm not a Christian because my parents were. My belief in the Bible as truth is my own, not a mindless buy-in to an archaic world-view. Jesus changed my heart and gave me back my brain. Being Christian means the love of Jesus has forever ruined my appetite for lesser truth, cheap love, and plastic religion. I have real reasons for how I am and what I believe, as Pascal said, "The heart has reasons reason knows not of." The bottom line is this: because of who I am and whose I am, I determine what I must do. At the deepest level of my being I have found Jesus to be exactly everything He claimed to be. He has made Himself real to me—heart, mind, and soul.

As a Christian, I'm not just a truth seeker; I'm a product of the truth. My heart has been recreated. My hunger for real life is met in the reality of Jesus. I'm no longer into religion because I'm free and unafraid. Unlike before, when I lived my life to please other people or to make up for what was lacking in me, I determine what I must be, because of whose I am. I am a Jesus guy so I can't be boring, predictable, or narrow-minded. On the contrary, since Jesus is truth, I fear no truth wherever I find it. Since Jesus is love, I fear no person, place, or thing. I am fully and creatively alive and along with Paul I shout, "All things are yours, whether Paul, or Apollos, or Cephas, or the world, or life or death, or the present or the future—all are yours" (1 Corinthians 3:21–22).

CRAZY IN LOVE

I love Eugene Peterson's translation of 2 Corinthians 5:13: "If I acted crazy, I did it for God; if I acted overly serious, I did it for you. Christ's love has moved me to such extremes. His love has the first and last word in everything we do." What a concise, precise explanation of what it means to live like a Christian. We are crazy in love with Jesus because He is crazy in love with us. Love, real love, will do weird things to you. And don't you dare dismiss this as religious quackery. We love going crazy over stuff all the time.

Going crazy for love is one of the coolest human experiences there is. I remember when I was courting my wife, Paula, like it was yesterday. I'd drive by her house just to see if she was home. We would park in the driveway and spend hours just talking. When I'd get home my mother would be waiting and ask me where I'd been. I said, "I've been with Paula, and we've been talking for hours." Mother said, "What did you talk about?" I said, "I don't remember." Because I was crazy in love, the conversation flowed like a river. When we weren't together talking about nothing, we'd be on the phone talking about everything.

That was back during the day when we had the old rotary phones. I remember pulling the rotary dial around to the metal stop and letting it go. I loved the sound each click made as I dialed her number. We would talk endlessly for hours and hours over anything, over everything, and over nothing. I'd lie on the floor, stand, roll over and stand on my head. And when I finally got off at the behest of my parents, they wanted to know what we'd talked about all that time. My response was always, "I don't remember."

How can this be? It's because when you're in love, you live at a place beyond reason and logic. The following observation attributed to Napoleon Bonaparte illustrates this point well:

> *I marvel that whereas the ambitious dreams of myself, Caesar, Alexander, should have vanished into thin air, a Judean peasant, Jesus, should be able to stretch His hands across the destinies of men and nations. I know men; and I tell you that Jesus Christ is no mere man. Between Him and every other person in the world there is no possible term of comparison. Alexander, Caesar, Charlemagne, and I myself have found empires; but upon what do these creations of our genius depend? Upon force. Jesus alone founded His empire upon love; and to this very day millions would die for Him.*[1]

THREE PURSUITS OF THE J-LIFE

Recently, I was watching the *Today* show. One of the hosts, Matt Lauer, was doing a piece on Easter Island. They were discussing the huge Moai statues which weigh many tons each. Matt asked the guide why the people carved the huge rocks in the quarry and then risked breaking them on the way to the building site (which often happened). "Why didn't they move the rocks to where they would be erected and then carve them?" The guide said, "It would probably be very difficult to motivate people to move rocks that had no meaning."

Moving rocks with no meaning describes everyday life in

America. There is no joy in a job you hate, a family you don't see, and a lifestyle you can't afford. After a while you ask, "Why am I doing this? What is my motivation?" These are good questions and they need great answers. I believe they can only be answered in Jesus, which means I need to be able to tell anyone anywhere what's so cool about the J-life. When you see R4G's living free, having fun, and making a difference in the world, you want to know what fills them up with joy and sends them out to the far corners of the world to try to change the world. What kind of life are we advocating? What are we so enthusiastic and excited about? R4G's love their three sacred pursuits. Each one is inexhaustible in its scope and ever-expanding in its allure. They keep drawing me forward into the mystery and the majesty of the J-life (the life Jesus gives).

The first pursuit of the J-life is to know God's heart. It sounds crazy to claim that the infinite God wants me to know Him. Yet that's exactly what He wants. The goal is not information about Him (facts, figures, and probabilities do have their place), but to know the "whys" of His heart. David said, "Open your mouth and taste, open your eyes and see how good God is. Blessed are you who run to Him" (Ps. 34:8, The Message). It's overwhelming to think God wants me, little ole' me, to know His big heart. That He would beckon me into this kind of life is sometimes more than I can contain. It is crazy to contemplate the Lord of Glory would want me to know Him or think He would want to know me. Herman Melville said, "The reason the mass of men fear God and at bottom dislike Him, is because they rather distrust His heart and fancy Him all brain, like a watch." God is love and this reality is at the core of all He does. You can trust His heart even when you cannot trace His hand. With confidence, you can still believe God even when you can't believe what just happened.

God invites you to run to Him to discover for yourself the secret places of His heart. As you do, you will know that "The Lord is good and his love endures forever; his faithfulness continues through all generations" (Ps. 100:5). And though I walk daily through the land of the dying, I will fear no evil, because I know God has me on His heart and will never abandon me. It's when I can't understand circumstances or predict outcomes that I need the confidence of God's motive.

I received a semi-panicky phone call recently from one of my best buddies. He was calling from Buffalo, New York, where his baby daughter was hospitalized with second and third degree burns. A steaming mug of coffee was accidentally dumped on her little head. I wanted to reach out to him and make it right. I asked God, "Why?" and He had the gall to say, "You know why!" I said, "God, I don't know why, that's why I'm asking You why." He said, "You know accidents happen. The laws of physics are going to apply every time scalding liquid falls on tender skin. In the real world, babies get burned, wives get abused, sons die with AIDS, and cancer cuts good lives short. But in the midst of it all, David, you do know My heart. I grieve with you, but it is impossible to suspend the laws of life and for there to be any life left to live." If God intervened and suspended all cause and effect relationships this wouldn't be the real world, it would be heaven. And believe me, God is getting around to that.

In a few days, my buddy's daughter was transferred to the burn unit at Vanderbilt Hospital. His sweet baby girl looked pitiful wrapped up like a miniature mummy. They left enough skin uncovered around her eyes so she could see out. Even though she had plenty of pain medicine, she was fitful and fidgety. She wanted her daddy to pick her up and then put her down. She wanted her pacifier, and then she'd throw it across the room. There was no position she got in which didn't make her squirm, cry, or pitch a fit. But when her daddy laid back and let her crawl up on his chest and snuggle, she calmed down. As long as he cradled her in his arms, with her head dug into his chest, she stopped crying and drifted off to sleep. I was blown away by his daddy patience. He is normally a wild, fun-loving, ready-to-party kind of guy. I saw a side of him I didn't know existed. He has the heart of a father. That day, watching this young dad caring for his burned daughter reminded me again of the calming, healing power of a Father's heart.

So when religious creeds feel like cold stones and Christian platitudes sound like a hollow gourd, God bids me to press deep into His heart. As John R. MacDuff said, "Trust God where you cannot trace Him. Do not try to penetrate the clouds He brings over you. Rather look to the bow that is on it." When I can't understand what's going on around me or see my way ahead, I crawl up onto His mighty chest, lay my head on His shoulder and listen for His heart. His motive is love. His method is grace. His arm is mighty to save, for through experience we have come to believe, "God is our refuge and strength, an ever-present help in trouble. Therefore we will not fear, though the earth give way and the mountains fall into the heart of the sea" (Ps. 46:1–2).

The second pursuit of the J-Life is to trust His love. Logically, one builds on the other. If I know God's heart (His nurture and predictability) I will be more apt to trust His love (His nature and unpredictability). Using my friend as an example, I couldn't have predicted his daughter would be burned, but I could predict he would have acted like a father. When you know the Father's heart you don't hesitate to cry, "Abba-Father." When life hurts and smothers your soul, you know He's already on the move. To know God's heart is to trust His love. To trust His love is to live courageously.

Love is the most powerful force on the planet. God's love created you and me and Jesus' love has redeemed us. Trusting His love is your power to live a bold courageous life from the inside out. As Jesus promised the woman at the well, "Anyone who drinks the water I give will never thirst—not ever. The water I give will be an artesian spring within, gushing fountains of endless life" (John 4:14, The Message). Read that again. The J-life is like having a well dug deep down inside your heart. Out of that well gushes an endless supply of real life. That's why the J-life can't be imitated. It can be experienced and expressed, but like Jena's doubts, surface faith only disappoints, because it has no deep place which can't be stirred or poisoned by surface conditions.

In the outback of Australia, the farms are too big to build fences around. So instead of fences, they dig a well at the dead center of their territory. The well has the one thing their livestock can't live without—water. Isn't it interesting that Jesus claimed to be the water of life? He's the source of our love and our daily bread. He is our rest, our refuge, and our relentless lover. Isn't that what we're craving? Someone to love us most when we deserve it least? In Christ, you've found someone to trust with reckless abandon, "the LORD is good and his love endures forever; his faithfulness continues through all generations" (Ps. 100:5). C. S. Lewis said, "When I have learnt to love God better than my earthly dearest, I shall love my earthly dearest better than I do now. Insofar as I learn to love my earthly dearest at the expense of God and instead of God, I shall be moving toward the state in which I shall not love my earthly dearest at all."[2]

What a beautiful order to the J-life. God invites me to raise the hood, so-to-speak, and know His heart. Then I get to kick the tires as I learn to trust His love. Then after I raise the hood and kick the tires, God welcomes me to the revolution.

The third pursuit of the J-life is to follow wherever He leads. Knowing the heart of God builds faith. Trusting His love creates courage to follow His lead whenever to wherever. The place He wants is my favorite place to be. It may not be the safest. Maybe you've heard people say, "The safest place to be is the center of the will of God." But they would be wrong again for this is a religion's way of relieving you and me from trusting God with the results. All I know is following His lead will mean I need never fear living a wasted life.

Around every corner I turn there is another thing to know, another reason to trust. Follow Jesus wherever He may lead and do whatever He may ask. Wherever God leads me, His love covers me. Whatever I face, He is with me. He's won the battles, but I must act to claim the victory. He has slain the dragons and chained the demons, but I must still get up and walk out onto the field of battle. Though fear may haunt me it can never hurt me unless I give into it. Jesus is my champion, my warrior, and my full-time occupation. He is my ultimate white knight. He leads me onto victory in His name as He whispers in my ear, ". . . take heart. I've overcome the world" (John 16:33).

What's so great about being Christian? Every day is a new adventure. Every moment is a chance to know His heart, trust His love, and follow His lead.

SEVEN SURE SIGNS OF THE J-LIFE

The J-life can't be put on and taken off like a football jersey. It's not going to church, then checking the God-thing off your list for the rest of the week. It's not about "putting on airs" or worrying about what other people might think, like Jena's parents do. It is the alive life; the authentic, loving, integrated, and visionary life. It is Renegade Jesus living in me and through me producing the fruit, which flows up from the root. It is the truth of Jesus' promise.

> *Live in me. Make your home in me just as I do in you. In the same way that a branch can't bear grapes by itself but only by being joined to the vine, you can't bear fruit unless you are joined with me. I am the Vine, you are the branches. When you're joined with me and I with you, the relation intimate and organic, the harvest is sure to be abundant. Separated, you can't produce a thing.*
>
> —John 15:4–5, The Message

The J-life is about being who you really and truly are. It's not fake or forced, it is real. I saw this illustrated when Oprah Winfrey was a guest on *Late Night with David Letterman.* Oprah recounted a story about wanting new glasses when she was thirteen. Her mother said, "No." But Oprah wanted the new glasses so much she faked a robbery, where she was hit in the head, her old glasses were broken, and she was taken to the hospital where she faked amnesia. When Oprah's mother arrived at the hospital and talked to the doctor, he told her, "Someone broke into your home, hit your daughter in the head, and broke her glasses." With suspicion she asked Oprah, "Do you know who I am?" Oprah says, "No, Ma'am, I don't." Her mother said, "I'll give you three seconds to remember, one, two. . . ." Oprah said, "Mother, is that you?" She was busted.

R4G's must never forget who and whose we are. Jesus identified the core sign of the J-life as love. He said, "Your love for one another will prove to the world that you are my disciples" (John 13:36, NLT). In Christ we become authentic and real. The proof of our authenticity and the depth of our reality is seen in how we love people and in not being threatened by them. Love is what makes me look like Jesus. What He looks like in you and me here in America is what He looks like in R4G's living in England, Africa, Asia, or Russia. If Jesus looks like love, what does love look like? There are at least seven sure signs of love expressed in the J-life. They are: honesty, trust, freedom, joy, generosity, humility, and hunger.

HONESTY

The first sign of life is honesty. I'm not talking about the kind that keeps you from stealing my car. I'm talking about the kind of honesty which borders on the heroic because it dares expose the deep, dark places of my heart to God. Without this gut-level openness and honesty, God cannot enter my heart or forgive my sin. Of all the things God can do, creating the world and holding the stars in place, He cannot enter my heart uninvited. I alone hold the key to the one space He longs to occupy most. Coming out of the closet of denial gives God access to the awful feelings of being unloved, unwanted, and unimportant. Instead of being revolted by what He sees, He fathers my orphaned soul.

December 8, 2005 was the twenty-fifth anniversary of the murder of John Lennon. A nobody named Mark David Chapman gunned Lennon down in front of the Dakota building in New York without warning or provocation. All Chapman had to say at the scene was, "I just shot John Lennon." Twenty-five years later Chapman was asked what he thought about on that fateful day. Chapman said, "It was like two trains barreling down the same tracks full-speed. My utter nobodiness collided head-on into his utter somebodiness." How well that describes what lies at the core of our deepest fear. We are petrified that we might be nobodies. So we avoid God and try to fill that void, with all sorts of things legal and illegal, moral and immoral. Over time we accumulate secrets. But here is the problem; we weren't made to keep secrets from God. There is at our heart a God-shaped vacuum and no one or nothing else can fill it.

When I get honest with God the healing begins. As I open up my heart and invite Him in, I experience His love and forgiveness. When that happens I begin to be able to accept Jesus. As I confess my sin and agree with God about how unacceptable my sin is, it begins to lose its grip on me. When I keep secrets, the well dries up. When I get real and come clean, the river flows again. David said, "Create in me a new, clean heart, O God, filled with clean thoughts and right desires. Don't toss me aside, banished forever from your presence. Don't take your Holy Spirit from me. Restore to me again the joy of your salvation, and make me willing to obey you" (Ps. 51:10–12, LB).

R4G's hate pretending to be something we're not. We are genuine souls who jump at the chance to throw away the mask of religious pretense. We're not proud of our own sins and temptations, but we don't hide them from God in shame and self-loathing. Assured of His love, we are free to bear all and not hide in the shadows of deceit like a coward. God knows what a selfish jerk you can be, so the minute you feel overwhelmed with the old desires, confess them to God and trust Him to change your thinking. Honesty is the open door where Jesus' love forgives my sin and stills my inner demons. Forgiveness is freeing. Freedom loves realness and transparency. The R4G's cry is, "if God is for me, who can be against me."

TRUST

The second sign of the J-life is trust. As we will see in the next chapter, trust is the key to everything. Trust grows in the heart that harbors no secrets from God. Since there are no secret sins, hurts, or wounds I'm nursing, trust grows. And where trust grows, there will be courage. Not the lack of fear or intimidation—I'm afraid that never goes away. But if God knows all my dirty little secrets, loves me anyway and accepts me in Jesus, trusting Him for daily bread or mountain-moving intervention is both a privilege and a thrill. Come clean. Take off the mask. Trust God's love. Adam did and God clothed him. Moses did and God used him to rescue a nation. David did and he unified a divided nation. Peter did and he was returned to effectiveness. Paul did and he shook the world. Honesty means that God knows me. Trust means that I know God; they go hand in hand and feed on each other.

FREEDOM

The third sign of the J-life is freedom. Honesty leads to trust and produces freedom. In Christ we are free from the dread of the past, fear of the future, or ulcers in the present. Whatever comes tomorrow has to get through Jesus before it gets to me. Why wouldn't we want to come in nice and close to our loving Savior who forgives our sin, promises His love, and sets us free?

The Scriptures warn us that the fear of man can prove to be a snare. The person living the J-life doesn't use fear or intimidation to get his way. Since Jesus is my peace and my provision, my joy is extending the same grace to others that He so freely extends to me daily. One of the true signs that Jesus is living in and through me is that I love what He loves, hate what He hates, and I want what He wants. Jesus loves people; imperfect people, rich people, poor people, white people and black people, religious people and irreligious people. If that's what He loves, I do too. His love for people as they are then frees me from judging people or defining them by their net worth or lifestyle.

Jesus hates sin. He hates it when a man loses his way and sells his soul for a job, an affair, and the bondage of an addictive habit. He hates it when people choose shame over grace and settle for religion when a relationship with the living God is within reach. He hates it when preachers with personal agendas charge for the free gift of the gospel. But He loves it when people turn from their sin and find love, acceptance, freedom.

This life is too short to waste it pursuing your own agenda. While we're here, let's set as many other people free as possible. Freedom is our joy. You can't contain the J-life to a Sunday morning while sitting in rows of pews looking at the backs of the heads of other people. That's why religious rules and empty tradition hold no sway over us. That's why we dare and dream and aspire. That's why the J-life informs everything we do and empowers how we do it.

JOY

Joy is the fourth sure sign of the J-life. In today's vernacular, we would use the word fun. Call it what you like, joy is attractive. No one wants to hang around sad dogs spreading gloom. Joy is a deep, core presence of wonder and excitement. It's the ability to accept the acceptance of Jesus and feel it actually welling up inside. In Christ there is no condemnation; all is right with the world. Since God knows me by name, loves me without boundary or breaking point, and is at work in my life at this very moment, no wonder I stand a little straighter, exude a gentle strength, and reach out my hand to greet people with a smile. Jesus lives within my heart, therefore, I have no one I fear and nothing to prove. This is the day that the Lord has made and I'm going to honor Him by enjoying it. Storms will come, but they can't steal my joy. Today, a promise made may be broken, a partnership dissolved, but my joy is secure and my soul is intact.

GENEROSITY

The fifth sign of the J-life is generosity. The first Bible verse I learned as a kid was John 3:16, "For God so loved the world that He gave . . ." God is by His very essence generous. In Genesis 1, I learned that God's generosity is displayed in His creative power. He created the world to be an abundant place for you and me to live in and enjoy. His lavish love and faithful generosity are evident every day in a brilliant sunrise or a golden sunset. He gives the rain to refresh the earth and makes life possible.

In John 10:10, Jesus promised us abundant life. Every day without exception, Jesus meets our needs according to His riches in glory. Since He is a giver and I am to be like Him, generosity is the hallmark of my everyday life. The spirit of generosity within stimulates your imaginations so that you can dare live free, have fun, and be agents of change with a message of hope to a world in pain.

Wherever the spirit of greed reigns, you'll see godlessness. Wherever the spirit of scarcity reigns, you'll see the fruits of fear. Wherever the spirit of generosity reigns, you'll see the evidence of Jesus teaching, "Give away your life; you'll find life given back, but not merely given back—given back with bonus and blessing. Giving, not getting, is the way. Generosity begets generosity" (Luke 6:38, The Message).

It's not that we are supposed to be generous; the whole point is that we are able to be generous. Giving, not getting, is our new nature. Generosity includes but is not limited to money. R4G's are generous with time, talents, and treasures. We invest our lives in worthy causes and high ideals. What we don't invest and send on ahead will eventually go back into the box and be left behind. And because generosity is God's nature, nothing can be taken from us that He cannot redeem or restore.

HUMILITY

The sixth sign of the J-life is humility. One of Jesus' most compelling qualities was His steadfast humility. Here was the Lord of Glory, who had legions of angels ready to move on His command, yet He was humble in every situation. He humbled Himself in the midst of His disciples to wash Peter's feet. He humbled Himself before kings and paupers alike. He showed humility in the way He responded to prostitutes caught in the act. He was gentle to tax collectors whose practice of fraud was scandalous and well known. Jesus moved into every situation with great humility. It wasn't that He wasn't strong and capable. It was that His strength was under control.

One of the most beautiful characteristics of the J-life is the humility it produces. Humility is not an insipid niceness or limp-wrist weakness. The humility that characterizes the J-life is the God-given self-confidence which eliminates the need to prove to people the worth of who you are, and the rightness of what you're doing. Jesus was confident in who He was and what He stood for.

As an R4G, I am strong and confident, but these qualities come from Jesus through me, not from me. Humility eliminates egocentricity, because its center of gravity is Jesus, not the approval or applause of people. It's the ability to go in every situation without fear of the people. It's a total freedom that comes to the life of the person who knows the heart of God, trusts His love, and has learned to follow His lead, wherever that may be.

R4G's live with the conviction that no one can keep from them or take from them what God wants and has planned for them. They have a big-time belief in the promise, "For I know the plans I have for you, declares the Lord, plans to prosper you and not harm you, plans to give you hope and a future" (Jer. 29:11). Humility is the inner assurance that I don't have to fight for my rights or demand my privileges, because God's got my back.

HUNGER

The seventh sign of the J-life is hunger. Jesus said, "Blessed are those who hunger and thirst after righteousness for they shall be filled" (Matt. 5:6). The kind of hunger I'm talking about is a hunger that lasts all your life—a hunger for God. R4G's hunger for Jesus, for the person He is, for the life He gives. We hunger to plunge into the depths of His heart. We are like kids on Christmas morning ready to trust His love for great adventures we can only imagine in our sleep. We are like a racehorse whose every muscle aches to break out of the gate and run whatever race He might lay before us. The divine scandal that every life matters to God occupies my heart, my head, my time, and my life. Things that once seemed all-important have now faded into the background.

I'm hungry to live the abundant life that His death made possible. My ambition is to live like He lived, love like He loved, and leave behind what He left behind. I'm thirsty to see the whole world drink from the living water that gives life. I hunger to be a wave maker in this crazy, dangerous, uncivilized, risk-taking movement called the church. I'm hungry to live for God's glory and the good of all mankind. I am a man on a mission whose sole aim is the fueling and funding of a global revolution where the love of Jesus renovates the human heart and builds the kingdom of God on earth.

On a practical note, it's not the lack of hunger that gives us victory over sin in the J-life. We are hungrier than ever, but our tastes have changed. What we once craved to the point of obsession, we no longer care for. Jesus changes the desires of your heart. In religion, you must muster up the strength to say no to the very things you want most. A businessman is out of town on business and because he lusts in his heart, he'll have to fight the urge to visit a prostitute or the temptation to watch the in-room adult movie channel. But the guy whose heart is filled with love for his wife doesn't have hunger for the old ways. When temptation does come, his heart takes him back to the love he has in Jesus and at home. Remember, the goal of the J-life is not to stop eating the garbage, but to lose the taste for it all together.

WALK HIS WAY

Too much of the history of Christianity has been devoted to domesticating Jesus, of diluting Jesus the renegade, revolutionary, into Jesus the civilized. Andrew Greely wrote in the *Chicago Sun-Times*, "Much of the history of Christianity has been devoted to domesticating Jesus—to reducing that elusive, enigmatic, paradoxical person to dimensions we can comprehend, understand, and convert to our own purposes. So far it hasn't worked."[3]

Jesus can't be contained in a building, labeled for safe consumption, or stuffed into religious pigeonholes. As a follower of Jesus Christ, I have a life worth living and I'm going to live it. I will walk the way He walked. By His grace, I will realize His promise to do even greater things. And while I don't completely understand it, I do embrace and dare to believe the audacity of the promise. After all, you and I live in this wonderful, new, wireless, wall-less, flat world. We have tools available to us that were unheard of ten or twenty years ago.

How different would Jena's life have been if instead of being taken to church to be made safe from the real world, she could have confronted the truth about Jesus early? If her church were a gathering place for renegades, maybe the truth about the J-life would have prepared her for the real world.

How much different would her experience have been if she was able to give an answer to her suitemate? It wasn't an unreasonable request. Nancy wanted to know what was at the core of her church going. Do you know what is so cool about being a Jesus-person? Wouldn't it have been different if she could have understood and been able to articulate to those around her that she didn't follow a religious Jesus but a renegade Jesus and that her commitment to the J-life wasn't something that pleased her parents or fit within the expectation of those around her, but that she truly knew and loved Jesus as an actual fact and experience?

5

THE SINGLE KEY TO EVERYTHING ELSE

DISCOVERING THE ONE AND ONLY THING YOU'VE GOT THAT GOD WANTS

In God we trust, all others we virus scan.

—*Unknown*

Faithless is he that says farewell when the road darkens.

—*J.R.R. Tolkien*

Chapel was required for everyone who attended Mid-America seminary. So I went, though I didn't want to. I was mad at God and the last thing I wanted to do was stand alongside a bunch of do-gooders singing about how good God is. They had no clue how wrong they were. I felt like a flaming hypocrite standing next to these naïve, tie-wearing wanna-be preachers singing praises to a God who didn't give two hoots about them, me, or the world they were learning how to save. Like I said, I was good and mad.

After the music part was over, I sat there listening to the seminary president preach about, of all things, the faithfulness of God. The more verses he quoted the angrier I got. I was trying to concentrate, but my mind kept rehearsing the last six months of hell I'd just been through and was still going through. I was hurt. I was mad. I was angry, but mostly I was afraid. My head was filled with big questions and dark doubts. I lost my way and was very close to losing my faith too.

The voices echoing in my empty soul said, "You're too dumb, too stupid, and too defective for God to care about what happens to you. Why don't you just quit all this nonsense and rejoin the real world? There's nothing to this Jesus stuff anyway." I sat there stewing in the juices of resentment while demons drew me deeper into my own private hell. I was lost and I had never felt farther from God than I did in that moment in, of all places, a seminary.

Nine months earlier I had announced with great aplomb that I was leaving my position to attend seminary. It didn't come as much of a surprise to anyone; though many had hoped I would opt for staying at the church and driving back and forth from Louisville. To my face, people said they admired me for picking up and moving to Memphis with a wife and two small children. But behind my back, and to my wife, they questioned whether or not this could possibility be the will of God. I was leaving a secure job where people loved me, to move to a place where I knew no one; I only knew that Elvis lived there. God had to show up quick or I was toast. I had no fall back plan. It was do or die and that was what I was doing by degrees—dying.

But God did not show up, at least not in any way I expected. My wife and two daughters were back in Kentucky living with my in-laws; how humiliating! I couldn't find a job. I ended up sleeping on the apartment floor of a guy from Mobile, Alabama, who I met in my first period Greek class. I tried to find a place to preach, but all I could get was a little church in the poorest county in the state, which had just gone through a horrible church split. I couldn't afford to call home except on the weekends. Everything I touched turned to crap. I was broke, confused, and wondering where God was in all this. I remember thinking things couldn't get worse, and then they did.

I woke up the next day with what felt like a slight groin pull. It persisted through the day. I thought it might be from sleeping on the floor. I got up the next morning still feeling not bad or sick, just strange. It was late Friday afternoon and hardly anyone was left in the seminary offices when I went to inquire about seeing a doctor. I had no insurance, but heard there were some physicians who would see seminary students for free. The secretary flipped through her Rolodex, found a doctor nearby, dialed the number, and handed me the phone. I explained my symptoms. He assured me it was nothing to be too concerned with. I set an appointment to see him the next Monday afternoon.

I felt better, but on the way to my car I couldn't shake this nagging dread. It said, "don't get in that car. Go back and make another call." I ignored it at first. I sat in the car just feeling a heavy weight pressing down on me. For some reason, I went back and asked for another name. The nice lady dialed the phone again and connected me with Dr. David Dunavant. He asked me a few questions and then he said, "I was just about to leave, but if you'll come on over right now, I will stay and see you." As luck would have it, his offices were not far away.

Upon entering his office, the nurse motioned for me to go straight back. This was the royal treatment for a change and I liked it a lot. Dr. Dunavant came right in and asked me to lie down. He started pressing around on my stomach. Without even looking at me, he walked over to the phone on the wall, lifted the receiver, dialed three numbers only and in a low, somber voice said, "This is Dr. Dunavant from across the street (another lucky coincidence that his office was just across from the Baptist Hospital) and I need an operating room ASAP." He hung up the phone, turned to me and said, "You have an inflamed appendix and we need to get it out." I said, "right now?" He said, "Yes, the sooner the better." And with that I lost it. My anger, hurt, and feelings of failure all collided at that moment. I screamed, "There ain't no way in hell you are going to operate on me here in this God-forsaken city. I will get in my car and go home to Kentucky." He sensed that I was about to lose it when he put both of his hands on my shoulders, leaned in real close, and nose to nose calmly said, "David, you will not last long enough to drive home. Your appendix is more than likely ruptured and every second counts. This is about life and death." With that I wilted. I lost control and wept like a baby.

The next thing I remember was waking up in the ICU. My appendix had indeed ruptured. I stayed in ICU for over a week and in the hospital for a month. When they released me, I went back to Kentucky and moved in with my parents to recuperate. There I was—homeless, penniless, and with medical bills stacked to the ceiling. To add to the load, I received a notice from the seminary that I failed all my classes for lack of attendance. I didn't know whether to cry or laugh. Couldn't someone cut me some slack?

Fast forward a few months to my moment in the chapel. I had

moved back to Memphis, I was back at seminary and ready to tackle this thing again. It was January, cold, and there I sat, in chapel, utterly not wanting to be there. God let me down. But I needed to know why. What had I done so horribly wrong to deserve this constant sorrow and pain? What could I do to get God on my side again? As I sat there brooding, the seminary president said, "Many of you are sitting here in need of a miracle." That got my attention, so I leaned in. He said, "If you need a miracle today, right this minute you're probably going to be disappointed, but if you will trust God over time regardless of outcome, He will do great things for you and through you." And with that, something in my heart leaped. It was like the last tumbler falling in place so the door to my self-made prison could be unlocked and I could be freed.

God wanted me to trust Him rather than try to figure Him out or predict His behavior. At that precise moment, the lights came on; God wanted me to trust Him without knowing the outcome. Right then and there I understood that trusting God is the single key to everything. I went from someone who had faith in God to a guy who was determined to trust God no matter what the outcome. Whatever my reality was at the moment, I would trust God and be free. And it was that discovery that kept me going on this amazing non-religious road to getting real with God. That was the day I started framing reality from God's perspective. It has made all the difference.

FRAMING REALITY

At a news conference the morning after the Iraq war began in 2003, Secretary of Defense Donald Rumsfeld was asked by a reporter "what do you have to say about your apparent failure to follow the war plan?" Rumsfeld replied with a smile and a wink, "I don't believe you have the war plan—do you?" How often I've begged God to give me a glimpse at His war plan. Too often I don't have a clue of what's really going on. You know by now that life can get hard without warning. When that happens, you can't bend reality to your will. God created the world to work by certain laws—realities. Thankfully, He created the world to sustain life. He created a generous world and if you know how to step into it you will discover its abundance. Remember, all reality is God's reality, or a dysfunctional departure thereof.

God is real; therefore, His existence creates and defines reality. Encoded into this reality is a core set of principles. All change revolves around these changeless realities. They are timeless and prevail through all cultures, countries, dynasties, and kingdoms. These keys to understanding life in God's world are simple as well as self-evident. Master them and the rewards are endless. Ignore them and you lose big time.

Let me explain how simple and self-evident they are by making this statement—you are now here. You're reading this book *now*. Later you may have dinner, watch TV, or sit in a coffee shop, but wherever you go is now and *here* for you. When my children were young and we were traveling, their favorite question was, "Are we there yet?" My favorite response was, "You can never be there. You can only be here." I used to drive them crazy with this response. But, this silly little game illustrates the simple, self-evident principle of reality called now-here.

Congratulations, you are here. You exist. There was a time you didn't exist, but now you do. Your being *here*, *now* guarantees that you will never be nowhere. It may sound simple, but it is actually very profound. You are here. You are the possessor of God's greatest gift—life. How often do we just stop and savor the reality that God decided that you and me being here now, meeting in the pages of this book would be a good thing? Maybe even a life-changing thing?

The fact that you are infers intentionality and awesome creative power. You are unique in every way. Your DNA is yours. Your fingerprint is one of a kind. You think, feel, laugh, and cry in your own way. You are self-aware, and have an inner dialogue. You are a spiritual being having a human experience. All of you here and now were willed into being by God. He is the great exception to the laws of cause and effect. He is the uncaused cause. And since the cause must be greater than the effect, God too is a thinking, feeling, loving, and creative being who is obviously in love with life and you. Why else would you still be here now?

God loves being. Maybe a better way of saying it is that God loves hanging out. And because He has the power of "being," you are endowed with that gift. He intends that you be here now experiencing what you're experiencing so you too can be alive, free, and having the time of your life.

The real question is, "why are you here?" What are you supposed to be and do that makes your existence of any consequence? What is the key to making sure that your brief time here now is well spent? As I said at the beginning of this journey, the greatest fear we all face is the fear of being insignificant and/or squandering this divine moment. A wasted life is tragic, sad, and unnecessary. The life worth living is yours if you know the key principle.

The greatest threat to your life is the voice inside that keeps you from being fully present here and now. As you try to read this book, your mind will tend to wander. You'll get distracted. Your eyes will continue to scan the words, but they're often mere images, disconnected from your head and heart. This is no accident, and you're not the only one. Each of us bears the wound of the orphan, which says that we're alone, abandoned, unloved, and unwanted. No one truly knows who we are, understands what we're going through or cares. You are looking for a protector, a provider—someone who sees you, understands you, cares about your pain, and has a plan.

We scan the horizon for someone who, rather than dwelling on our deficiencies, will help us embrace our more noble selves and better angels. Who can quiet the inner demons and turn on the light so we can see clearly our *now* moment?

We long for home where things were simpler, when our parents paid the bills and kept away the things that went bump in the night. We fight off the dread of being unworthy and unloved. As you age, the fear of waking up old and obsolete, relegated to the scrap heap of time dogs your days. Therefore, F.U.D. (fear, uncertainty, and doubt) rob us of the here and now so much so that your life can be over before you actually begin to live.

Another simple reality is that we exist in a world of scary, stark contradictions and extremes. This was brought home to me during the recent hurricanes in the coastal states of the United States. Spending time on the coast, in the refugee camps, walking through the most devastated areas, seeing the lives of people literally blown away in the span of a few hours was sobering. You wondered where God was on August 29, 2005. As you drove from street to street, you felt the desolation viscerally. I shuddered at the utter futility of life itself. Why build back what will be blown away in a few hours?

I took a digital photo of a barren lot. I learned later that the house that was on it fourteen days before was over 100 years old. Two weeks after Hurricane Katrina, this lot was scraped completely clean. The house that housed generations, the cars that took kids to school, and all other signs of life were gone. Even the shrubs were gone and the mighty trees were mere toothpicks. All that remained were the concrete front steps. It was weird seeing a set of steps leading nowhere. It was as though a giant vacuum cleaner sucked the place clean—no debris—no life—no hope. On the top step was a set of house keys, a set of car keys, and the deed to the property with a brick on top of it. It was a surreal picture of utter hopelessness. Who can you trust? What can you trust? This reality changes everything except for the fact that we were *there* in that new reality still existing—still *here*. But what *now* and what for?

Once I was back in Nashville, I felt weird. Who was I to drive through the beautiful streets and experience the lush foliage as summer turned into fall, and feel the abundance of blessings, the convenience, the luxury and prosperity all around me? I see these two stark contrasting realities everyday, everywhere. On one hand, life is good and generous and tranquil and majestic. On the other hand it's messed up, full of misery, with pain and immeasurable loss. Something has gone badly wrong with the world. We fail to realize that oftentimes what is wrong with the world is actually what has gone wrong within each of us.

In the midst of this maddening duality we search for solid ground. To guard against the harsh realities, we load up on power, position, and control. We clutch tightly to the symbols of status that remind us we're important. We live in a world of complexities seeking simple answers. We're left swimming in a sea of questions surrounded by a desert of simplistic answers that won't work.

FACING REALITY

James Baldwin said, "Not everything that is faced can be changed. But nothing can be changed until it is faced." One of the best ways to face reality is to ask great questions. Asking the right question leads to the discovery of meaning. Asking the wrong question over and over again is like the ostrich that hides his head in the sand hoping that if he ignores reality, it will go away.

So what are the right questions that lead to freedom and life? It helps me to place questions into two categories: questions of means and questions of meaning. Questions of means are preoccupied with how things are done or acquired. Questions of meaning deal with the big why and what questions of life. If you get the two confused, you'll get lost and hurt.

We love "how" questions best. How do I make a living? How do I get married? How do I buy a house? How do I live the kind of life that surrounds me with all the assurances that I'm a person of significance? But to live fully and freely as God intends, we must begin with the questions of meaning. So we must learn to love asking, "Why am I here and what does God want from me?"

There will come a day, it came for me when I was seventeen years old, when you stop trying to avoid God and you'll be forced to ask, "What do you want from me?" What you hear back may surprise you. Because of all the religious indoctrination that we've gone through, we may think that God wants something far different than what He actually does.

For example: God doesn't want your permission. God is God and He does whatever He chooses. It doesn't matter whether you like it or not. You cannot judge God. As the Scriptures proclaim, "The LORD reigns, let the earth be glad; let the distant shores rejoice. Clouds and thick darkness surround him; righteousness and justice are the foundation of his throne. Fire goes before him and consumes his foes on every side. His lightning lights up the world; the earth sees and trembles" (Ps. 97:1–4). Now, when I read that, I do get a sense of my own smallness next to His expansive self-importance. You and I can breathe easy knowing He is on the job. Has He left anything to chance? Not a chance.

God does not require, nor is He impressed by our futile attempts at self-reformation. I've lost count of the numbers of people who have told me over the years, "Dave, I'm going to get serious about God and I'm going to start going to church as soon as I get some things in my life straightened out." I want to shake these people and say, "What, are you crazy? Is that what you think God wants? You're going to live and die and miss God all together, because you're never going to get your life straightened out on your own." This is a slap in the face of God. It's a lie dressed up as an excuse used to avoid the truth. You're broken deep inside. It's not a slight crack or flaw either. You are shattered into a million little pieces. And like Humpty Dumpty, all the king's horses and all the king's men cannot put you back together again.

Trying to make up for your past sins is like trying to glue a shattered lightbulb back together. You can't straighten what is bent. If human effort could save us, Jesus would be a joke. Even sincere attempts at self-reformation push real life with God into some future place and time. Fixating on our personal flaws just make you more aware of how many of them there are. Self-help salvation has two fundamental flaws. First, it underestimates the seriousness of my sin. Second, it woefully over-estimates my ability to change. The Scriptures put it this way, "A dog returns to its vomit," and, "A sow that is washed goes back to her wallowing in the mud" (2 Pet. 2:22). Graphic to be sure, but it makes the point. The bad news: you can't change yourself. The good news is you don't have to. When the J-life starts, appetites change.

God isn't interested in your compliance with His commands. I was raised in a religious environment where compliance and obedience were the seminal Christian virtues. To comply and obey were the keys to the kingdom, or so I was told. God isn't interested in your *being,* only in your *doing.* Whether your heart was in it or not didn't enter into the equation. Long before Nike came up with "Just Do It," church people were *just doing it* with little joy in it or much to show for it.

Attend church every week even if it is perfunctory, rote, and routine—just do it. Read the Bible every day. Just open it up and dip in anywhere and though what you're reading may be disjointed, confusing, and incoherent—just do it. Do it, check it off, and expect credit for it. That's why churches are filled with people who are good and mad about it! And it's also why most church services are more like funerals than parties. Every Sunday the saints gather to sit and soak wondering, *God, I've been good. What's gone wrong?*

OK, let's get real and bottom-line this whole deal. Get this straight; God doesn't need your good works, your blind obedience, or your vote. To listen to some of the "religious right" (whatever that means) you'd think God is more interested in politics than He is in people. Religious experts tell us that what God wants is a moral, social revolution or we're done for. To listen to them you'd think God created the world and then left the building. We've boycotted Disney and retreated into our expensive, exclusive private Christian schools. Hey, we've elected men who claimed to be Christians plenty of times only to be disappointed. Whether it was Jimmy Carter and his depressing speeches, Bill Clinton and his repeated sexual trysts, or George W. Bush and his leadership into a controversial war; I would argue these are good men, but they are men and that is the point. Good government, the church, the family, and all the social movements combined have not saved us and they never will. Our hope is in Renegade Jesus, His Renegade love, and His Renegade Nation.

THE SUPERIORITY OF TRUST

Trust is the single key to everything with God. It is vastly superior to every other human effort. It is the single key that unlocks the gates of heaven. It is the one ingredient that releases God to do great things for you and through you. It is the code that activates the love of God and it is the bulwark against sin, death, and the grave. Jesus said, "Do not let your hearts be troubled. Trust in God; trust also in me" (John 14:1). Trust is the key that unlocks all the treasures of heaven here on earth.

This may not be as evident as it should be because of our current way of looking at trust. To simply trust God seems too easy, but let me assure you it is not. Trust is not passivity. It's not giving lip service to the idea of God. It is not a miracle mantra, which turns God into my own private genie. Trust is the place where God's part and my part meld into a mysterious union. It is the divine dynamite created when God's intention and my free will are mingled. It's like the Persian proverb which says, *"Trust in God, but tie your camel."* I can't do God's part in creating the camel, the rope, or the post to tie her to. And God won't do my part—tie the camel to the post.

This is illustrated beautifully in the story I heard about a young girl who was upset when she discovered her brother set traps to catch songbirds. When asked what she did about it she said, "I prayed that the traps wouldn't work." Anything else? "Yes, I asked God to send the birds away from the traps." Anything else? "Yes, then I went out and stomped the traps to pieces." She got it!

Trust is not religious hocus-pocus. I was up late one night watching TV and I saw a guy hawking sacred prayer clothes on one channel. On another, a preacher was holding up a tiny blue bottle of holy water that he had prayed over. It was healing water and could be had for a donation of any size. Of course the larger the gift, the more potent its healing properties. I even saw "prosperity" wristbands which were "guaranteed to bring the blessings of God" on anyone who wore one. How gullible are we? Why is any of this more attractive than the way of trust?

Trusting God is not religious magic and neither is it the last resort. I've heard people proclaim that they're trusting God in such a sad, somber tone that I felt sorry for both them and God. Trust is not a guarantee of success in advance. It does not guarantee predetermined outcomes except ones like, "When I am afraid, I will trust in you. In God, whose word I praise, in God I trust; I will not be afraid" (Ps. 56:3–4).

Trust is where Jesus and I meet. It is the glue of our mysterious, non-religious union. For example, to *believe* in Jesus is to *know* certain facts. To have faith in Jesus is to act with confidence on the basis of that belief. A good example of this is the promise in Romans, "if you confess with your mouth, 'Jesus is Lord,' and believe in your heart that God raised him from the dead, you will be saved" (Rom. 10:9). This is God's contract. There is no doubt about its outcome. If you believe and exercise faith, the outcome is guaranteed.

Trust on the other hand is to say, "I don't know about this situation or its outcome, but I do know Jesus and that's enough." Trust leaves the ultimate outcome up to God. Belief and faith lead to certainty, while trust allows us to embrace mystery when certainty is not possible. As we'll see in Chapter 9, it hardly ever is.

God says, "This Good News tells us that God makes us ready for heaven—makes us right in God's sight—when we put our faith and trust in Christ to save us. This is accomplished from start to finish by faith. As the Scripture says it, "THE MAN WHO FINDS LIFE WILL FIND IT THROUGH TRUSTING GOD" (Rom. 1:17, LB, emphasis mine). The single keystone of life with God is trust. It is the converted heart's courage and the new man's ambition. It dreams new dreams, imagines outrageous possibilities, and dares to be the change God wants in the world.

Trust is the power that translates theory into reality, truth into transformation, and morphs missions into movements. It is the best thing, for it is the closest thing to heaven on earth. How does it do all that? Let's consider a few of its many benefits.

Trust acknowledges my total dependence on God. It renders all other effort unnecessary, except the glad chore of joining God where He is already moving.

Trust recognizes that . . .

> *God made the world and everything in it, and since he is Lord of heaven and earth, he doesn't live in man-made temples; and human hands can't minister to His needs—for He has no needs! He himself gives life and breath to everything, and satisfies every need there is. He created all the people of the world from one man, Adam, and scattered the nations across the face of the earth. He decided beforehand which nation should rise and fall, and when. He determined their boundaries. His purpose in all of this is that they should seek after God, and perhaps feel their way toward him and find him—though he is not far from any one of us. For in him we live and move and are! . . .*
>
> —Acts 17:24–28, LB

Charles Haddon Spurgeon said, "When you have no helpers, see all your helpers in God. When you have many helpers, see God in all your helpers. When you have nothing but God, see all in God. When you have everything, see God in everything. Under all conditions, stay thy heart only on the Lord."[1] This is the power of trust. When all trust is in Jesus, then you can trust that Jesus will be found in all things.

Trust accepts the sole sufficiency of Jesus as the full, finished, and final proof of God's love for me as I am, not as I ought to be. There exists no greater freedom or no more sublime joy than to trust God's love offered through the life and work of Jesus. God finds great pleasure in our acceptance of His acceptance of us in Jesus.

Because of who Jesus is and what He did, we trust God's love above all other loves. And when we trust His love without fear or regret, we give Him the one thing we have He wants—our heart. As Brennan Manning said, ". . . the splendor of the human heart which trusts that it is loved gives God more pleasure than Westminster Chapel, the Sistine Chapel, Beethoven's Ninth Symphony, Van Gogh's *Sunflowers*, the sight of ten thousand butterflies in flight or the scent of million orchids in bloom. Trust is our gift back to God, and He finds it so enchanting that Jesus died for love of it."[2] Trust God and be free.

Trust relocates the center of self. Nothing is more roundly condemned by God than self-centeredness. It is like a leech sucking the soul dry. The Scriptures warn, "wicked men trust themselves alone . . . but the righteous man trusts in me and lives!" (Hab. 2:4, LB). All great men and women have acknowledged their total dependence on God's good hand to save. George Washington, alone, cold, and discouraged at Valley Forge penned these words to his favorite chaplain, Rev. Israel Evans: "It will ever be the first wish of my heart to aid your pious endeavors to inculcate a due sense of the dependence we ought to place in that all wise and powerful being on whom alone our success depends." Trust acknowledges that it is God who has made us and He alone gives victory or causes defeat. He raises up and brings low. He is wise and does all things well. And like Roy Rogers riding up at the last minute to save the day, He is never early, never late, and always on time.

Trust doesn't stave off fear or even starve all doubt. But it does relocate the center of your universe from self to God—as it should be. A guest at an official reception once told President Abraham Lincoln that in his home state people said the welfare of the nation depended on two things—God and Abraham Lincoln. "At least they're half right," the President humbly responded. In the gospel, Jesus is the one who says "I've got your back; now turn and face life with courage and audacity. You may lose some battles along the way, but trust me and you will win a final, full and glorious victory."

One of the most compelling aspects of trust is that it demands the same thing from every participant. The command to everyone, in every age, and at all times, "Trust in the LORD with all your heart and lean not on your own understanding" (Prov. 3:5).

Trust is our gift back to God and God finds it so enchanting that Jesus died for the love of it. Trust grows within the heart an unshakable confidence that it is loved without limitation, liability, boundary, or breaking point. As Emerson once said, "All I have seen teaches me to trust the Creator for all I have not seen." For the R4G who trusts God, great things are possible.

When my girls were little, I would pretend to be a bear chasing them through the house. I'd get down on all fours and chase them from room to room. They would scream and squeal, pretending they were running for their lives. When I would corner them, their squealing would turn into nervous laughter. They would turn and say, " 'top it daddy, 'top it. You're not a bear, you're my daddy." They'd run out of the corner and into my arms. It was sweet because it was trust. I've often thought that is how we treat God. Once we ran from Him for fear of judgment, but now we run into His arms. We are learning to trust His love even when it is hard to understand His ways.

I am learning to understand the radical trust in Job's confession, "Though he slay me, yet will I trust in him" (Job 13:15, KJV). He has been too good for too long for me to want to run from Him. I have trusted Him and I am glad. Yes, I have scars and I walk with a limp, but I can say along with Thomas à Kempis, "Oh, how great peace and quietness would he possess who should cut off all vain anxiety and place all his confidence in God."

Trust converts the heart from the fear of abandonment. The core fear of children is the fear of being left alone, unloved and unwanted. It is also a secret fear harbored by us adults too. We fear being abandoned by our spouse or our good friends. This fear chains us to meaningless, joyless jobs. We hate the work, but stay because it pays the bills. Rather than trust God for work that matters, we trade our souls for the false security of a dehumanizing job.

Trust creates confidence that if God is for me, who cares who aligns against me. Trust calms the terror of abandonment by embracing the promise of God to never leave me or forsake me. By cruel and brutal experience, the great missionary Paul came to this heart conviction, ". . . I am not ashamed, because I know whom I have believed, and am convinced that he is able to guard what I have entrusted to him for that day" (2 Tim. 1:12). Trust means that no one can take from me what God wants for me. The only wild card in trust is *me*. That's why the way of trust is the key to everything else with God!

The way of trust is the key to surrender and submission. Convinced of God's love we surrender to His commands. Assured of our place in His plan, we submit to divine providence. This simple story illustrates the superiority of trust. A cheerful five-year-old girl was waiting with her mother at the grocery checkout. She saw a string of white plastic pearls in a pink foil box. "Oh please,

Mommy. Can I have them? Please, Mommy, please!" Her mother checked the price and said, "They cost one dollar and ninety-five cents. If you really want them, I'll think of some extra chores for you and in no time you can save enough money to buy them for yourself." As soon as Jenny got home, she emptied her penny bank and counted out twenty pennies. After dinner, she did more than her share of chores. She went to the neighbor and asked if she could pick dandelions for ten cents. On her birthday, Grandma gave her another new dollar bill and at last she had enough money and bought herself a necklace of plastic pearls.

Jenny loved her plastic pearls. They made her feel grown-up. She wore them everywhere—church, school, even to bed. The only time she took them off was when she went swimming or had a bubble bath. Her daddy loved her very much and every night at bed time, he would stop whatever he was doing and read her a story. One night when he finished the story, he asked, "Jenny, do you love me?" "Oh yes, Daddy. You know that I love you." "Then give me your pearls." "Oh, Daddy, not my pearls. You can have Princess—the white horse from my collection; the one with the pink tail. Remember, Daddy? The one you gave me. She's my favorite."

"That's okay, Honey. Daddy loves you. Good night." And he brushed her cheek with a kiss. About a week later, after the story time, Jenny's daddy asked again, "Do you love me?" " Daddy, you know I love you." "Then give me your pearls." "Oh Daddy, not my pearls. You can have my baby doll. The brand new one I got for my birthday. She is so beautiful and you can have the yellow blanket that matches her sleeper." "That's okay. Sleep well. God bless you, little one. Daddy loves you." And as always, he brushed her cheek with a gentle kiss.

A few nights later when Jenny's daddy came in, he noticed a single tear rolling down her face. He said, "What's the matter Jenny, why are you crying?" Without saying a word, she raised up her hand. He held out his hand and into it she dropped her prized plastic pearl necklace. She looked up at him and through her tears she said, "Here, Daddy. Here's want you've wanted." With tears streaming down his face, Jenny's dad took the cheap plastic necklace with one hand and with the other hand he reached into his coat pocket. He pulled out a blue velvet case and pressed it in Jenny's hands. She looked at him and then opened the box to find a genuine strand of pearls. They were exquisite. She was breathless. Her daddy said, "Jenny, I have had these pearls waiting for you all this time. I wanted you to trust me enough to give up the plastic pearls you loved for something I knew you would love even more." With that they hugged and Jenny learned a valuable lesson about trust she never forgot.

Out of love, God offers us the real thing. But we must trust Him enough to willingly hand over our fake and phony attachments for the real treasure. He longs to give us beauty for brokenness, love for lust, and freedom for fear. All he asks is, "Trust me." All that is left for us to do is hand it over. The dad had the real pearls all the time. He was just waiting for Jenny to give up the dime-store stuff so he could give her his best. Just like our heavenly Father. What are you hanging on to?

God will do great things for anyone and I do mean anyone (and that includes you) who dares give Him the one thing He wants—absolute, unwavering trust. Therefore, He begs you today, right now in this never-to-be-repeated "now-here" moment, to dare and attempt something so big and so scary great that you're doomed for failure if He doesn't show up. I have dared trust Him for great things and I have seen God come down and do miracles. I have had visions and then watched them materialize right before my eyes.

DARE TO TEST GOD

Since God calls us to trust Him, He also dares us to test Him. F. B. Meyer said, "You do not test the resources of God until you attempt the impossible." Don't be afraid to believe the words of Jesus when He said, "if you have faith as small as a mustard seed, you can say to this mountain, 'Move from here to there' and it will move. Nothing will be impossible for you" (Matt. 17:20). Imagine, nothing is impossible to the person who dares trust God enough to actually call Him out on His promises. And if you dare become the great soul you were created to be, you only need two things to thrive—trust and endurance. One will sustain you when the other is in short supply. As Norman Vincent Peale said, "Never be afraid to trust an unknown future to a known God."

Face this fact and never, never forget it; *everything great that God wants to do for you, He waits to do through you.* No exceptions. No exemptions. If you won't move to trust Him, He will find someone else who will. His will is going to get done on earth as it is in heaven, just not through you.

Spoon-feeding time is over. For as E. M. Forster said, "Spoon feeding in the long run teaches us nothing but the shape of the spoon." It is time you move into full-bore Renegade status. Step out and trust that either there will be something solid to stand on or else you will be taught to fly.

Trust is the key that unlocks the door to everything worth having. It breaks the bondage of sin and shame because it accepts my acceptance in Jesus. It uncorks my courage and opens my mouth to speak words of help and healing. Like Abraham who God called to leave home for an unknown destination, trust will take you where you've never been. Like Moses who spoke to the mighty Pharaoh, trust will require you to do what you're convinced you can't.

Putting God to the test creates things that could never be created. The early Christians did that when they formed the church.

Trust will shut the mouths of the lions as with Daniel; it will slay giants with slingshots like David. Trust will starve your doubts and feed your faith. It seizes opportunities. It builds hospitals for healing. Armed only with trust in God, great universities have been founded and social movements have moved forward.

Nothing happens without trust. There are no movements moving ahead without someone at the lead armed with a vision for change, and trust that God will show up and move mountains when they need to move. Trust doesn't eradicate fear, but it does defy it. Trust is power to believe what you don't feel, knowledge of what you can't see, and the ability to hold onto the invisible hand of God and wait with invincible trust for the morning.

Remember the words of St. Francis de Sales, "The same everlasting Father who cares for you today will take care of you tomorrow and every day. Either He will shield you from suffering, or He will give you strength to bear it. Be at peace, then, and put aside all anxious thoughts and imaginations."

6

THE MORPHING POWER OF CONVERSION

SOMEWHERE BEYOND MERE BELIEF SOMETHING AMAZING HAPPENS

It is in changing that things find purpose.

—*Heraclitus*

He who made us also remade us.

—*Saint Augustine*

One of my prized possessions is an old wooden cane. I keep it leaning in the corner of my office so I can see it first thing each day. It's not much to look at, to be sure, but to me it gets better looking every day. I paid seventy-five cents for it at an estate auction over twenty-five years ago. And although it's not worth much, it remains one of my most valued possessions.

Upon close examination, its rather crude carvings aren't much to brag about. It's charred about eight inches up from its tip, no doubt from stirring the ashes of one too many fires. But each time I look at the blackened tip, I remember my roots. This simple cane over time has morphed from a crooked stick to a priceless family heirloom because it belonged to my grandfather, or pap-pa, as we used to call him.

The purpose of my pap-pa's cane doesn't make it all that unique, but our relationship makes it precious to me. I've learned that the same kind of conversion happened when I (a common, ordinary, bent stick) entered into an epic, life-changing, heart-converting, joy-filled relationship with Jesus.

Jesus described this morphing moment as being "born again." When He described this conversion relationship to one of the elite teachers of His day, the reaction was typical.

> *"With all the earnestness I possess I tell you this: unless you are born again, you can never get into the kingdom of God." "Born again!" exclaimed Nicodemus. "What do you mean? How can an old man go back into his mother's womb and be born again?" Jesus replied, "What I am telling you so earnestly is this: Unless one is born of water and the Spirit, he cannot enter the Kingdom of God. Men can only reproduce human life, but the Holy Spirit gives new life from heaven; so don't be surprised at my statement that you must be born again."*
>
> —John 3:3–8, LB

New birth is the entry point into the J-life. It is the *only* entry place. It is the place and moment in time where we pass from death to life. Therefore the J-life can't be joined, studied, or agreed to. It is a life-changing experience, much like physical birth.

Jesus used this encounter with Nicodemus to introduce a radical, new non-religious paradigm into the equation. Traditionally a man's relationship with God was about accepting certain "God-facts" as true. The emphasis was then on what you believed. Your faith was the various opinions about God that you held in your head. Believing things is the litmus test of religion, but Renegade Jesus moved the focus of reality from head to heart.

According to Jesus, intellectual assent to religious ideas about God isn't enough. It's not a relationship with the information that Jesus came to achieve by a radical change of heart, which in turn would free the mind. He came, not to enlighten the mind, but to renovate the heart. Jesus called for and accepted nothing less than the radical conversion of the human heart because He knew all too well that nothing changes until the heart changes. And no man can resurrect or renovate himself.

Radical conversion based on a relationship is not all that hard a concept to grasp. A great artist like Picasso could take a fifty-cent stretch of canvas and convert it into a masterpiece worth millions by painting on it. Rockefeller could sign his name to a piece of paper converting it into millions of dollars. Longfellow could place ink images on a worthless piece of paper and instantly transform it into literary genius. Einstein could scribble an unknown formula on a chalkboard and change the world we live in forever. A common wooden cane attached to my pap-pa is a priceless point of connection to someone I love and miss very much.

Jesus the Christ can take a broken, sin-stained soul, wash it in His cleansing blood, put His Spirit in it, and convert it into a valuable trophy of God's grace. We call a vital experience you can't live without Christian conversion.

Jesus is not a myth. He was a man who lived in time and space. Tacitus, the great Roman historian of the first century, wrote of Jesus the man. Josephus, the noted Jewish historian, tells of the crucifixion of Jesus. I heard a professor say once that the *Encyclopedia Britannica* uses over 20,000 words in describing the life and enduring impact of Jesus. His description took more space than was given to Aristotle, Cicero, Alexander, Julius Caesar, Buddha, Confucius, Mohammed, or Napoleon Bonaparte.

It was St. Augustine who said, "Our hearts are restless until they find their rest in thee." Only Jesus can fill the God-sized hole in the center of your heart. He's the only one who takes you beyond mere belief to a place where something amazing and eternal happens. It's called conversion and you can't be free without it.

Many men have inspired, conquered, enslaved, freed, gained, and lost power. Great figures have moved on and off history's stage, but Jesus won't go away. Why? It's because He alone dared claim the power to convert the human heart.

Conversion is not a set of promises, reforms, or stipulations you make to God. It's what God in Jesus, the Messiah, does for us. It is a divine process whereby God does the work of reviving, redeeming, and renovating a stony heart, making it new again. As Jesus said, it is heaven's life bestowed on a person by invasion of the Holy Spirit.

As Paul said to his young converts, "You were dead in your transgressions and sins" (Eph. 2:1). What do dead men do? They do nothing, unless or until God makes them alive and able to respond. And that is what Jesus died to do. This is accomplished when the power of Jesus converts the heart from dead to alive. It is a wonderful experience. Those of us who have had this experience are still searching for words to explain it adequately. I've seen thousands of people converted by Jesus. The change that results can defy explanation. And maybe that's what makes finding life outside conventional Christianity so radically different from mere religion. While personal conversion searches for words, religion on the other hand is a collection of creeds, prohibitions, and obligations for which no experience is forthcoming, except for guilt, shame, and condemnation. Religion is like trying to swim with a rock around your neck. Conversion is like conquering gravity.

THE PROBLEM OF BELIEF

All my life, I've been told what to believe. Belief is important, but it's definitely not enough. At some point, what you believe has to be experienced. As Jim Wallis points out in *The Call to Conversion*,

> *The recovery of the centrality of conversion is essential to genuine renewal. Monastic movements of the Middle Ages, the radical Reformation of the 16th Century, and the Evangelical revival of 18th Century England and 19th Century America were each marked by a primary emphasis on conversion. . . . Our Scripture, confession, and creeds are all very public, out in the open. Anyone can easily learn what it is supposed to mean to be a Christian. Our Bible is open to public examination; so is the church's life. That is our problem. People can read what our Scriptures say and they can see how Christians live. The gulf between the two has created an enormous credibility gap.*[1]

Conversion has fruits and evidences, otherwise it is mere religion. Religion is sterile because it, at best, stimulates the mind while ignoring the heart. Religion is focused on assent and compliance. It says you must believe. And believe we do. If modernity was the age of unbelief, postmodernism is an age of ultra-belief. Unlike modernity where we demanded proof, today we're willing to entertain anything that makes us feel good, true or not. Our problem is we believe everything, but with little effect. Maybe that's why you tell a man there's 400 billion stars in the sky above him and he'll believe you, but tell him a bench has wet paint and he has to touch it. Why? We want a truth that we can touch, taste, and experience.

Martin Luther said, "Just as no one can go to hell or heaven for me, so no one can believe for me." The belief of which Luther speaks lives in the depths of a converted heart. Christian belief dares to do what is logically impossible. It dares to promise that finite beings can know and relate to the infinite on a personal level. The scandal of the gospel is that our Creator regards the plight of His creation. This is possible because Jesus is the link, the life that brings the transcendence of God to us in the form of faith, hope, and trust. It is faith in Jesus *the man* married to trust in Jesus *the God* that makes loving Him transformational. To experience Him is to be changed by Him. If there is no change, you merely hold various opinions about Him.

An eager graduate student once asked Albert Einstein, "Dr. Einstein, how many feet are there in a mile?" To the utter astonishment of the student, Einstein replied, "I don't know." The student was sure the great professor was joking. Surely Einstein would know a simple fact that every schoolchild is required to memorize. But Einstein wasn't joking. When the student pressed for an explanation for this gap in Einstein's knowledge, he explained, "I make it a rule not to clutter my mind with information that I can find in a book." Einstein didn't rock the world by obsessing over trivia. He pressed into the deep realities of life. His passion for truth made him a pivotal fixture in modern world history.

Too many people see the Bible as information to be argued over. Even those who claim to have a "high view" of Scripture often use it to push their own agenda. As propaganda, it therefore divides and degrades rather than redeems and restores. J. I. Packer warned, "If we pursue theological knowledge for its own sake, it is bound to go bad on us. It will make us proud and conceited. The very greatness of the subject matter will intoxicate us, and we shall come to think of ourselves as a cut above other Christians because of our interest in it and grasp of it."[2] Of this I am sure: the Bible wasn't given to stimulate your brain, but to transform your heart.

Belief can just be traditionalism. I'm not saying that tradition is a bad thing. But I do make a distinction between tradition and traditionalism. Traditionalism is the dead faith of living men. It has no power, no life, and no ability to inspire and enliven the spirit. The only reason people still believe it is because they're either too bored or too afraid to think outside the little God-box they've inherited. As Søren Kierkegaard once said, "the majority of people are not so afraid of holding a wrong opinion, as they are of holding an opinion alone." Quentin Schultze, professor of communications at Calvin College said, "We human beings are social creatures who tend to go along with what other people believe rather than venture courageously in an unpopular direction. We are more fearful of being thought crazy than wrong, as long as we have the comfort of being mistaken with others. Ignorance loves company. We are creatures of fashionable, even if sometimes foolish, ideas."[3]

Belief can just be sentimentality. Many religious people believe in a hand-me-down faith. It's like the old gospel song, "it was good enough for grandma, it's good enough for me. So give me that old-time religion." That's a nice sentiment, but hardly one worth hanging your eternal hopes on. As J. C. Ryle said, "You cannot enter the kingdom of God on the credit of your parents' religion. You must eat the bread of life for yourself, and have the witness of the Spirit in your own heart. You must have repentance of your own, faith of your own, and sanctification of your own."[4]

James, the half brother of Jesus, cut to the chase when he said, "Faith by itself, if it is not accompanied by action, is dead. But someone will say, 'You have faith; I have deeds.' Show me your faith without deeds, and I will show you my faith by what I do. You believe that there is one God. Good! Even the demons believe that—and shudder" (James 2:17–19).

A TOTAL ME MAKEOVER

Humanity is hurting big time. We are in a major mess. How do you go about changing culture? How do you change government? Even with the radical overthrow of one oppressive government means the rise of another in its place. The truth is that governments don't change, schools don't change, educators don't change, and families don't change until people change. People are the problem as well as the solution. People can't change until their heart changes and the heart can't change on its own.

We don't need a little nip and tuck here and there. An attitude adjustment by itself won't do. We need a total "me makeover." We need a new heart, which longs to be made right so it can do right for the right reason. As T. S. Eliot said, "The last temptation is the greatest treason; to do the right deed for the wrong reason." We need a new "want to."

In Ecuador the celebration of a new year has significant meaning. During the week proceeding January 1st, people create and decorate scarecrow-like dummies. Then at midnight on December 31st, they take these dummies out and set them on fire. It's called "Burning the Old Man." This tradition marks a new beginning and represents the burning away of their sins and shortcomings. It doesn't matter how you celebrate the idea of new beginnings, the most important thing is that you actually have one. This is conversion—a whole new you.

We don't need reforming; we need resurrecting. We don't need a religion; we need a new hook-up. We don't want to make life work; we want to make it dance. Remember, Jesus did not come to make bad men good, but to make dead men live.

When I was a kid growing up in church, we ended every service singing "Just As I Am." The preacher would beg people to come down front. Later, when I became a pastor, I learned that a minister's job could be in jeopardy if enough people didn't respond to the invitation. So we'd sing sadly while the preacher pleaded mournfully sounding at times like a used car salesman for God. People came down front to make their decision for Jesus public, but most of the time it began and ended right there.

THE MECHANICS OF A CONVERTED HEART

Christianity is not a club you join; it joins you. It is not a set of rules by which you live your life. It is a relationship that attaches itself to your insides. When it happens to you, you change. But when Jesus enters your heart, mere belief is morphed into a new life. As the Scriptures promise, "if anyone is in Christ, he is a new creation; the old has gone, the new has come!" (2 Cor. 5:17).

Let me admit from the get-go that trying to explain the mystery of conversion is kind of like the Lifesavers commercial I've seen on television. It begins with a dad and his son sitting on a rock watching the sun set over the ocean. It is a clear day and the sun is brilliant against a translucent sky. It appears the sun has been dunked in the ocean like a giant donut in a sea of blue-green coffee. The scene is gorgeous. The little kid leans over to his dad and whispers, "Do it again." How do you explain the realness of a sunset or the way a great song moves you or how the words of a poem can make you cry? But I'll try, because there are certain conditions that need to be present for conversion to be possible.

CONFRONTATION

The first pre-condition for conversion is confrontation. That may not sound like a great place to start. No one wants to "pop the hood" of his or her heart and let God poke around inside. There is no telling what kind of dark sins He might uncover. But look at it this way; the good news is only good in relation to the bad news being bad. The good news is tremendous, because the truth of the bad news is so terrifying.

Let me illustrate with a story about two brothers. One brother dies and the other brother goes to the pastor of the largest church in town. He says, "Pastor, my brother and I never went to church. Neither of us had much use for religion. But appearances are important to us, so if you'll agree to do my brother's funeral and somewhere during the eulogy you say he was a saint, I'll donate $100,000 to your building program." The pastor thought about it for a moment and said, "Double it and you've got a deal." The brother said, "OK."

On the day of the funeral the pastor gave this eulogy, "The man who lies before you was a very rich man. He wielded great power in our community. But to my knowledge he never darkened the door of a church. He never gave a dime to ease the suffering of another. If the newspaper accounts can be believed, he was a cheat and a scoundrel. But compared to his brother over there, he was a saint." Paying someone to lie about your life is dumb, but avoiding God for fear of confronting what He already knows is as stupid as it is unnecessary. Better the ugly truth than a beautiful lie.

King David confronted his adultery and conspiracy to murder by saying, "Against you, you only, have I sinned and done what is evil in your sight, so that you are proved right when you speak and justified when you judge" (Ps. 51:4). David sinned against a whole host of people, but he knew until he made it right with God, he couldn't hope to make it right with anyone else.

Leon Morris said, "God has no need of marionettes. He pays men the compliment of allowing them to live without him if they choose. But if they live without him in this life, they must also live without him in the next." I understand all too well what it's like to try to avoid something unpleasant and painful. Change is hard, confession is scary, and coming clean can be traumatic. We wonder what will happen if we get honest before God. What if He turns His back on me? It is that moment of disclosure, where we're naked to the world, where we wonder—will God kill us or clothe us?

Confronting the truth means accepting the undeniable fact that I am more sinful than I've ever dared imagine. It's one thing to say, "all your righteousness before God is as filthy rags" and a whole other thing to say mine are. You and I are utterly bent, but at the same time we are more loved than we could ever dare dream. But until we're broken over our sin, we'll forever stay bent and beyond saving.

Your problem is not that you sin occasionally. Your problem is that you can and do sin at all. It is not the practice that has gotten us into trouble; it's the propensity to sin that drives a wedge between a holy God and us. Confronting the bad news is the front door to the good news.

CONVICTION

The second condition for conversion is conviction. It's not enough to say "Well you know we're all sinners. After all, nobody's perfect." Confrontation of sin must be personal and convictional. My sin is not someone else's fault. I am the one who spits in the face of God. I am the one who sits smugly on the throne of my heart crowing about my own self-importance. I alone am to blame for growing accustomed to a spiritual diet of slop and vomit. It's like the little boy who was overheard praying, "Lord, if you can't make me a better boy, don't worry about it. I'm having a real good time like I am." That's me in a nutshell. I'm not what I ought to be, but all I need is a little fixing. After all, I know a lot of people worse than me. God, I don't need invasive surgery, just a little adjusting here and tweaking there and I'll run just fine. We are never more optimistic than when we overestimate our own goodness compared to other people's badness.

I remember coming home from a long day at the office and Paula telling me that our new vacuum cleaner was on the blink. Priding myself as a Mr. Fix-it, I took the machine to my workbench in the garage for an "expert diagnosis." I checked all the obvious causes without uncovering the problem. "It must be in the motor," I thought to myself, so I took off the cover to get a closer look. Within twenty minutes I had the entire vacuum scattered over the top of my workbench. After three hours, I decided to take it back to Sears, but I couldn't reassemble the blasted thing.

I am fairly mechanical, so this predicament became a personal challenge. After four hours, it escalated to an all-out war. I was determined to put the darn thing back together. Since the plastic pieces would no longer slide back into place, I forced them. The more pressure I applied; the more pieces I broke and splintered. I ended up with a very expensive, broken beyond repair vacuum cleaner. I was powerless before this unyielding hunk of plastic and metal. After five hours of slinging and slamming things around, I admitted that I couldn't fix the problem. Not only could I not fix the original problem, but I messed things up to the point that this vacuum cleaner had to be put to sleep. This broken machine lying before me was another vivid reminder that some things can't be fixed by me. A skinned knee can be mended with a kiss and a Band-Aid, but no Band-Aid made can mend a broken heart. I am not a machine who can be fixed with spare parts or good intentions.

Let's face it, we're bent and broken. It's sometimes hard to see because we've learned how to cope. We're like ducks on a pond. On the surface, we glide around serenely, but underneath, our webbed feet are churning a mile a minute. So on the outside, we put on a happy face, but inside we're suffocating under the blankets of fear, frustration, and futility. We are suffering from bondage so real and painful that it threatens our very existence. This bondage knows no race or creed. It is no respecter of class or achievement. It does not honor education or position. It is bondage of the human spirit and soul. It is the human condition for which there is no human antidote. It squeezes until we die, explode, or surrender.

America guarantees us personal liberty, but it cannot grant us spiritual freedom. While we all have liberty, we are certainly not free in the truest sense of the word. Real freedom is only possible for those who confront their sin with the conviction that I cannot fix myself.

CONTRITION

The third condition for conversion is contrition. This is what Peter felt when he fell at Jesus' feet and said, "Go away from me, Lord; I am a sinful man!" (Luke 5:8). When I confront the truth about my sin and am utterly convinced I can't fix what's broken, all that is left to do is come to God for mercy. Contrition is the place where indifference dies.

I was listening to then Tennessee Titans cornerback Samari Rolle on a Nashville sports call-in show one day. A caller asked, "Samari, is it true you sleep with your lucky T-shirt every night?" Samari said, "Yes, I've slept with that same lucky, unwashed T-shirt for over eleven years." The host asked, "How can you stand it?" Samari said, "You get used to it. It doesn't smell too bad." That's how it works in our spiritual lives too. Over time we learn to live with our unwashed, unclean selves. It's not great, but it's what we know.

To sin is to be human, to boast about it is to be blind, but to grieve before God over it is to be saved. Jerry Bridges said, "Your worst days are never so bad that you are beyond the reach of God's grace. And your best days are never so good that you are beyond the need of God's grace." In his mesmerizing best-selling autobiographical novel, *A Million Little Pieces,* James Frey describes a test given to a young man who has just been admitted to a rehab program. After years of repeated drug and alcohol abuse, his parents, as a last ditch effort before certain death, have him committed. He is forced to take a true-false test. He reads, "My sins are unpardonable. I stare at the question. My sins are unpardonable. I stare at the question. My sins are unpardonable. I leave it blank. I finish 566 of 567 true or false questions of the test and I close the booklet."[5] To confront the truth about yourself with conviction and contrition is the first step away from self-loathing and into the new life Jesus promises. As the Bible promises, "The sacrifices of God are a broken spirit; a broken and contrite heart, O God, you will not despise" (Ps. 51:17).

Contrition is the "Godly sorrow [that] brings repentance that leads to salvation and leaves no regret" (2 Cor. 7:10). You must be bothered enough by your brokenness to bare it all to God and cry, "Lord have mercy." Contrition owns up to my guilt as I hold onto the promise, "God gives grace to the humble."

CONFESSION

The fourth condition for conversion is confession. Confession is much more than a statement of the fact; it is a cry for help in light of the facts. It is how I lose the awful weight of guilt and dread that's collected around my heart. Confession is like letting the air out of a balloon before it bursts. It is like coming out of hiding to step into the warmth and brilliance of a brand new day. When we say, "I need to get something off my chest" we're talking about confession.

Frank Warren got the idea for *PostSecret.com* as a project for an art exhibit in November of 2004. It is a public place where people confess their private thoughts and remain anonymous. Every week Warren receives confession postcards from around the world. Most of the postcards express politically or socially incorrect ideas, detail abuses both past and present, or articulate body image issues that people have never told others. As evidenced by the comments posted at the bottom of the page, many visitors to the site have found a sense of camaraderie as they read secrets that they themselves have. For most of them, shame and guilt kept them from talking about their own secrets. *PostSecret.com* provides an anonymous space for disclosure, and both the contributors and visitors are finding that these confessions remove their sense of shame and isolation.

The surprisingly vulnerable confessions on these cards display and evoke a wide range of emotion. For example, one postcard states, "I don't care about recycling (but I pretend I do)," while the card beneath it reads, "His temper is so scary that I've lost all of my options." The submitters say they find a sense of release and freedom when they finally drop their card into the mailbox. As he found when he confessed his own secret, Warren says, "Sometimes, we believe we are keeping a secret, but it can be just as true that the secret is keeping us."[6]

Warren's last comment gets to the heart of why confession is essential to conversion. Confession isn't for God, it's for us. Because He's God, He already knows all your deepest, most shameful deeds and thoughts. He knows the pain you bear for the sin that others have perpetuated against you. Confronting the truth allows you to feel your feelings (contrition) and take responsibility (conviction) for your part and then agree with God that it's never going to heal on its own (confession).

It may sound too good to be true; the price of admission into God's family is admission that you can never earn your admission! But that is exactly how simple and yet hard it is to get into God's Kingdom. The Scriptures make it plain too, "If we confess our sins, he is faithful and just and will forgive us our sins and purify us from all unrighteousness. If we claim we have not sinned, we make him out to be a liar and his word has no place in our lives" (1 John 1:9–10). As easy as this might appear, remember that the two hardest words to pronounce in the English language are "I'm sorry!"

Confession can be seen in two parts. First you repent, then you receive, take hold of, to possess forgiveness and the conversion it brings. One of the most moving pictures of repentance that I have ever read is in C. S. Lewis' book, *The Great Divorce*. In one scene Lewis and his spiritual guide are looking at a man whose sin is lust. It perches on his shoulder in the form of a lizard. An angel offers the man a chance to go to the mountains to live in the Kingdom of God.

"I saw coming towards us a Ghost who carried something on his shoulder. What sat on his shoulder was a little red lizard,

and it was twitching its tail like a whip and whispering things in his ear. As we caught sight of him he turned his head to the reptile with a snarl of impatience. "Shut up, I tell you!" he said. It wagged its tail and continued to whisper to him. He ceased snarling, and presently began to smile. Then he turned and started to limp westward, away from the mountains.

"Off so soon, said a voice. The speaker was more or less human in shape but larger than a man, and so bright that I could hardly look at him. Yes. I'm off, said the Ghost. Thanks for all your hospitality. But it's no good, you see. I told this little chap, that he'd have to be quiet if he came—which he insisted on doing. Of course his stuff won't do here: I realize that. But he won't stop. I shall just have to go home. Would you like me to make him quiet? said the flaming Spirit—an angel—as I now understood. Of course I would, said the Ghost. Then I will kill him, said the Angel, taking a step forward. Oh-ah-look out! You're burning me. Keep away, said the Ghost, retreating. Don't you want him killed? You didn't say anything about killing him at first. I hardly meant to bother you with anything so drastic as that.

"It's the only way, said the Angel, whose burning hands were now very close to the lizard. Shall I kill it? Well, that's a further question. I'm quite open to consider it, but it's a new point, isn't it? I mean, for the moment I was only thinking about silencing it because up here—well, it's so embarrassing.

"May I kill it? Well, there's time to discuss that later. There is no time. May I kill it? Please, I never meant to be such a nuisance. Please—really—don't bother. Look! It's gone to sleep of

its own accord. I'm sure it'll be all right now. Thanks ever so much.

"May I kill it? Honestly, I don't think there's the slightest necessity for that. I'm sure I shall be able to keep it in order now. I think the gradual process would be far better than killing it. The gradual process is of no use at all. Don't you think so? Well, I'll think over what you've said very carefully. I honestly will. In fact I'd let you kill it now, but as a matter of fact I'm not feeling terribly well today. It would be silly to do it now. I'd need to be in good health for the operation. Some other day, maybe. There is no other day. All days are present now."[7]

Repentance is the death that leads to life. It's saying to Jesus, "Here is everything I've been holding onto for my own security. I hand it over. You take it and kill it. I am sorry I ever loved it, longed for it, and lusted for it more than you."

The Call to Conversion offers this insight into the call to repentance:

Jesus inaugurated a new age, heralded a new order and called the people to a radical conversion of the heart. Repent. . . . Conversion meant "turning" to "convert." In the King James Bible, conversion is translated "to turn." In Hebrew, conversion (shub) means "to turn, return, bring back, or restore something to its original state." It occurs more than a thousand times and always involves turning from evil to the Lord. . . . The first evangelists did not simply ask people what they believed about Jesus. They called upon their listeners to forsake

> *all and to follow Him. To embrace His kingdom meant a radical change, not only in outlook but in posture, not only in mind but in heart, not only in world view but in behavior. Conversion for them was more than a changed intellectual position. It was a whole new beginning.*[8]

Repentance is both hands out, fingers wide apart, releasing everything back to God. Some will be killed but all will be resurrected to newness of life. It's like letting go of a piece of maggot-infested meat and taking hold of the delicacies of heaven.

Once we repent to God, we then open up and actually receive, take hold of, and possess this promise, "But to all who received him, he gave the right to become children of God. All they needed to do was to trust him to save them" (John 1:12, LB).

Let's say I have a bottle of medicine containing a proven cure for cancer. I give you my word that it is able to completely cure anyone who takes it. Because you have cancer, you come and buy an entire case of this miracle medicine. In a few weeks I receive the tragic news you've died. I inquire as to the cause of your death—cancer. I'm so distraught over the news that I go to your home and ask your family what happened. Upon entering your kitchen, I see the carton of cancer medicine sitting unopened. I ask, "Why didn't you open the medicine and take it?" Your family says, "Well we talked about it, we prayed about it, we even had others come over to study the literature regarding its claimed efficiency, but we just never got around to opening it up and taking it." How sad to die with the cure at arm's reach!

The same is true of salvation. Although Jesus has provided it, it means little to you until you repent and receive it as a gift. What

He accomplished on the cross will do us no good unless we take Him inside.

The four conditions of conversion are confrontation, contrition, conviction, and confession. Jesus said, "there will be more rejoicing in heaven over one sinner who repents than over ninety-nine righteous persons who do not need to repent" (Luke 15:7). Charles H. Spurgeon said, "The grandest fact under heaven is this—that Christ by his precious blood does actually put away sin, and that God, for Christ's sake, dealing with men on terms of divine mercy, forgives the guilty and justifies them, not according to anything that he sees in them or foresees will be in them, but according to the riches of his mercy which lie in his own heart."

THE CONVERSION EFFECT

A small-town druggist overheard the following conversation of a teenage boy talking on his cellular telephone. "Hello, sir, I was calling to see if you needed a lawn boy. Oh, you have one. Well, is he adequate? Oh, he is! Thank you, sir, for your time," said the young boy. The druggist said to the boy, "Sorry you didn't get the job, son." "Oh, no sir," said the boy. "I've got the job. I was just calling to check up on myself."

It would do you well to check up on yourself from time to time. As the Scriptures suggest, "Examine yourselves to see whether you are in the faith; test yourselves" (2 Cor. 13:5). While conversion cannot be easily dissected, it is an experience whose effects can be seen. When Jesus comes in and renovates your heart, you feel different, but there is much more than a feeling, because feelings pass, but the conversion effect endures forever.

PEACE

One of the first effects of conversion is the experience of peace that passes understanding. At my conversion I remember feeling this amazing peace sweep over me. The Scriptures promise, "Since we have been made right in God's sight by faith in his promises, we can have real peace with him because of what Jesus Christ our Lord has done for us" (Rom. 5:1, LB).

There is no peace for the unconverted heart, only periods of calm between the storms.

CLEAN

I remember feeling clean after my conversion. It was like I'd been washed from the inside out. I felt free knowing all was right between me and God; all accounts were up to date and there was nothing to fear. I looked back and knew the past was forgiven. I looked ahead and knew the future made sense and I looked around to see I was not alone, but a part of this great Renegade Nation.

At the moment of conversion I felt a lightness come over me. It was as though a mighty weight had been lifted. No longer was the weight of the world's woes crushing down on me. The dread of what was ahead had morphed into an excitement to see what new possibilities my God was planning for me. I was saved and I felt it. I was redeemed and I knew it. I now had a new heart that made me alive and free. I noticed I tended to laugh more, pray more (not because I should, but because I couldn't help it), and see the world as a bigger, brighter place.

The converted heart anticipates tomorrow with the hope of better days. Why? Because the reality of the sun rising in the east and setting in the west suggests there is work to be done. Jesus said He was always at work doing His father's business. Now that you and I are members of the family, we too join God in His work. My converted heart beats strong and fast after God's agenda. I am no longer me-centered, but Jesus-centered. I love Him. I long to prove the depth of that love by dedicating my life to serving His agenda. Every day is a clean slate, waiting for me to rise up and seize my divine moment.

NEW EYES

The converted heart sees life differently. The eyes of our understanding have undergone a kind of spiritual Lasik surgery. We see life as a gift and every day as a sacred moment. We look at people and see those who Jesus loves and pursues. You've heard people say. "I'll believe it when I see it." The heart converted from doubt and cynicism to love and trust sees it first, and then believes it can happen. We see the impossible as possible. Ours is much more than religious optimism. It is an abiding, growing sense of destiny and divine timing. As Paul said, "I pray also that the eyes of your heart may be enlightened in order that you may know the hope to which he has called you" (Eph. 1:18).

NEW DESIRES

The converted heart is filled with a new drive and ambition. Contrary to what religious people say, Christianity is not the denial of desire. Jesus used the metaphor of hunger to explain the conversion effect. "Blessed are those who hunger and thirst for righteousness, for they will be filled" (Matt. 5:6).

The converted heart has a passion for the life of divine intention.

Since God sought me, saved me, called me into this new life, and left me here, there must be work for me to do. I'm not talking about religious fanaticism here. We have enough of those. These are people who have forgotten their purpose, but have doubled their efforts. They run around making a lot of noise and like a cap pistol, their "pop" signifies nothing. They are like basketball players without a basket, tennis players without nets, or a golfer without a green. What I'm talking about is the purpose-focused life.

One of my favorite verses is, "For when David had served God's purpose in his own generation, he fell asleep; he was buried with his fathers and his body decayed" (Acts 13:36). How cool is that? David served God's purpose. This made his life timeless, for it is God's purposes alone which will prevail in the end. But he did it in his own generation. This gave a timely effect to David's life. There are two qualities a converted heart seeks. We long to live a life that is timeless and timely. This is our goal and driving ambition—to live free, have fun, and dedicate our lives and fortunes to changing the world driven by the conviction that every life matters to God.

As an R4G (a loved, converted, qualified, gifted son or daughter of God), I carry in my heart a definite sense of design and destiny. These may sound like hokey ideas in our current society of cynics, but they are epic ideas to, those with a converted heart. We believe God when He dares us to, "Call to me and I will answer you and tell you great and unsearchable things you do not know" (Jer. 33:3).

Obviously this is not an exhaustive list of all the effects that are present in the converted heart but I hope they're enough to give you a sense of whether or not you possess one. This is really important because too often people just imitate the religious behavior they're told to do, without realizing that just imitating the action of religion really doesn't change anything at the end of the day. Whatever good works you do that don't proceed from a converted heart is counted as outward compliance. And for all the things God will tolerate, heartless obedience is not one of them. You can do all the "do right" things and still miss God. Remember Judas, the man who kissed the door of heaven and went to hell?

PROOF OF NEW LIFE

As we close out this discussion, let's just take one more broad overview about the morphing power of conversion. Remember we're talking about change here—a deep, pervasive renovation of the human heart. We're not talking about adopting certain habits or lifestyle restrictions. We're not talking about a biblical worldview or Christian moral values. We're talking about the greatest, most important thing that can ever happen to a human being—when the heart is converted by the presence and the power of the living Jesus. And for that conversion to have any credibility, it must produce real results in the real world. We must be able to see the change. Wherever the spiritual root is good, spiritual fruit will be forthcoming. As Jesus said, "A good tree cannot bear bad fruit, and a bad tree cannot bear good fruit. Every tree that does not bear good fruit is cut down and thrown into the fire. Thus, by their fruit you will recognize them. Not everyone who says to me 'Lord, Lord,' will enter the kingdom of heaven, but only he who does the will of my Father who is in heaven" (Matt. 7:18–22).

As I said before, Jesus did not come to make good men better. He came to make dead men live. Has He made you alive? Has He resurrected your heart so you don't just feel different, you *are* different? Dallas Willard said "Spirituality in human beings is not an extra or 'superior' mode of existence. It's not a hidden stream of separate reality, a separate life running parallel to our bodily existence. It does not consist of special 'inward' acts even though it has an inner aspect. It is, rather, a relationship of our embodied selves to God that has the natural and irrepressible effect of making us alive to the Kingdom of God—here and now in the material world."[9]

We are free but we're not freewheeling. We're not floating on a cloud like a feather, but our freedom leads us into a sweet bondage where we willingly become slaves of Jesus. Whatever righteousness we commit is an expression of our love for God. He died for us. We gladly live for Him. We submit and bow the knee to the One who purchased our freedom at an awful price. We pledge allegiance to Jesus and no other. We love our country, but our dual citizenship means God's kingdom comes first. We cannot be co-opted by the Republicans or the Democrats. We are now the blood-bought property of Jesus; the One who loves us and gives us no reason to fear slavery to Him as our Lord and Master. And while our relationship with Jesus is very personal, it is never private. And as the following poem suggests, we look forward to the day when all the sinners from every age gathers in a place populated with the most unlikely cast of characters.

I was shocked, confused and bewildered as I entered Heaven's door,
Not by the beauty of it all, by the lights or its décor
But it was the folks in Heaven that made me sputter and gasp
The thieves, the liars, sinners, alcoholics, and the trash.

There stood the kid from seventh grade who swiped my lunch money twice.
Next to him was my old neighbor who never said anything nice.
Herb, who I always thought was rotting away in Hell
Was sitting pretty on Cloud Nine looking incredibly well.
I nudged Jesus, What's the deal? I'd like to hear your take.
How did all these sinners get up here? God must have made a mistake.
And, why is everyone so quiet and somber? Give me a clue.
Hush child, He said, they are all in shock, no one thought they would see you.[10]

7

THE OUTRAGEOUS JOY OF AN XTREME FREEDOM

WHY THE MORALITY POLICE NEED TO LIGHTEN UP AND LEAVE US ALONE

Joy is the most infallible sign of the presence of God.

—*Léon Henri Marie Bloy*

They may take our lives, but they will never take our freedom.

—*William Wallace*

In January of 2004, police were shocked by what they found inside an old house outside the town of Durham, Ontario. Responding to complaints from relatives, police entered the ramshackle house and discovered two teenage boys locked in wire cages. Their biological aunt adopted the teens more than a decade before. Through the years, the boys (now 14 and 15 years old) were repeatedly abused at the hands of their adoptive parents. Ontario officials learned that though the boys did attend school during the day, they were sent to their cages at night.

On weekends and holidays, they were allowed downstairs for a small bowl of cereal in the morning and then sent back to their cages wearing diapers, where they would spend the rest of the day. The adoptive mother was described in court as a domineering, controlling woman whose husband was an illiterate and dyslexic handyman, who beat the boys on her command for fun. Detective Kate Lang and Constable Tim Maw released the fifteen-year-old from his makeshift cage. They told him he would never be locked in there again. The teen response was, "Really?"[1]

This story makes my blood boil. How dare these people deny what is most fundamental to the human spirit—freedom. I love freedom. I need freedom. I was made by God to be free, live free, and die free. I oppose anyone who wants to deny it or take it away from me or anyone else.

In the land of the free and the home of the brave, the fight for freedom has mobilized armies, fought back tyrants, spilt blood, and galvanized the might of an otherwise divided people. Who will soon forget watching senators and congressmen from across the political spectrum standing on the Capitol building steps singing, "God Bless America," on that dastardly dark day—September 11, 2001. Freedom won is epic. Freedom lived is heroic. Freedom lost is catastrophic. Freedom denied is intolerable. But freedom surrendered is tragic.

Jesus has prevailed because He is the author of what we want most—freedom. He launched His mission on earth by saying, "The

Spirit of the Lord is on me, because he has anointed me to preach good news to the poor. He has sent me to proclaim freedom for the prisoners and recovery of sight for the blind, to release the oppressed, to proclaim the year of the Lord's favor" (Luke 4:18–19). I never read these words without feeling a burst of energy pumping through my veins. Because of this single statement, my life makes sense here and now. I have all I've ever wanted and no one can ever take it from me. It is my birthright and I cherish it always.

Because Jesus is the great liberator, the world is not lost and we are never hopeless. I need never fear abandonment or destitution for I will never be unemployed. Freedom is my mission. My goal is to set the captives free in every way you can be free. My weapons are not mean and hateful words, but unconditional love and forgiveness. The stakes are high. The enemy is stealthy, subtle, and sly. But we are well equipped for this fight. And no matter how bad goes the battle all is never lost nor can it ever be as long as Renegade Jesus is afoot ripping doors off cages and resigning our would-be captors to the outer regions of hell.

Speaking of our captors, don't dismiss them lightly. They are out there and they have an uncanny way of finding you. And for some strange reason they know your weaknesses. Remember, as a R4G, your job is to get up everyday and live out of the joy (I like the word fun better) that flows from your freedom in Jesus. Fix your converted heart on knowing God's heart; then you're free to live the way you want. As Saint Augustine said, "Love, and do what you like." So trust His love and then do whatever stirs your heart that needs doing. Remember we're talking about the converted heart and what it now knows and is capable of now that Christ occupies the throne.

But get ready, for the minute you live this freely and passionately, the morality police get nervous. For once you live to love God and please Him only, you no longer need the rules. Therefore, you no longer need the keepers of the rules. Oh my, someone's out a job. And don't expect these self-appointed guard dogs to accept unemployment graciously. Under legalism they bite, but under grace all they can do is gum you.

Be brave. Be daring. Step out of line and march to freedom's rhythm. Arise every morning and express your joy filled and freed up aliveness. Smile. Skip. Be happy. Have fun. Hug the unhuggable. Love the unlovable. Let God be God and every man a liar. Be joyful and playful, especially at church. Ignore denominational loyalties if they give off an air of religious snobbery. Rip away irrelevant labels, which slot you as "religious right," "moderate," or "liberal left." These dividers have no relevance to the current redemptive dialogue. In the Renegade Nation, Jesus is our unity, our freedom, and our common ground.

Be big for God. Live with guts, gusto, and grace. Be a mighty R4G who loves God, loves life, and loves people without regard to label, liability, or lifestyle. But do it with your eyes wide open knowing there is a hoard of religious zealots awaiting you who see themselves as God's watchdogs. I call them the morality police. They get up every morning worried you'll go overboard and besmirch the family name. Curtailing your freedom and fun is their full time calling. And while they may be wrong, they are exceedingly good at what they do. You must fight for your right to live as you were meant to live—freed up, joy-filled Renegade on a mission for God.

R4G's are free from the fear of a wasted life. We don't worry about the size of the house we live in, the kind of car we drive, or how many people we boss around at work. We use our freedom to commit to the "big rocks" that matter in this life and the next. We shy away from the easy life. Tom Hanks, in the movie *A League of Their Own* and in response to the complaint that professional baseball is too hard, said, "It's supposed to be hard, it's the hard that makes it great." Yes, living a great life is hard, but so is a wasted one. At the end of my days here I want to look back and say, "It was worth it all. I served God's purpose for my life. I loved, I encouraged, I inspired, and I promoted the good. My life mattered. I made a difference and left the world an appreciably better place." This only comes to those who live free by conquering the one who hates your freedom most.

BEWARE BEELZEBUB

Someone hates you. His name is Satan. To him, you are the enemy. His hatred for you cannot be ignored. He cannot be bought off and the fact that you don't believe he exists just makes his job that much easier.

Like it or not, you are in his crosshairs. Read this alert carefully: "Keep a cool head. Stay alert. The Devil is poised to pounce, and would like nothing better than to catch you napping" (1 Pet. 5:8, The Message). In most other translations it says Satan is stalking you like a lion lays in wait for its next meal. You may ask, "Why does he care about little ole me?" I am not the Pope, or Billy Graham, or some mega important person. How could I possibly pose a threat to him?

I can tell you what he doesn't fear about you. He doesn't fear your faithful attendance at church or Bible Studies. As a matter of fact he's quite glad you're there, because he'd just as soon you go to hell from church as any other place. He's a church-goer himself.

He doesn't fear your half-hearted prayers or your wandering thoughts in God's general direction. He doesn't fear your sacrificial giving. He doesn't fear your philanthropy. He doesn't fear your theology or your orthodoxy. He doesn't fear your organizational skills. He loves it when you give out of guilt, serve out of duty, and overextend yourself simply because you don't want to let anybody down.

The only thing he fears about you is your freedom. He fears it because it's what he had, but can never have again. And like the spoiled brat he is, if he can't have it, he doesn't want you to enjoy it either. He longs to put the doors back on the cages and stuff you in them. His sole mission is to steal your freedom and your soul. He loves it when you define your life by your defects. He laughs with glee when the morality police arrest your progress and steal your joy and stifle your dreams. He wants you safe, not dangerous. He wants you tied up, not freed up. He loathes you for you remind him of what is lost to him forever—freedom. He can't be pacified, but he can be defeated.

ALL I WANT TO DO IS . . .

If post-modernism had an anthem it would be, "*All I Wanna Do.*" It is written and sung by one of my favorite artists, Sheryl Crow. The song is an observation she made while sitting in a bar sipping a beer next to an ugly guy named William. She looks out at the car wash across the street. It's packed with people on their lunch break washing their cars while wearing their work clothes. As she sits there sipping her beer she says, tongue-in-cheek, that she's nothing like those clean-obsessed young professionals, for all she wants to do is have fun. Working hard at a meaningless job or rushing to wash your car only to get it dirty again on the drive home seems futile to her. She suspects she is not the only one looking for happiness in life, for even those across the street seem caught in the pursuit of a life worth living.

I agree with Sheryl, I want to have fun. But why does admitting that sound so foolish to us serious religious types? Would it sound any more spiritual to use the word joy? Hey, I'm up for joy. It is a great word, but so is fun.

God as an act of joy created us to be filled with joy—fun—happiness—wonder, or whatever you want to call it. Nehemiah, the great leader and movement shaper in the Old Testament said, "the joy of the LORD is your strength" (Neh. 8:10). How dare we live another moment with sadness in our eyes or anger in our voices—we're loved and forever free. Act like it!

This is a day of great gladness and joy. As the angels heralded at Jesus' birth, "Do not be afraid. I bring you good news of great joy that will be for all the people" (Luke 2:10). Jesus is either good news of great joy or He's a joke. He knows me, wants me, loves me, lives in and through me, or He doesn't. There is no middle ground here. Because He lives and loves, we are free to have fun.

It's not wrong to wanna have fun—is it? It is OK to sing about fun, make funny movies, and create an entertainment empire touted as the happiest place on earth, but to bring fun into any conversation about God seems strange to the religious. But why?

Why is fun foolish and God so serious? The Scriptures shout, "in your presence there is fullness of joy; at your right hand are pleasures forevermore" (Ps. 16:11). Does that describe the average Sunday morning church service in America? I'm afraid not. Is it because we want to appear more sophisticated and civilized than we are? What's wrong with being crazy, head over heels in love with the coolest person who ever walked the planet—Jesus?

Maybe He's the real rub—Jesus. We hardly ever actually say His name in church. We talk about God and the Lord, but feel a little foolish saying we're here to worship Jesus. I hear passionate pleas to reinstate a biblical worldview in government, entertainment, and society at large. And, honestly, if I hear another sermon on the virtues of Christian values, I am going to scream. Let's face it right now—Jesus is either dangerous or foolish or maybe both. Paul said, "the message of the cross is foolishness to those who are perishing, but to us who are being saved it is the power of God" (1 Cor. 1:18).

If it is foolish to love Jesus out loud then let's be foolish and let's be the biggest, best fools we can be for God. I know it sounds a little out of order, doesn't it? We are more comfortable with civilized Jesus. But whom can He save? Who has He freed? Why in Jesus' name do we dare linger at the altar of civilized religion hoping to kiss their ring or gain their approval? I will not serve or pay homage to their limp-wristed Jesus. I serve a Savior who was born in a barn, lived a simple, sinless life and who was wrongly accused, and convicted. He died on a cross and thereby purchased for me an atonement I couldn't earn. He loved me when I was an embarrassment to Him. He set me free and I will be his fool to the day I die.

Don't worry about the Elite; be a Renegade for God and join

the Renegade Nation, the only hope of the world. We're a growing group and we're everywhere. Don't be ashamed to appear foolish for God. Who knew Associate Supreme Court Justice Antonin Scalia would dare say out loud to a group in Baton Rouge, "God assumed from the beginning that the wise of the world would view Christians as fools . . . and he has not been disappointed. . . . If I have brought any message today, it is this: Have the courage to have your wisdom regarded as stupidity. Be fools for Christ. And have the courage to suffer the contempt of the sophisticated world."[2]

JAILERS FOR JESUS

Oswald Chambers said, "God who made the birds never made birdcages; it is men who make birdcages, and after a while we become cramped and can do nothing but chirp and stand on one leg." Why do we love building jails, real or imagined? Maybe it is because men tend to deny others what they themselves long to possess but don't. I think that is at the heart of why people, good people, feel the need to act as though they're God's Gestapo. Let's look at two of the jailers you need to watch out for.

First, watch out for the ordained jailers for Jesus. These are the professional clergy who are specially trained to talk for God. They are well educated in the tools of their trade. They have studied Greek, Hebrew, and Latin. They read systematic theologies for fun and while most are good, godly, selfless, and dedicated people, many are the most uptight and unhappy people I've ever met. Either way, surveys tell us that the vast majority of clergy are miserable. They are chronically overworked and unappreciated. They feel trapped in dead-end churches and at the mercy of mean-spirited, small-minded people. I heard one speaker say recently that an estimated five thousand clergy per month are leaving the ministry for good. That's sad, but not unexpected. Religious people are hard to please and easily ticked off. So if you're scared to tell the truth for fear of losing your job, you toe the party line, give them a sweet sermon, take their money, and live with the shame of being the equivalent of a religious prostitute. Either way you look at it, this can easily compromise the messenger and the message.

I enjoy blogging and the dialogue it provokes. Recently a fellow blogger objected to something I said. He ended his comments by saying, "Who does this guy think he is?" A good friend of mine e-mailed me and apologized for this guy's rude remarks. This is what I said to my friend, "The best thing Jim said, was, 'Who does this guy think he is?'" I said, "The best thing you will ever do is question anyone who dares to tell you they speak for God, especially me." Amen! Just because a person is ordained, and seminary-trained doesn't mean he or she is necessarily right. You are responsible to "test the spirits to see whether they are from God, because many false prophets have gone out into the world" (1 John 4:1).

Most ordained people who speak for God mean well. But some don't. There are charlatans and cheats among us. Jesus called them "wolves in sheep's clothing" and said, "You blind guides! You strain out a gnat but swallow a camel. Woe to you teachers of the law and Pharisees, you hypocrites! You clean the outside of the cup and dish but inside they are full of greed and self-indulgence" (Matt. 23:24–28). Not a very nice thing to say, but definitely needed.

Second, be on guard for the orthodox jailers for Jesus. These are the ones, the only ones, who are right. They have a corner on the truth market. And while they may be wrong, they are never in doubt. They've got God on their side and in their hip pocket. Sometimes they're kind and winsome, but most times they're rigid and demanding.

They're like a religious version of McDonald's. The great thing about McDonald's is that no matter where you go you will get the same food. I didn't say great food; maybe not even *good-for-you* food, but it will be the same food. It will be safe and edible. This is what the merchants of orthodoxy promise—a safe, comfortable place to worship a "God like us" with "people like us." We'll tell you what you need to know and should there exist an alternate view to ours, you don't need to know.

But alas, the religious world is not like a fast-food franchise; it's more like Heinz 57 or a fruit basket. It's like Forrest Gump's mama's sage advice, "Life is like a box of chocolates. You never know what you're going to get." That truth is even truer about religion in America on a Sunday morning. What is considered orthodox in one church is strictly forbidden in another. Entire denominational entities exist solely for the perpetuation of a single solitary, slender doctrinal distinctive. Some churches require baptism by immersion; others are OK with sprinkling water on the head, while others believe baptism is for babies. Still other churches divide up over the sacrament of Communion with both its mode and meaning. On and on the list can go from whether you can drink beer, wear shorts, or attend R-rated movies. I've even heard of people being turned away from a church service because they wore slacks, had tattoos, or failed to wear a tie.

If it makes you feel any better, Jesus didn't escape the ire of the orthodox either. He allowed His disciples to gather grain on the Sabbath. The Pharisees condemned Him for allowing an unlawful act. What did Jesus say? He settled it by teaching a greater truth. He said God made the Sabbath for man, not the other way around. Clear. Simple. To the point, but hardly safe. He would pay for this later.

Let me bottom-line it. Religion is divisive. It chops God up into little bite-sized preferences. Religion's only interest is your obedience and your wallet. That's why the Renegade spirit is stifled by religion. There's no freedom in religion. There's no freedom in law-keeping. There's no freedom in dry dusty orthodoxy. Freedom comes from Jesus. And that freedom is accessed through a relationship with Jesus. It is personal, powerful, and life changing.

ALL ACCESS FREEDOM

The heartbeat of the gospel is freedom. Freedom is precious because it is never cheap. It is the best of things, possibly because it is so expensive. Freedom in Christ is not cheap grace; it is extravagant love. It is not a free freedom. It is a costly freedom for it required an awful price. Only God Himself coming down from the land of the living to the land of the dying and perpetual pain could satisfy the debt we owed. As the great missionary Paul said, "It is for freedom that Christ has set you free," and it was the apostle John who promised, "If the Son sets you free, you will be free indeed" (John 8:36).

Stepping into God's great free-life, we discover for the first time what we were meant to be—free. What makes this freedom

Xtreme is its comprehensive, multi-faceted nature. This lavish freedom produces outrageous joy in the J-life. To understand this extreme freedom, you must understand its three movements. These include the freedom from, under, and to. Let's look at each one individually.

First, is the freedom FROM. Jesus died to pay my debt due a holy God. At His resurrection, the gates of the debtor's prison were opened and I was set free. Because of the redemptive work of Jesus on the cross, I am free from the bondage of the past and the dread of the future.

In the 1994 film, *The Shawshank Redemption,* Red—Morgan Freeman's character—spent his prime wasting away in prison because of a reckless crime he committed as a teenager. After forty years of incarceration, Red finally receives his release and is freed from Shawshank. However, he can't free himself from the habit of asking for permission each time he wishes to use the men's room. He's become "institutionalized." This newfound life scares him because he's grown accustomed to the structure behind bars. Walls, bars, and guards with guns became Red's sanctuary. He didn't have to exercise his own decision-making. Someone else did the thinking for him, and now, on the outside, he faces a prospect more daunting and terrifying than incarceration: freedom. Red confesses that he contemplates various ways to break his parole and return to the security of his prison cell. He sums up his dilemma in one line: "It is a terrible thing to live in fear."

People caught up in legalism are no different than Red—wishing for freedom but scared to death of the choices it demands. It's much easier to retreat to our lists of "do's and don'ts," of black and white categories than to think, pray, and struggle with thorny social, moral, and political decisions. The church, by erecting legalistic walls, trains up a generation of Christians who can't think or act for themselves.

The Xtreme freedom that Jesus offers begins with freedom from; a freedom from the bondage of past sins and degrading habits; a freedom from the emotional bondage of broken relationships. We all have hidden in the closet of our forgetfulness those incredibly painful and scarring moments when trust was violated and relationships were shredded. And no one is free who harbors unforgiveness for these unforgettable experiences. "For I see that you are full of bitterness and captive to sin" (Acts 8:23). It's only the grace of God that gives us the freedom from becoming bitter over betrayals. When I forgive someone who's hurt me, I'm the one I'm freeing.

There is also the freedom from needing to prove my worth by my work. I'm free from being chained to a job or a career just because it pays the bills, provides me a corner office, or earns legitimacy among my peers. It's the freedom from the need to please.

I'm free from the relentless, shrill voice of the people pleaser inside me using the fear of rejection to paralyze me. I'm free from forced fellowship and ungodly agendas. Let them lasso someone else's freedom with their rope of rules made of sand. R4G's can't be corralled into a tidy little kingdom of political correctness. I am free from the manipulation of a promised future favor if I'd just go along. I am free from the allure of power, privilege, or position. I'm free from a thousand tiny demons that come at the moment between consciousness and sleep that rob me of my peace. "For the power of the life-giving Spirit—and this power is mine through

Christ Jesus—has freed me from the vicious circle of sin and death" (Rom. 8:2, LB).

Saint Augustine said, "Trust the past to the mercy of God, the present to his love, and the future to his providence." Renegade Jesus frees me from the shame of the past and the fear of the future. I live free from condemnation and I'm more than happy to return the favor to those around me. How sweet it is to let go of anger and forgive the petty slights and thoughtless cruelties done to me long ago. Because I've been judged and set free, I never sit in judgment of others—period.

Praise God almighty, I am free from the need to control people, places, and things. Jesus has broken the chains of my self-destructive self-talk. Yes I am a sinner, but I am also a saint. Thanks to Renegade Jesus, I have a new heart, a new passion, and a new reason to get up in the morning. In the words of the old southern spiritual, "Free at last, free at least, thank God almighty, I'm free at last!"

Second, is the freedom UNDER. The first movement of freedom is away from the old, dead, decaying life. The second movement is like getting under the cover of a solid roof during a hailstorm. My converted heart loves it under the roof of Jesus' loving Lordship. Ours is a freedom under His authority and control. He is boss. He has the right to tell me what to do with my life. He owns me and I am glad He does. He alone thought I was worth dying for. I think I'll trust Him, love Him, follow Him, and obey Him. Call it dumb, but I call it smart, because as Bob Dylan wrote, "You're gonna have to serve somebody, it may be the devil or it may be the Lord." You are free, when the speed limit is 70, to drive

40, 43, 44, 45, 69, or 69½. But you have no freedom to drive 90 and endanger my life. You don't have that autonomy. Freedom under is recognizing that my freedom has been bought, paid for and given to me under the lordship of Jesus Christ. His loving lordship, His sacrifice, His life, His intention for me is that I be loved and that I be free.

I remember the thrill of getting my first "all access" pass. I was out on the road with singer-songwriter Lionel Cartwright. We were in Charleston, West Virginia for a huge summer festival. As I got off the bus, I was handed an "all-access" pass on a lanyard to place around my neck. With it, I gained access to walk out among the crowd of 20,000+ screaming fans. As I started to go back stage, I was confronted with the huge, tattooed, triple-X T-shirt-wearing bouncer. He snarled at me until he saw the pass hanging around my neck. When he saw that little piece of plastic, he smiled and waved me through. All because of that laminated ticket, I got to go anywhere and everywhere I wanted. I could stand on the stage and talk to the guitar techs or I could go over and chow down at the catering truck. No one ever questioned who I was or what I did. I didn't contribute one thing to the success of this festival. I just had an "all access" pass. It was a gift and with it I had total freedom.

That's what Jesus does for us when He converts our heart and makes us a citizen of His new kingdom. We have been transferred from one kingdom to another kingdom. We now have "all access." We're the King's kids! We are still in the world, but no longer of it.

The grand paradox of our freedom in Christ is this; we are most free when we are most bound. The bond of which I speak is the bond of love that ties us hopelessly to the one who has our highest good as His most noble intention. Ravi Zacharias said,

"In an attempt to be reasonable, man has become irrational. In an attempt to deify himself, he has defaced himself. In an attempt to be free, he has made himself a slave. And like Alexander the Great, he has conquered the world around him but has not yet conquered himself."[3]

The athlete who is unwilling to discipline his body is not free to excel on the field of competition. His failure to train diminishes his performance no matter how hard he tries. He may try to run with speed and endurance, but failing to train is training to fail. Discipline is the price of freedom. As Dietrich Bonhoeffer said, "The demand for absolute liberty brings men to the depths of slavery."

The Christ-centered worldview can be expressed in two circles. The larger circle represents God who is personal, self-sufficient, and wholly other than His creation. The small circle represents us. We exist apart, separate, and other than God, but certainly not independent of Him. He is my shield and fortress. He is my advocate, my prophet, priest, and king. As prophet, He has the authority to tell me what to do. As priest, He is ever present, ministering mercy and grace when I walk around the rim of hell. As King, He is ruler of my heart. My affections and ambitions are tied to His revolutionary agenda. He is either Lord of all or not Lord at all. That's why he was puzzled when he asked, "Why do you call me 'Lord, Lord,' and not do what I say?" (Luke 6:46).

Paul, the loudest advocate of freedom in the New Testament said, "You my brothers, were called to be free. But do not use your freedom to indulge the sinful nature; rather, serve one another in love" (Gal. 5:13). Freedom is the opportunity to serve God by serving people. R4G's do not flaunt their freedom or stick out their tongues. They roll up their sleeves and use their freedom to serve God's redemptive agenda. As Saint Augustine said, "To my God, a heart of flame; to my fellowmen, a heart of love; to myself, a heart of steel."

Third, is the freedom TO. Jesus' aliveness living in me gives the freedom to become an authentic version of who He created me to be. I am no longer bound by my inner demons, dumb habits, or the insane need to prove my worth to the world. Paul warned the early believers: "It is for freedom that Christ has set us free. Stand firm, then, and do not let yourselves be burdened again by a yoke of slavery" (Gal. 5:1). We are free from the dread of the past and the fear of the future. Under the loving leadership of Jesus, I have authority and standing. I bow to the loving Savior who is a kingdom builder and cosmic problem-solver. Right here and now, He is calling us to engage our wild imagination to dream of the people-helping, need-meeting, world-changing possibilities before us. Consider this outrageous promise, "Now to him who is able to do immeasurably more than all we ask or imagine, according to his power that is at work within us" (Eph. 3:20). I don't know about you, but I have a big, vivid imagination. Yet Jesus says, *Think of your biggest, best, most amazing future and I can top it. You are free to be absolutely amazing, if you can turn a deaf ear to the naysayers and negative nellies. Fix your gaze on the Lord of Glory and you'll hear, is there anything too hard for me?*

Henri Nouwen said, "The great spiritual task facing me is to so fully trust that I belong to God that I can be free in the world—free to speak even when my words are not received; free to act even when my actions are criticized, ridiculed, or considered useless;

free also to receive love from people and to be grateful for all the signs of God's presence in the world. I am convinced that I will truly be able to love the world when I fully believe that I am loved far beyond its boundaries."[4] Do you get the sense that freedom is a big deal? It is at the heart of all things good and noble. To be free politically and socially is a costly privilege bought with the blood of many, but to be free spiritually is the greatest gift of all purchased on the cross by the offering of The One.

Because Renegade Jesus died to set me free, I am now and forever free to choose my attitude, knowing my attitude isn't everything, but it almost is. Gratitude leads to wonder which leads to joy. In Christ, I am free to dream a great dream and dedicate my life to pursuing it to its completion. I know that the size of my dream will determine the size of my life.

I am free to love people and welcome them into my life. I will smile when I meet people and make them my priority. People are not interruptions on the non-religious road to real, they're always the agenda. I am free to associate with people who are smarter than me, better than me, and who have more wisdom than me. They will always make me better.

As a lover of truth wherever I find it, I am free to read great books and listen to great music as sources of endless inspiration and personal growth.

I am free to interpret my circumstance in light of who I know God is. I will NOT define God by my difficulties. I can live anywhere in the world I want and do anything I want as long as it brings me joy and makes the world a better place for the people around me.

Because I am free from fixing the world, I have fun everywhere

I go. I enjoy every sandwich and sense the sacred all around me. I recognize the goodness and greatness of God in all I see and experience. Because wherever I am is worship, I can turn a car into a chapel and an airport terminal into a scared space as long as I am aware of the overwhelming generosity of God I am experiencing in the very moment.

I am free to turn my J-O-B into J-O-Y. For me, work is play. God made me to live free and have fun. Armed with that knowledge, I do what I love and I love what I do. And because it's fun, it looks easy to onlookers even though it's not. For Jesus, I bring everything I am to everything I do. Because I live within my calling, it's like play for me, therefore I can do it better than I can do anything else and I can do it with renewable energy and genuine excitement. My work is my joy and my offering back to God and the world around me. I am living the freed up, joy-filled life and I'm contagious!

What a joy to be free. As R4G's, ours is a hard-fought, blood-bought freedom, as are all true freedoms. But our warrior is the champion of love. Jesus is the author and finisher of our freedom. We are His trophies and we will never be the same again. We are the prize and we are forever changed by His victory.

Our Xtreme freedom breeds a gentleness of spirit. That's why laughter and fun are one of freedom's sweetest fruits. Under the lordship of Jesus, we run, play, and dance like those who have no worries. Kindness is our freedom's new habit. We love listening to others' joy and sorrow because we understand both are a part of the symphony of grace. Courage is freedom's power to choose. When confronted with the dark enemy of pride and prejudice, we choose love. Patience is freedom's intelligence and unhurried life is its sweet pleasure.

Stop apologizing for who you are. Stop apologizing for your strength. Stop apologizing that within your well-healed heart there's a renegade who wants to be free, have fun, and change the world. Stop apologizing because you can't please every "goober" who doesn't like what you do or the way you do it. Just stop it! Be who you are, in Christ. It seems like we're always being stretched beyond our comfort zone. Wherever He leads, I can feel rest assured that He has my back. There is fullness of joy in His presence, even though we're being stretched beyond measure.

The film *Braveheart* tells the story of William Wallace (Mel Gibson), a common man who led Scotland to freedom from English rule. With a great sense of destiny, Wallace commands a ragtag band of farmers and villagers to defeat their oppressors, forcing them back to England.

The turning point for Scotland comes at the battle of Sterling. The Scots are vastly outnumbered and begin to flee before the battle even begins. Wallace rides onto the scene and reminds the Scots who they are and what is truly important. "I am William Wallace. I see a whole army of my countrymen here in defiance of tyranny. You've come to fight as free men, and free men you are. What will you do without freedom? Will you fight?"

A soldier answers, "Against that? No, we will run, and we will live."

Wallace replies, "Yes, fight and you may die. Run and you'll live, at least for a while. And dying in your beds many years from now, would you be willing to trade all the days from this day to that for one chance—just one chance—to come back here and tell our enemies that they can take our lives, but they'll never take our freedom?"

He has given you true, glorious, eternal freedom. You have no condemnation. Your guilt is gone, never-to-be-remembered against you again. God intends that you *feel* forgiven. Your freedom was purchased at an awful price, so act like it, talk like it, pray like it, teach like it and most of all—love like it. I end this cry for freedom with the words of an ancient Franciscan Blessing:

> *May God bless you with discomfort at easy answers, half truths, and superficial relationships so that you may live deep within your heart. May God bless you with anger at injustice, oppression, and exploitation of people, so that you may wish for justice, freedom, and peace. May God bless you with enough foolishness to believe that you can make a difference in this world, so that you can do what others claim cannot be done.*

8

SAVORING THE SACRED NOW

NEVER, NEVER, NEVER SAVE ANYTHING COOL FOR COMPANY

Every ordinary day given to God and touched by God is a sacrament.

—*Bertha Munro*

Life is what happens to us while we are making other plans.

—*Thomas la Mance*

When I was a kid there was a secret closet at the end of our main hallway. It was always locked up tight by direct order of my mother. I wasn't even to touch the doorknob, much less dare try looking inside. Every day, there it was like forbidden fruit calling—"open me, open me up and discover the hidden treasure inside." What could possibly be so important, so valuable, so mysterious, and so fun?

For added protection, I thought, there was a metal grate in the floor in front of the closet. It seemed to protect the contents like a moat protects an English castle from hostile invaders. Actually it was the cover for the gas furnace. In the winter, it was too hot to step on. I thought, what a perfect way to guard the goodies—hey, I was a kid!

I'll never forget the day I came home and caught my mother getting something out of the forbidden closet of mystery. I'd never seen into the closet before. It was wondrous. There were shelves, neatly filled with plates and glasses, the likes of which I had never seen before. And I asked my mother, "What are these?"

She said, "This is my crystal and fine china." She took down one of the glasses and held it out for me to touch. It was tissue paper-thin, rose-colored, and had a long-stemmed pedestal. Each glass was meticulously etched with decorative designs. They were gorgeous, and fragile enough to shatter in the hand of a firm grip. Then she took down the plates. She held one out and said, "This was my mother's fine china." It had roses painted around the edges and silver around the rims. Then she took out a big, square, mahogany box. She opened it up revealing a red velvet lining and the shiny forks, spoons, and knives all perfectly aligned.

It was amazing! I didn't know we owned stuff like this. And I asked her, "What is all this stuff for?" She gave me a one-word answer—company. I asked. "What's company?" She said, "They are the special people we have over on special occasions." That's what we were saving our fine china for—for company! To my recollection, we never had any company. We never used those plates and glasses—ever. And with time, my brother and I moved away still waiting for company. My father and brother are dead, but the china remains unused, waiting for the company that never came.

I implore you to take the door off the hinges of whatever it is in your life that you're saving for "company" and use it every day. Today is God's gift to you. This moment, this place (a prison, a hotel, a hospital, your house, out on the beach), this "now" is sacred. Forget about tomorrow. It may never come. Be here right now! Today! Smell the smells. Hear the sounds of life calling you to engage. And never, never, never save anything really cool for company.

The outrageous joy of our freedom in Christ is the privilege to wake up and "be here"—here and now, embracing whatever this now is—good or bad. The Scriptures command, "Give thanks in all circumstances" (1 Thess. 5:18). *All* circumstances? When life goes your way, give thanks. When work is going wonderfully well, give thanks. When the relationships are on a greasy rail, give thanks. When your income is rising and your blood pressure is falling, give thanks. And in those rare days when just getting up and putting your big hairy toe on the floor is victory, give thanks. God wills that you savor the sacredness of this moment, this here-and-now, and this never-to-be-repeated moment in the sun.

The greatest poverty is to arrive at a moment in time where you have everything for which to be grateful except the power to be so. Last summer my family and I vacationed at our favorite place, Disney World. Out of all the amazing things I saw and enjoyed, one of the most unbelievable and stupefying sights I see each time I go is angry, agitated, red-faced parents screaming at their kids. I'm thinking, *did you work all year, save, and make the trip all the way down here to be stressed-out, wound-up, and screaming your head off?* You hear, "Stop that! Don't get wet! The lines are too long. You can't be hungry. Sit down until you can learn how to behave!" Is this having fun? I shudder to think about what kind of life they are returning to when all this "fun" is over.

That's why renegades are repelled by uptight, religious types who say, "You're not supposed to run, jump, or be silly. You're not supposed to have fun. If there ever is fun, we'll tell you what it is, where it is, and how much of it you can have." Life is hard, God is touchy, so don't tick Him off!

The word savor comes from the Latin word *sapere* which means "to taste and enjoy." To savor a thing, anything, requires a joyful heart. Only the truly joyful can appreciate the gift and the giver. Living in the "now" moment is a sacred gift from the Giver of all good things. To savor is to gaze on the gift with appreciation and gratitude for the giver. It is squeezing, reveling in this exquisite "now." So ambitious is this idea of savoring that the Scriptures say, "Taste and see that the LORD is good; blessed is the man who takes refuge in him" (Ps. 34:8). Experiencing the goodness of God requires being fully present in the moment, to taste the grace and lavish goodness of God.

Just as sampling the delicacies prepared by a master chef honors the labor of love, savoring and drinking in the present moment honors God as my Master donor. Savoring this sacred "now" makes you aware of your life and the gift of being here, alive, and adding your chapter to God's redemptive narrative. You may not control vast amounts of wealth in the world. You may not be powerful and well connected. You may not have the resources to get on a plane and fly away to a sunnier, safer place, but you can turn the place you are right now into a chapel by choosing to find God's thumbprint on this today. He is here; feel His pleasure, sense His smile, and make His heart your mighty fortress.

Don't be fooled into thinking that what you really need is that deal to come through or to land that new, lucrative job, and then you'll have it made. Everything you crave is present in this moment. Here and now, admit that what you seek is not more stuff from God, but God Himself. You long for the touch of your heavenly Father reminding you that you're not alone and you will never be abandoned. He is not busy or elusive like earthly fathers can be. He is here in the sacred now. He's not in a hurry; so why are you? He will whisper prophecies in your ear if you're ready to listen. Loosen up, lean in, and listen for the still, small, sweet voice speaking of mysteries to come.

As a father, I tend to think that my children would rather have what I can provide than me. They don't really long for time with me—do they? Many a father has fallen victim to the provider syndrome. As a result, we are raising a generation of children who are experience-rich and relationship-poor. A great example of this is the 1958 film *Cat on a Hot Tin Roof*. Starring Paul Newman and Elizabeth Taylor, the movie is based on Tennessee Williams's play about a wealthy dying patriarch called Big Daddy. While his children and in-laws squabble about the family inheritance, Big Daddy and his second son, Brick, try to come to terms with his failed fathering and his misplaced priorities.

In the basement of their family home, Big Daddy (Burl Ives) and Brick (Paul Newman) talk honestly among the clutter of discarded paintings, sculptures, and boxes of family heirlooms. Big Daddy looks around the room and says, "You know what I'm going to do before I die? I'm going to open up all these boxes." He tells

Brick his wife bought most of the stuff during a trip they took years ago in Europe. He boasts he's worth ten million dollars in cash and blue chip stocks; not to mention, he owns 28,000 acres of prime land. Brick says in a cynical tone, "Well, that is pretty rich to be." Big Daddy removes the cobwebs from an old clock and says, "There's one thing you can't buy in a fire sale or any other market on earth. That's your life. Can't buy back your life when it's finished." Brick wonders why Big Daddy allowed Big Momma to buy all the stuff. Big Daddy, picking up an old suitcase, answers, "The human animal is a beast that eventually has to die. If he's got money, he buys, and he buys, and he buys. The reason why he buys everything he can is because of the crazy hope that one of the things he buys will be life everlasting."

Big Daddy asks Brick why he never came to him when he wanted something, why he didn't lean on the people who loved him. He asks angrily, "What was there that you wanted that I didn't buy for you?" Brick, raising his voice in anger, "You can't buy love! You bought yourself a million dollars worth of junk! Look at it! Does it love you?"

Big Daddy lashes out, "Who do you think I bought it for? Me? It's yours! This place, all the money, every rotten thing is yours!" Brick answers, "I don't want things!" He pushes a sculpture and large vase to the floor. With a steel rod Brick begins smashing things, including a life-sized photograph of himself in a football uniform. He laments, "Worthless. Worthless. Worthless." He stops smashing things and breaks down crying. Big Daddy pleads with Brick to stop crying. A moment later Brick stops and says, "Can't you understand? I never wanted your place, or money, or to own anything. All I wanted was a father, not a boss. I wanted you to love me."[1]

Here's the key to the J-life—let each day be about receiving God's love, then giving it away. You see if I love you and you don't return my love, I hurt for I have lost something. But when God says I love you and you don't love Him back, He too hurts not because He has lost something but because you've lost literally everything.

We R4G's are free to love and we stay free by giving as much of it away as we can. Every moment is a gift of love. The sky, the birds, the air I breathe, the abundance I enjoy is proof God loves me. Fretting and fuming are evidences that I don't know His heart or trust His love. That's why the surest predictor of your ability to savor the moment and enjoy your life is, "what do you think about when you think about God?" If you see God as distant, moody, and hard to please, then every moment is laden with suspicion, "where is God? Has He left the building? Did I say something wrong?"

WHAT'S BEEN LOST

A young couple had two little boys, ages eight and ten. They were always getting into some kind of trouble. Their parents were at their wits end. What should they do about their kids' behavior? The mother heard that a clergyman in town was wise in the ways of disciplining young boys. So they asked him to talk to the boys.

When the appointed day came, he asked to see the boys separately so he could assess each boy individually. The youngest brother went first. The clergyman sat the boy down and asked, "Where is God?" The boy gave no response, so the minister repeated the question in an even sterner tone, "Young man, I asked you, where is God?" Again, the boy made no attempt to answer, so the clergyman raised his voice even more and shook his finger in the boy's face, "WHERE IS GOD?" With that the boy jumped up, bolted from the room and ran directly home, up the stairs, and locked himself in his closet. His older brother followed him into the closet and said, "What happened?" The younger brother replied, "We are in BIG trouble this time. God is missing and they think we took Him!"

Who has taken God from us? He is disappearing from public life and, for a growing number of us He is hardly perceptible, even at church. We see the evidence that God was once here, but as the Scriptures explain, "People knew God perfectly well, but when they didn't treat him like God, refusing to worship Him, they trivialized themselves" (Romans 1:21, The Message). Isn't that interesting but so revealing of the present reality? The more we try to ignore God, the more we end up trivializing our own existence. We've lost a sense of the larger sacred story that makes "here and now" have meaning and context. As Pascal suggested, "God made man in His image and man returned the favor."

Why do we chase the sacred away or prefer to hide from God? When did we trade worship for worry? We did it when we traded our joy for jobs. Instead of doing what we love and loving what we do, the vast majority of Americans get up on Monday mornings already praying for the weekend. And because we have lost the power to enjoy what we have and where we are, we try to escape through pleasure. So we try to finance our happiness while sinking deeper and deeper into debt, which keeps us a slave to a job we don't love just because it pays the bills. We get up day after day singing the great American anthem, "I owe, I owe, it's off to work I go."

We've traded our soul for security. The same old routine, month after month, year after year, has etched a frown like a sagging scar across our faces. We hate our lives even though we have more luxuries than ever before. The only motivation is to get through another day. Sometimes we think of changing, but the fear of the unknown keeps us at bay and in line. After all, if my job is my God and if I lost my job, chaos would surely engulf me.

We've traded our humanity for hurry and because hurrying is all about not being present, we live mentally and emotionally in yesterday's regrets and grievances or tomorrow's unknowns, while our bodies are stuck in this here and now moment. How relevant is the Jesus warning, "Do not worry about tomorrow, for tomorrow will worry about itself. Each day has enough trouble of its own" (Matt. 6:34). If we're evolving, it must be slow, for after two thousand years, worry is still our nemesis.

Who is it you no longer see because of your hurry-blindness? Is it the person at the restaurant who serves your meal? Is it the guy at the mini-mart where you pump your gas and buy your coffee? Is it the cleaning lady at work or the lowly secretary who inhabits the cubical you whisk by everyday? Have you lost your sense of presence? Where is the fascination with life you used to wake up with? How sad to be bored with waking up to a new day. Stop. Think. Take stock of your life. Imagine you're alive, living in a rich world brimming with blessing and possibility. The signs and senses of the sacred surround you, right now, right here. God is near. Can you feel His breath? Feel His pleasure? Knowing He's here and now sustaining, surprising, and loving you is the key to living each day to its fullest.

Savoring the sacred "now" is reclaiming your wonder. When

you stop to listen and "be," you sense that God has adorned this place, whether it be a city street, crowded interstate, or a country lane, with life and love. Appreciate the beautiful balance between what is fading away and what is being born. Remember, the bend in the road is not the end of the road unless you fail to make the turn. This is a good moment; you're reading which means you've got eyes, and people who thought you were worth educating. Yea you! Yea them! Yea God!

ENJOY EVERY SANDWICH

Several years ago I was watching the *Late Show with David Letterman*. His guest that night was Warren Zevon. Zevon was also Dave's first guest when he moved to CBS.

This was to be Zevon's last public appearance. He died weeks later from a rare form of lung cancer. Letterman asked Zevon, "How has having cancer affected you?" He said, "Twenty years of not going to the doctor was a phobia that's not going to pay off for me." Letterman leaned in and in a rare moment of tender seriousness asked Zevon, "What are you learning?" Here was a rare chance to look at life from the viewpoint of a man staring at death, eyeball to eyeball. Without hesitation Zevon looked at the camera and said, "I'm learning to enjoy every sandwich." What an awesome answer from the lips of a dying man! Seize the joy in your life today as it is. To wait another day, another hour is to waste too much of your sacred time. Learn to treat time as life.

At the end of the day, when I'm done, I want to say, "I squeezed every ounce of loving and living there was. I enjoyed my family. I enjoyed my kids. I enjoyed my work. I enjoyed the people who came in and out of my life. I found joy in the pain that made the good times even sweeter. I enjoyed the nice car, new house, and I enjoyed the apartment, too. I enjoyed it all and breathed deeply every sweet breath of life. I savored it and I didn't let anything or anyone rob me of being alert to the privilege of being alive and knowing I am loved by Jesus totally and unconditionally."

Where does the power to savor the sacred moment come from? It resides in the heart. That's why the Scriptures warn us, "above all else, guard your heart, for it is the wellspring of life" (Prov. 4:23). Guard your heart against that dark place where you have everything for which to be grateful except the power to be so.

How do you guard your heart? How do you enjoy every sandwich? Each morning as you wake up and become aware of where you are take time to say, *Jesus, I surrender to your devastating, liberating love, I surrender my heart to your care. I acknowledge that,* "Greater love has no one than this, that he lay down his life for his friends" (John 15:13). *Thank you for choosing me, for marking me out for redemption, not condemnation. Thank you, Jesus, for anointing and appointing me to go out into this day to live a free, fun, fulfilling life. Because of You, Jesus, my life has meaning so that every task of this day carries a sacred significance to it.*

Knowing You love me will make rush hour into a time to meditate on your goodness. There is a day coming when I will beg to be able to drive, but can't. Whatever awaits me in the marketplace today will not overtake me. I will not be stunned by bad circumstances or swayed by good ones. I will not be stung by the abrasive, arrogant ways and means others employ to get their way.

Jesus, no one will jail me today. No one can derail my trust in Your loving presence. I will be like Job who cried, "Though he slay me, yet will I serve Him." *I've built a guard of love that sentinels the gates of my heart. You keep me safe and secure knowing no need will go unmet. Though I walk through the shadow of the valley of unemployment, I will fear no destitution. Learning to surrender to love is leading me into a bigger, more spacious world where abundance is mine.*

Every day, I submit my will to divine providence. I take courage and comfort in knowing that, "You didn't choose me! I chose you! I appointed you to go and produce . . ." (John 15:16, LB). *Today I will live a productive life, one that changes me and the world around me. I will not be the same tomorrow as I am today for I will gain strength from knowing wherever today takes me, Jesus is already there.* The great reformer Martin Luther said, "That little bird has chosen his shelter; above it are the stars and the deep heaven of worlds; yet he is rocking himself to sleep without caring for tomorrow's lodging, calmly clinging to his little twig and leaving God to think for him." How amazing to think Jesus is always thinking about me.

Submission is not blind subjugation. Subjugation turns a person into a thing, destroys individuality, and removes all liberty. Submission allows me to become more of what God wants me to be; it calls out individuality; it frees me to want what God wants for my life and ministry. Subjugation is weakness; it is the refuge of the coward. Submission is strength; it is the first step toward true maturity. It is the place of greatest desire for I long for Jesus to "teach me to do your will, for you are my God; may your good Spirit lead me on level ground" (Ps. 143:10).

A good example of surrender and submission is what happens when you drive a car. Driving is mainly about the gas pedal, gear shifter, brake, and the steering wheel. They either work in concert with each other or they'll wreck the car. The J-life is about handing the steering wheel over to God and allowing Him to take charge of the controls.

Trusting God seems like a good idea until people, places, and things block the way. When that happens the tendency is to push and bully our way through. But that's like over-steering a car in a sideways skid, it doesn't help. Riding the brake while slamming on the gas is exactly what we do when we're afraid. What should I do? Take your hands off the wheel and feet off the pedals and vacate the driver's seat. Jesus is only a co-pilot on a bumper sticker. Surrender to Jesus. Trust His provision. Humble yourself so He can lift you up at the proper time and place (see James 4:10).

As R4G's, our power is His love pulsating through our veins. We are not rebels. We are lovers. We reject religion solely because it is loveless and lifeless. It is His love that compels us farther along the non-religious road to real. Yes, we are a messed up motley crew who pinch ourselves every day wondering why we've been so lucky to be loved this way. Can it be that we are God's chosen ones? The Bible says we're saints. Maybe, but our halos are crooked and our wings don't work at all, but we do so hunger to know His heart. We choose to trust His love and we pray for the faith to follow His lead no matter where it takes us. It was David Livingston writing from the heart of Africa in the mid-1800s who said, "Cannot the love of Christ carry the missionary where the slave trade carried the trader?"

Submission is admitting God knows something I don't know and sees something I can't. The fruit of submission is to learn humility. Humility is the one quality you can't fake for it flies in the face of all we're taught from the moment we become self-aware.

The story is told of two brothers who grew up on a small farm. One went away to college, earned a law degree, and became a partner in a prominent law firm in the state's capital city. The other brother remained at home. One day the lawyer came and visited his farmer brother. He asked, "Why don't you go out and make a name for yourself so you can hold your head up high like me?" The brother pointed and said, "See that field of wheat over there? Look closely. Only the empty heads stand up. Those that are well filled always bow low." Humility is not the key to winning; it is the prize itself and it is a sweet tasting victory.

Thomas Brooks said, "God has in himself all power to defend you, all wisdom to direct you, all mercy to pardon you, all grace to enrich you, all righteousness to clothe you, all goodness to supply you, and all happiness to crown you."

Enjoying every sandwich means that I take nothing for granted. All R4G's who have walked the wild way of grace for any length can boldly declare, "I know how to live on almost nothing or with everything. I have learned the secret of contentment in every situation, whether it be a full stomach or hunger, plenty or want; for I can do everything God asks me to with the help of Christ who gives me the strength and power" (Phil. 4:12–13, LB).

Assuming I know what's best for me leads to pride and it's just plain stupid. Assuming I deserve "better than this" leads to arrogance. By savoring every moment I get to spend enjoying your company, a good book, or a beautiful sunset, is to be changed by this never to be lived again moment. It is a gift of providence given to enrich my life forever. Live in it. Breathe it in. If you can do that without looking at your watch, you are free, and you are real. Are we having fun yet?

What power, knowing this moment has meaning! What a pleasure to know that every person who enters my life has a purpose. Yes, even the loud messy ones with sharp edges and green teeth. Therefore, I choose to be in this sacred divine moment with you, overwhelmed with the pleasure to share a meal, a word, a song, a smile, or best of all—a cup of Starbucks along this road to life outside conventional Christianity.

Consider this. If you are healthy right now, you are more blessed than the millions who won't survive another week. If you have never experienced the scars of war, the loneliness of prison, the agony of torture, or the pangs of starvation, you are ahead of more than twenty million people around the world. Yea God!

If last Sunday you attended the church of your own choosing without fear of harassment, arrest, torture, or death, you are more blessed than almost three billion people who live on the earth at this moment. If you have a refrigerator with food in it, clothes on your back, a roof over your head, and a place to sleep tonight, you are richer than 75 percent of this world. If you have money in the bank, in your wallet, or spare change in a dish someplace, you are among the top 8 percent of the world's wealthy. If you can read this message, you are more blessed than over two billion people in the world that cannot read anything at all. Yea God—let's throw a party. Let's shout out loud! Send up a flare! Yell! Run! Leap! Preach! Prophesy and proclaim from the rooftops that this indeed is, "the year of the Lord's favor." God is good. Life is good. And living in this moment is better than a million "maybe" tomorrows.

Face it, hurrying is not a sign of significance. It is a chronic symptom of insecurity. To enjoy every sandwich you must find the courage to eliminate hurry from your life. There is nothing that is not damaged by hurry. Only in America could one of our national monuments be aptly named "Mount Rushmore."

Say it under your breath, "This is the day the Lord has made. We will rejoice and be glad in it" (Ps. 118:24, LB). Eliminating hurry borders on the heroic for us hard-charging Americans. It requires we be fully where we are, living in the muck and mystery of every seemingly mundane moment.

Why are we in such a hurry? Often, it's a way to cover up for the things that haunt us. For sure it is cover for worry and fear. We're afraid if we're not out there working hard to get our piece of the pie, someone will steal it. It wouldn't do to let anyone get ahead of us. When we read, "Be still before the LORD and wait patiently for him; do not fret when men succeed in their ways . . . do not fret—it leads only to evil" (Ps. 37:7–8), do we dismiss this as too spiritual a philosophy to work in the real world of cutthroat competition?

Hurry can also be a cover-up for doubt and self-doubt. If you doubt God will come through for you, you'll need a back-up plan. We keep hedging our bets just in case this whole "Jesus thing" doesn't work out. I'll never forget my father asking me what my fall back plan was if the whole "preacher" thing fell through. Maybe it was youth or hubris, or both, but I said, "Dad, I don't have a 'Plan B'." He said, "Well don't you think a married man with a child on the way needs a 'Plan B'?" I said, "Dad, if this 'plan A' doesn't work out, God will give me another 'Plan A'." I believed it then, and I believe it more now more than ever.

Enjoying the sacred "now" moment requires we stay in the moment until it is over. Addicted to hurry as we are, we blow into meetings and appointments late. We jog through the agenda to get it all in under the allotted time. With check marks placed beside the bullet-points, we rush out and onto the next appointment. If we're not careful, we blow in and out of people's lives so fast we can't enjoy them and they can't enjoy us. We end up living fast-food lives with strained relationships dotted with indigestion, indignation, and indecision.

Staying in the moment is learning to appreciate not only the people themselves, but also to feel the weight and importance of being together. Some moments and places are so painful we want to run in and out of them while holding our breath. But when you avoid hard moments of breaking you also miss the breakthrough. Learn to linger, push through, and don't try going around your fears and insecurities. Hang out in one spot. Stay put. Resist rushing onto the next thing, enjoying the moment without the need to bring about artificial resolution. Important issues cannot be resolved over night but only over time. Do this and it is the beginning of better days and bigger things for you.

This is illustrated well during the last meal Jesus had with His disciples. They enjoyed this long, leisurely meal together. After walking from meeting to meeting and dealing with the press of people, it must have felt great to have some downtime—just Jesus and His mates. They cherished mealtime. And remember, these were meals in the near-eastern tradition. They lasted for hours. They lounged on pillows on the floor, not chairs at a table.

It was Jesus who took the conversation to a deeper level. He was troubled, so there must have been a sting to His voice when He announced, "I tell you the truth, one of you is going to betray me" (John 13:21). The disciples began to look around the room to see if they saw a traitor's face hidden among them. The room was rife with high drama. Jesus had thrown a verbal hand grenade into the middle of the inner circle. What John, the beloved, did next shows the genius of staying in the moment.

Peter, true to his impetuous self, couldn't stand the strain of not knowing who it was. He leans over and insists John ask Jesus to collar the culprit. The Scriptures say, "Leaning back against Jesus, he asked him, 'Lord, who is it?'" (John 13:25). John illustrates the amazing ability to remain in the moment. He was secure and embraced the tension, using it to press into Jesus. How could he be so relaxed if he had not learned to stay engaged in the now moment? He trusted Jesus, because he knew he was loved. As the Scriptures teach, "Perfect love casts out fear." John was okay with what came next. Staying okay with whatever happens next is essential to savoring the sacred "now."

Sitting around passively waiting for God to appear like a rabbit out of a hat isn't waiting, it's being lazy. But running around at a frenetic pace trying to bend the world to your will is exhausting for you, annoying for those you're pestering, and a sign to God you've got a lot of growing up to do. Waiting is the art of striking a delicate balance between God's part and mine. Dallas Willard said, "The abundance of God is not passively received and does not happen to us by chance. The abundance of God is claimed and put into action by our active, intelligent pursuit of it. We must act in union with the flow of God's kingdom life that comes through our relationship with Jesus. We cannot do this, of course, purely on our own. But we must act. Grace is contrasted with earning but not with effort. Well-directed, decisive, and sustained effort is the key to the keys of the kingdom."[2]

It seems to me the key to waiting with anticipation is to heed this advice, "Anyone, then, who knows the good he ought to do and doesn't do it, sins" (James 4:17). To me this means, do today's "to do's." Get up, get out, and do the next right thing in front of you. Place yourself in the path of what God is doing in the world. Just because you can't do everything doesn't mean you can't do something today.

Doing today's "to do's" is investing this moment by focusing my attention on the doable tasks at hand. Achieving something meaningful no matter how small it may seem, gives me the right to say, "This is the day the Lord has made. We will rejoice and be glad in it" (Ps. 118:24, LB). If I am going to live, I must live today. If I am going to live the free, fun, fulfilling life of an R4G, it starts here and now!

Ernest Newman, the renowned British music historian, said, "The great composer does not set to work because he is inspired, but becomes inspired because he is working. Beethoven, Wagner, Bach, and Mozart settled down day after day to the job at hand. They didn't waste time waiting for inspiration." That's it; never waste time waiting for the mood to hit you, engage this wonderful, never to be lived again, now moment and squeeze it dry. You can't do everything today, but you can do something now. If your dream is to write a book, then sit down and think up a great title, subtitle, chapter-headings, write something. Why? Because writers write; they do today's "to do's." Singers sing. Builders build. Teachers teach. Leaders lead. And they all do it one word at a time, one note at a time, one brick at a time, and one day at a time.

Another core commitment of savoring the sacred now is to make today's decisions today. To do otherwise causes you to waste today worrying what might or might not happen tomorrow.

Jesus said emphatically, "don't be anxious about tomorrow. God will take care of your tomorrow too. Live one day at a time" (Matt. 6:34, LB).

Assuming life is going to be one long path of gain and glory is a sure fire way to lose sight of God. Assuming things will "work out" without thought, prayer, planning, and preparation is dumb, shallow, and insulting to God. At the core of what it means to be alive here and now is the power to choose. By using your brain, your heart, your imagination you can choose to shape the future today. How? Make the decisions today which will most directly shape your tomorrows. Decide what you must do and do it starting today.

Will Rogers said, "Don't let yesterday use up too much of today." We are promised nothing more than today. The Bible says, "The length of our days is seventy years—or eighty, if we have the strength; yet their span is but trouble and sorrow, for they quickly pass, and we fly away" (Ps. 90:10). Let's say you're thirty-five right now. If the average life is seventy then you are halfway to the end. You may have fifty years, fifty months, or fifty days.

As a R4G, the ability to savor the sacred "now" is potent and powerful. You handle every day as a gift from God. It is a sacred gift and wasting it is a sin. Awaken every day surrendered to God's love and submitted to His divine providence. See everything as a gift for which to be grateful. Resign from the rat race. Slow down. Stay in the moment. With great intentionality, do today's "to do's." Make today's decisions. Do these things today and every day thereafter, and you will be a formidable force for good. What else could you possibly need? Life finds meaning in the context of story. Life is about drama and drama requires actors. So, take time to hang with your mates.

Bono wrote, "The hardest thing to do is to stick together; mates, family, marriage, business, bands. It's like resisting gravity. It's like King Canute in his chair trying to talk back the tide, but you can, and we have, and we will turn the waves around. The alternative is too predictable. You rid the room of argument. You empty your life of the people you need the most."

Aldous Huxley said, "To his dog, every man is Napoleon; hence the constant popularity of dogs." Savoring the here and now moment means we use things and love people not love things and use people. As the Scripture teaches, "Love must be sincere. Hate what is evil; cling to what is good. Be devoted to one another in brotherly love. Honor one another above yourselves" (Rom. 12:9–10).

Hanging with your mates means you never eat alone. Eating isn't just for staying alive, it provides the social context for relationships to grow and develop. It is so important we will still be gathering to eat in eternity, "'Blessed are those who are invited to the wedding feast of the Lamb.' And he added, 'God himself has stated this'" (Rev. 19:9, LB).

The Scriptures are crystal clear when they remind us we brought nothing into the world and we will not take anything out when we're finished. But that's not entirely true. It is true about the mundane, profane, things of this life, but it's not true in relation to what's really important. You can keep the relationships you've enjoyed. "Pay all your debts except the debt of love for others—never finish paying that! For if you love them, you will be obeying all of God's laws, fulfilling all his requirements" (Rom. 13:8, LB). Savoring the sacred "now" means I understand the difference between the urgent and the important. Things are urgent, but people are important.

If this moment calls for trusting then take your sticky hands off the wheel. If it is time to act, then screw up your courage, stand up, and take the first step. TAKE HOLD OF EVERY MOMENT. Savor it. Squeeze all the essence of sweet existence you can out of it. In this scared now, if it is pain then feel it. If it is joy, then express it. If it is a song then sing it. If it is a risk then take it. If it is a loss then grieve over it for this moment so you can move onto the many others on the way.

A friend of mine opened his wife's underwear drawer and picked up a silk paper wrapped package. He said, "This isn't any ordinary package." He unwrapped the box and stared at both the silk paper and the box. "Lori got this the first time we went to New York, ten years ago. She never wore it; saving it for a special occasion. Well, I guess this is it." He placed the box on the bed next to the other clothes he was taking to the funeral home. Lori, his wife of forty-two years had just died. He angled his head at me and whispered through the tears, "Never save anything new for a special occasion. Make every day, every moment, and every person a special occasion."

I understand life is a sacred gift to be lived up to, not gotten through or merely survived. I no longer keep anything. I use crystal glasses every day. I'll wear new clothes to go to the supermarket, if I feel like it. I don't save my special cologne for special occasions; I use it whenever I want to. The words "Someday . . ." and "One Day . . ." are fading away from my dictionary. If it's worth seeing, listening or doing, I want to see, listen, or do it now. I don't know what my friend's wife would have done if she knew she wouldn't be there the next morning, this nobody can tell. I think she might have called her relatives and closest friends, put on that new dress, hired a band, and thrown a party.

Never delay, postpone or keep anything for company, which can bring laughter and joy to your life or someone else's. Remember, all days are here in this day. All moments are these moments. Promise me you'll never, never, never save anything cool for company. I will use the fine china at every meal knowing the people around my table today will soon be at tables of their own. I will use the best wine every day and pour grape juice for company. Serve filet mignon on toast with chips during every football game and should company barge in, they'll have to settle for leftover meat loaf.

9

TRADING CERTAINTY FOR MYSTERY

GOING FROM AN ARROGANT, AGITATED "KNOW-IT-ALL" TO A HUMBLE, HAPPY "KNOW ENOUGH"

Mystery is but another name for our ignorance; if we were omniscient, all would be perfectly plain.

—*Tryon Edwards*

The heart has reasons reason knows not of.

—*Blaise Pascal*

Ken Jennings was just your average Joe until he became the all-time winner on the wildly popular TV quiz show—*Jeopardy*. He appeared on seventy-five shows straight, giving over 2,700 correct responses. He won in excess of 2.5 million dollars in prize money. The answer which ended his amazing winning streak was, "Most of the firm's 70,000 seasonal white-collar employees work only four months a year." Jennings answered, "What is FedEx?" The correct question was "What is H&R Block?" How could he have missed that one? Even I knew the answer to that question. To me this was a no-brainer. The moral of this story; not even a guy as smart as Ken Jennings has all the answers all the time! The more we know, the more we know we don't know.

I cringe every time I see the bumper sticker, "JESUS IS THE ANSWER." It's not that I don't believe that Jesus is exactly who and what He claimed to be, "the way and the truth and the life" (John 14:6), Jesus is just too big to fit on a bumper sticker. He is the answer to all things, but that does not mean all the answers are available to me. One of the keys to growing up in the J-life is to learn that certainty and mystery are friends not foes.

It's not that we R4G's [I wish I could use the label "Christians," but I can't] aren't forever settled on the full and final sufficiency of renegade Jesus. It's that we have traded the fear of what we don't know for the certainty of what we do. We trust Him for what we see as well as for what we don't know. Even when moral dilemmas drive us out of our comfort zone of easy answers and pat formulas we trust we know enough.

We don't insist on certainty; for we have learned with God things are seldom as they seem. Divine providence and the promise of His love assure us that though He may be silent, He is never still and though He may be invisible He is never far away. Trying to be smart as God is not our goal. We will never know it all, but we do know enough, and that's why we love mystery. We loathe intellectual laziness and the deadly religious assumptions it breeds. Thinking about God blows our minds and expands our little world.

To illustrate how easy it is to assume you know the answer, take "The World's Easiest Trivia Quiz." This is a "no-brainer" because the answers are simple and self-evident. Here, take it for yourself:

1. How long did the Hundred Years War last?
2. Which country makes Panama hats?
3. What is a camel's hair brush made of?
4. The Canary Islands are named after what animal?
5. What was King George VI's first name?

When you read questions like these you may be tempted to think you're pretty smart, that you know everything—or at least you can find all the answers. Craving certainty, religion promises all mysteries will yield to fervent prayer and arduous Bible study. But the fact is, for all the Bible study we've done and for all the time and money we've spent doing it, often the best to be said is that we've become smarter sinners. Pretending to have all the answers hasn't made us happier. Do Bible thumpers have the reputation of being more humble? Are we more freed up? Are we more joy-filled or more passionate about the plight of the poor and the disenfranchised?

Are we displaying more and more of the signs of the J-life? The brutal truth is those who claim to know the Bible best can be some of the meanest, maddest, most messed up people you'll ever run up against. I've actually heard people justify racism, hatred, segregation, the "thing-a-fication" of women, and a whole host of godless myths all based on their interpretation of the Good Book. And if you dare disagree with their views on anything, they'll call you names and seek to discredit you. I know, for I've had my share of threats from Bible-quoters and mean-spirited know-it-alls.

We've all heard arrogant, agitated, self-righteous know-it-alls who insist they have the absolute, one and only, true "Christian view" on all things pertaining to politics, economics, science, social justice, and just about everything else. Some are so bold as to think they know more because they claim, "God spoke to me." They assure us all the answers are available in the Bible. But they would be wrong because even if everything were covered, we'd still be left to someone's interpretation. Some of the most confusing days I ever spent on the planet have been in seminary arguing over the theological hair-splitting minutia. Small-minded, mean people with their heads full of Bible facts do not a happy person make.

Reducing all truth to simplistic religious statements is arrogance pure and simple. Rather than reflecting profundity and sophistication, a flat rejection of mystery as a way of experiencing God in the "now" is a sure sign of mistrust. It renders null and void all claims of love and devotion made pubic or otherwise, because it demands a certainty we can't handle and God won't give.

HAPPY KNOW ENOUGH

One of the sure signs you're making progress with God is the day you morph from an arrogant, agitated "know-it-all" to a happy, humble "know enough." It is not what I don't know about Jesus which keeps me in hot pursuit of the J-life. It's what I do know.

Here is what I do know; He has done me good. I am a satisfied customer. I have tasted that the Lord is good. He loves me as I am, not as I ought to be—of this I am certain. I want more of this mysterious Jesus, the Lord of Glory, and lover of my soul.

Not knowing why Jesus allows certain things makes me want to give up my R4G status if I could, but I can't. I know too much, I have come too far. I've walked too many times through the valley of the shadow of death to doubt He is with me. My child-like trust is my certainty. It is the single key to everything God promises for it is the only certainty which binds us together in the divine mystery—redemption. Here's what I know for sure; I love Jesus and I know He loves me. After all these years, it feels so freeing and frightening to just blurt it out loud—I love Jesus!

God cannot be dissected and dismissed, that's why He demands trust. He will not be pinned down for labeling or observation like a butterfly on a Styrofoam board. The kinetic nature of His progressive self-revelation defies reduction to a stagnant doctrinal statement. He will not be owned, analyzed, or sanitized. That is not to say we can never make doctrinal statements about Him, but what statements we do make are descriptive, not exhaustive. And once we make them, they are not static and by no means represent all that can be said. Indeed they may be a logical starting place, but most certainly are a lousy stopping place. As John said, "Jesus did many other things as well, if everyone of them were written down, I suppose that even the whole world would not have room for the books that would be written" (John 21:25).

As R4G's we must find better ways of bringing forth the beliefs we hold dear. We must move the conversation from certainty to mystery and back again. By doing so, we will switch from strict one-way communication to open, winsome, two-way dialogue. We will assert and affirm without becoming aggressive and dogmatic.

Awakened from our dogmatic slumbers by the conversion of our hearts by Truth, we will be like, "the men of Issachar, who understood the times and knew what Israel should do" (1 Chr. 12:32). Lean in; "let's talk" will be our invitation to the inclusion of anyone attracted to the abundant life Jesus promised. If you're still preaching and waving a big Bible, trust me, nobody's listening but the chairs, and even they look sleepy.

KNOWN YET UNKNOWN

Ever heard the old axiom, "a picture is worth a thousand words?" It is one of those sayings which seems true, but isn't. A picture, a portrait, a painting is worth way more than a mere thousand words or emotions. This hit home to me the morning I stood in the Louvre in Paris staring for the first time at the actual Mona Lisa. I was a mere ten feet away. What an epiphany. I wondered what all the hubbub was about. What was so great about a painting of a girl with a smile? But now I knew for myself. I was experiencing the painting for the first time, visually, viscerally, and emotionally.

Standing there in its presence, I sensed a great treasure revealed to me in that glorious moment. Yet, I knew a greater story remained concealed. It was as though the painting was smiling only at me with a knowing look, which said, "If you only knew what I know." I had a thousand questions dancing in my head like fireflies. Who was she? What was going on outside that day? Was it hot or cold in the studio? Did she want to pose or not? Where did she go afterward? Did she think the painting made her look fat? Did she like the smile or think it was forced on her? So much I now know I didn't know before I knew. How maddening! How sweet! How much like God to show enough, but not all.

A work of art offers us a type of knowing. Its existence is a revelation, but only hints of all it actually knows and means. This is not to say the message it is sending in the now is not real. But it won't tell us everything. He leaves much to be discovered. For all it is willing to tell me, it withholds far more. If it is a good work of art it bids me closer, if it is great it draws me in, if it is a masterpiece it almost sucks me into the canvas itself. It is as if I can breathe into my lungs a bit of its own time and history. It engages me, changes me, and then bids me leave to reenter the real world a richer soul.

If a painting, a song, a piece of prose or poetry can transport us to a different place and time, what might we expect of an encounter with Jesus—the creator and sustainer of life itself? Yes, trading certainty for mystery is to confess I can never know God exhaustively. But by embracing the *mystery of certainty* I can actually and truly claim to have experienced God meaningfully and with profound effect—resurrection.

Special revelation [the Bible for example] neither makes God known nor leaves God unknown but rather renders God as the known and unknown. This is not to say we cannot know what we know for sure. Why else would we be told ". . . to contend for the faith that was once for all entrusted to the saints" (Jude 1:3). The Gospel is truth. It is settled in heaven, but the drama of redemption is still being played out in the drama of our every day lives.

We are the created not the Creator, the redeemed not the Redeemer. What we contend for is "the faith"—neither my faith nor my version of it. And it is this admission (our redemption is His idea not ours) which makes us hopeful our creator, who created me and you as an act of love, will continue to redeem the world in love and not throw it back on the cosmic junk heap because we've screwed it up so badly. Thank God for rainbows and second chances.

Bill Bryson in his book, *A Short History of Nearly Everything*, offers us a glimpse into the majesty and mystery of our Creator:

> *In a single blinding pulse, a moment of glory much too swift and expansive for any form of words, the [universe] assumes heavenly dimensions, space beyond conception. In the first lively second (a second that many cosmologists will devote careers to shaving into ever-finer wafers) is produced gravity and the other forces that govern physics. In less than a minute the universe is a million billion miles across and growing fast. There is a lot of heat now, ten billion degrees of it, enough to begin the nuclear reactions that create the lighter elements—principally hydrogen and helium, with a dash (about one atom in a hundred million) of lithium. In three minutes, 98 percent of all the matter there is or will ever be has been produced. We have a universe. It is a place of the most wondrous and gratifying possibility, and beautiful, too. And it was done in about the time it takes to make a sandwich.*[1]

As mind-boggling big as creation is, it cannot contain its Creator. God is big. He is huge. He is larger-than-life and all the marvels you see are but a shadow of His greater glory. And to think when He thinks, He thinks of me, is thrilling and frightening all at the same time. Anything less is religious shouting. Religion is too inflexible to contain the mystery.

DESPERATELY SEEKING CERTAINTY

In an uncharacteristically combative interview, Tom Cruise engaged in a verbal shouting match with NBC's Matt Lauer. Cruise was out promoting his new movie, *War of the Worlds*. Lauer challenged Cruise on his recent statements about psychiatry. Cruise challenged the validity of it as an actual science. Lauer asked Cruise what made him an authority on the subject. Cruise responded in a way which arrested my attention. He said if he wanted to know about something he would take the time to study it and find out all about it. I was fine with that. Then he said, "I don't talk about things I don't understand." When I heard that, I thought, "Wow, that would leave me out of just about everything." I don't understand how electricity works or how my cell phone can bounce a signal off a satellite and then back down into my daughter's phone three miles away, but I use them gladly. Not using or appreciating something I don't understand until I understand it is indeed a high standard; actually an impossible one.

Isn't it logically impossible that we as finite creatures could ever fully understand the infinite? Think about it, at its maximum size, your brain weighs about 46 ounces, about the size of a big gulp at 7-Eleven. If it's true that on our best day we only use about 10 percent of our available brain capacity, then we're only using about a McDonald's quarter-pounder with cheese amount of our brain. How would we ever dare think we could comprehend, catalog, and codify infinite mysteries of time and eternity with a hamburger-sized brain? This shouldn't discourage you; it should drive you onward and upward to discover all which can be known, embraced, and celebrated. God is here and He is not silent.

Celebrate the certainty that God chooses to be known. Not just known *about,* but actually and authentically known. Known as in the way I can know my wife. What a mystery! What a privilege! If all He intended is knowledge of His existence, He would have stopped at natural revelation. The scandal was His coming down to be one of us. As Joan Osbourne sang in her wildly popular ballad, *If God Was One of Us,* "if God had a face what would it look like?" I love it though when she poses the penetrating question, "Would you want to see the face of God if seeing meant you had to believe in Jesus?" That's what Jesus did. He took on the limits and liabilities of human flesh so you could have a certainty on which to hang your hopes. He was the real revelation of God's heart and passion for you.

God's love makes certain assertions about Him possible, even essential, but never think for a moment the words, ideas, and concepts we use to convey His love in any way limit Him or even come close to fully revealing the breadth, depth or height of His love. As Paul said to the Roman renegades, "Oh, the depth of the riches of the wisdom and knowledge of God! How unsearchable his judgments, and his paths beyond tracing out!" (Romans 11:33). You've heard the old saying, "If it sounds too good to be true; it is." With Jesus, He is far more wonderful than tongue can tell. Our problem is not making Him sound too good, but failing to make Him sound good enough.

What is this certainty we seek? It is the confidence we have in the relentless, boundless love of Jesus for me, not as I should be, but as I am. There is a certainty in my converted heart which assures me I will never face another sunrise afraid, nor another sunset alone.

It is with great certainty I embraced the mystery that God is infinitely great yet limited. He can do all things, but there are many things He chooses not to do. He does not stop all evil before it happens. He doesn't cure all cancers or fix every marriage. He doesn't stop every car from colliding with another, though He could if He chose. He is great enough. I embrace the mystery that God is good, yet restrained. He could stop all wars and cease all hostilities. And though we have the hope He will do so in the future, "He will judge between the nations and will settle disputes for many peoples. They will beat their swords into plowshares and their spears into pruning hooks. Nation will not take up sword against nation, nor will they train for war anymore" (Isaiah 2:4). We wish it were today.

I embrace the mystery God is now here breathing on me. He is here with me as I write these words in Nashville, Tennessee. He is here with you as you read them, wherever you are—at home, the office, the United States, Korea, South Africa, Brazil—wherever and whenever. While He is there with you, in this moment, meeting you in these written words, in this space and time experience, He is also out there running the world, keeping the stars in space and the planets from colliding; making sure His world is running according to His plan and purpose. He's not out of breath or in a hurry. He has time to listen. Spill your guts for He is the only one who truly understands. And He's got time to listen.

Jesus taught the disciples to pray, *Our Father, Who art in heaven, hallowed be Thy name. Thy kingdom come, Thy will be done on earth as it is in heaven.* God is here and there all at the same time. While He is there, working out His will in heaven, He is here preparing earth for the new day which will certainly dawn soon. He promised us a new heaven and a new earth. But until that day, this is the day of salvation where trust is the key to the Kingdom. This is the day of God's good favor. And Jesus is here, now fueling and funding His wireless, wall-less, worldwide revolution.

The Renegade Nation is burgeoning, growing and spreading around the world. It is an international movement with branch offices in every country. And while He is here redeeming the world, He is also there running it. I take great comfort in knowing while He is way over here He is no less there. And while He is there, He is no less here, at all times. This is a mystery but also a certainty.

This is not true for you and me. We can only be here in this moment, savoring the sacred now. If I'm not here I'm literally nowhere. My body is here, the heart is beating and the blood is flowing, but the real me is A.W.O.L. As the old saying goes, "Wherever you go, there you are."

God is here and there. He is in the tomorrows of my life already. He is preparing the way and according to Jesus, a place as well. "Do not let your hearts be troubled. Trust in God; trust also in me. In my Father's house are many rooms; if it were not so, I would have told you. I am going there to prepare a place for you" (John 14:1–4). He knows exactly what I'll need when I get there. So I am certain His plan will prevail. All that is required of you and me is to trust Him.

And to trust Him, you must love Him. To love Him you must have been loved by Him, therefore the necessity of a converted heart.

These affirmations are mysteries. They come to me through the love of Jesus Christ. They are planted in my DNA as an R4G at the moment my heart is converted. My old heart of stone has been replaced with a new heart; a heart which aspires and dreams, a heart which embraces mystery with as much joy as it does certainty. For those who only know the cold, concrete hardness of certainty, there arises in their hearts, their lives and their rhetoric a cold, ugly orthodoxy.

UGLY ORTHODOXY

Let's go back to our no-brainer quiz and see how you did. The first question was, "How long did the hundred years war last?" The correct answer, 116 years from 1337 to 1453. The second question was, "which country makes panama hats?" The correct answer is Ecuador. The third question was: "what is a camel's hair brush made of?" The correct answer is squirrel fur. The fourth question was "the Canary Islands are named after what animal?" The correct answer is: dogs. (The Latin name is *insularia canaria*—"island of the dogs.") The fifth question was, "what was King George VI's first name? And the correct answer is: Albert (when he came to the throne in 1936 he respected the wish of Queen Victoria that no future king should ever be called Albert). This silly little test proves while answers are available they are not always as easy as they appear.

How often have you been absolutely sure of something only to find out later you were big-time wrong? Here is where humility is a big help. We need to admit there are a ton of things we don't know, can't know, and don't need to know. Don't feel obligated to explain away all the inequities of your life with God. Your life is only a part of the larger drama of redemption. Don't let anyone make you feel like you should have all the answers. For me, I would settle for just knowing a few of the right questions.

Does this mean we cannot be sure of anything? Of course not. I can't explain why God allows hundreds of thousands to die in a South Asia tsunami but I know God cares about their suffering.

I read and hear religious "experts" bemoaning the fact we live in a day and time when we no longer believe in absolute truth. Really? I've thought about this assertion a lot, but I don't accept it. Why? We still drive cars, we still use electricity, and we still go to hospitals when we're sick. We still live in a world of amazing order in spite of what should be total and utter chaos. I'm not shocked at the violence in the world; I'm amazed there's not a lot more. People are obeying laws of nature every single day without giving it much thought. So I reject the idea that people reject the reality of absolute truth.

What I think has changed is people reject those who claim to have cornered the market on absolute truth. They reject the attitude and the mentality of those who take absolute truth and use it to exclude, abuse, or shut out people they don't like.

God gave truth to us. And by definition, truth given by God is simply a verbal definition of reality. What is true is always true, always has been true, always will be true. It's real. That's the road we're all on—the road to real. What is real is true. What is true is reality. Reality is God expressing His aliveness.

To illustrate the relationship between belief and doubt, think about a balloon. Blow it up just a little and let the air inside represent your belief or faith. The outside of the balloon's circumference represents your doubts. The more you believe, the larger the surface of your doubts grows. So for all I do know, there is more I don't.

The father who brought his son to Jesus beautifully illustrates this idea. From birth, the boy was plagued with violent seizures. The father asked Jesus to heal his son. Jesus said, "Everything is possible for him who believes." Immediately the boy's father exclaimed, "I do believe; help me overcome my unbelief!" (Mark 9:24).

Here is our dilemma. We believe and we don't believe. Believing more leads us into more we don't believe. And when our faith grows and we believe more, we go to the next level where it is a challenge to believe all over again. Voltaire is reported to have said, "If a miracle occurred in the market place of Paris and in the presence of two thousand men, I would rather disbelieve my own eyes than the two thousand." It seems to me it's after we get "*smarter*" we complicate our lives with notions of absolute seeable, knowable wonder.

When I was a kid I used to watch TV programs, which seem in today's world not only simplistic, but otherworldly. Shows like *Leave It to Beaver* promised a world of sanity, simplicity, and a place where all problems were solved in thirty minutes or less. This no more reflects the world of today than it did then. We live in a world of increasing complexity where there are indeed answers, but not simplistic ones. Problems are complex and rigid religious rules are hard to apply. The only thing an ugly orthodoxy knows for sure is who is to blame. While there are things which are definitely black and white, right and wrong, we live in a world where the application of truth and non-truth, right and wrong, ethics and morality, become more and more complex as life becomes more and more fragmented and disjointed, and disconnected.

We need fewer fingers pointing and more honest, respectful dialogue. Seekers of truth, beauty, love, and honor have nothing to fear from seeking together. Dialogue and conversation are good for us. Albert Einstein said, "The important thing is not to stop questioning." I would add it's important to ask questions of one another. It's easy to characterize and demonize people you don't know. It's another thing all together to walk together in respect and love. If God has spoken and decreed His will be done on earth as it is already being done in heaven, why are religious people so jaded and jacked-up?

Religious obscurantism solves nothing. I remember hearing preachers pound the pulpit and proclaim. "God said it, I believe it, and that settles it." That still makes the hair on the back of my neck stand up. It seems to me if God said it that alone settles it. I know God has spoken and has not stuttered, but He leaves much to be learned here on this non-religious road to real. And though there is much still left to learn, His love draws me to Him and compels me forward. I feel like Brennan Manning who said, "I could more easily contain Niagara Falls in a tea cup than I can comprehend the wild, uncontainable love of God."[2]

HOW BIG IS GOD?

A little boy came to his father and asked him, "Dad, who made God?" The father, engrossed in the evening paper, responded,

"Beats me, son." The little boy would not be put off. "Dad, why is the earth round?" The dad answered, "I don't know, son." The boy played around for a minute, and then asked, "Dad, is there life on other planets?" The father patiently answered, "Nobody knows the answer to that." Finally the boy asked his father, "Dad, do you mind me asking you all these questions?" The father put down his paper, "Why, not at all, son," he said, "how else are you going to learn?"

When you think about God, His origins are shrouded in mystery. The Bible reveals very little about where God came from. No ink is spent in the sacred Scriptures trying to explain where God came from or trying to prove He exists. Right out of the box in Genesis One, we're told, "In the beginning God . . ." There is no explanation other than the divine assumption that God's existence would be self-evident.

When Moses, the great leader of the nation of Israel, was given his commission to lead them out of bondage, he asked God to tell him His name. A name gives you an idea of a person's authority and importance. The response Moses got was, "Tell them 'I am' sent you." God used the Hebrew verb "to be." Translated into our language it means, "I am, I always have been and always will be." God is self-sustaining. God is authentic. He is original and real. And since God created you in His image, you too are an original with the potential to be real; this is why you need a redeemer.

As we said earlier, Jesus too is totally authentic, self-contained, and real. He needs nothing outside Himself to be fulfilled or validated. He is more than enormous. He fills more space than the entire universe. What a beautifully revealed mystery God is!

Not only are God's origins mysterious, so are His ways. As the prophet Isaiah quoted, "As the heavens are higher than the earth, so are my ways higher than your ways and my thoughts higher than your thoughts" (Isa. 55:9). God is a planner and a master connector of cause and effect to accomplish His will on earth.

The story is told of a man in China who raised horses for a living. When one of his prized stallions ran away, his friends gathered to mourn his great loss. After they expressed their concern, the man raised this question: "How do I know whether what happened is bad or good?" A couple days later the runaway horse returned with several strays following close behind. The same acquaintances again came to his house—this time to celebrate his good fortune. "But how do I know whether it's good or bad?" the old gentleman asked. That very afternoon the horse kicked the owner's son and broke the young man's leg. Once more the crowd assembled to express their sorrow over the incident. "But how do I know if this is bad or good?" the father asked again. Well, only a few days later, war broke out. The man's son, however, was exempted from the military service because of his broken leg. You guessed it, the friends gathered again and the father asked. . . . But we'll stop the story there. You can see how this debate could go on and on. This tale points out that from our limited human perspective, it's impossible to know with certainty how to interpret every seemingly random experience of life. But God knows. Experience assures us for certain, God is at work in all things and for our good and His glory.

If you use just your rational mind, you wouldn't do things the way God does them. For example, in creation, why would you create two human beings destined to disobey, fall into sin, and need to be redeemed? Look at all the pain and suffering in God's creation simply because He created us with the power to choose love or non-love. But the decision to create us human beings, not religious robots, gave us the power to choose life or death, trust and mistrust, fear or faith.

So what are we to do with this wild, loving, ever-living Jesus? Let's join in the chorus with Renegade Paul, "Let God be true, and every man a liar. As it is written: 'So that you may be proved right when you speak and prevail when you judge'" (Rom. 3:4). Let's live with the breathless expectation of what He will do once we abandon certainty for trust.

GRACIOUS UNCERTAIN CERTAINTY

Brennan Manning said, "Mystery is an embarrassment to the modern mind. All that is elusive, enigmatic, hard to grasp will eventually yield to our intellectual investigation, into our conclusive categorization—or so we would like to think. But to avoid mystery is to avoid the only God worthy of worship, honor, and praise. It is failure to slake the thirst of seekers and believers alike—those who reject the dignified, business-like Rotary Club deity we chatter about on Sunday morning in search for a God worthy of awe, silent reverence, total commitment, and wholehearted trust."[3]

The nature of the J-life is we know what we know and trust God for the rest; consequently we do not crave clarity. We possess a growing inner confidence and though we can't predict His methods, we do know His motives. Demanding clarity and certainty means doubt reigns on the throne of your tormented heart.

Gracious uncertainty is the mark of the spiritual life. Trusting Jesus means I do not know what a day may bring forth, but I trust the One who brings the day forth. I am uncertain of tomorrow's realities, but I am certain of today's "to do's" and today's decisions. We are deeply and unashamedly mystical. We are connected on a deeply mystical level with the Creator of the universe.

Immersing ourselves in the richness of the J-life, we emerge with God's best gifts. By faith we are able to see the invisible. The eyes of our understanding are open. We dare to dream of great things for we know things are always created twice—once in the heart and then in real time.

Because we have a new heart, we are able to hear things inaudible to the human ear. We can hear God speaking to us. It doesn't need to be an audible voice. We vibe to the vibration of the spirit. Not just the Holy Spirit, but also the spirit of our fellow man. Because of the Holy Spirit dwelling in us, we are in tune, in touch, and in rhythm with the movement of the spirit. Worship is a wonderful, wireless, wall-less everyday experience. We do not need go to a church building to worship. We gather to worship to learn how to experience God everywhere else. Our worship allows us to know what we know, but it also allows us to know what others might miss. We sense God afoot. We are big-picture people. We are not arrogant, self-righteous, know-it-alls. We are happy, humble, know-enough's.

A country girl from rural Georgia won an all-expenses-paid weekend in New York in a radio contest. She had never been more than a hundred miles from her home and had never flown before. When her Delta jet touched down at New York's LaGuardia airport she found herself in a bold, bright new world.

Her next first was the ride in a long, sleek, black limousine with a uniformed driver. She was still bug-eyed when they pulled up to the entrance of a posh hotel. Bellhops rushed to open doors and handle luggage.

Her first disappointment came when the bellhop showed her to her room. The room was very nice, but her luxury suite was smaller than she had imagined and apparently she was sharing it with the two people already in it when she arrived.

Sensing something bothering her, the bellhop asked, "Is there a problem? "Well, I don't mean to complain, since this is free and all, but I thought my room would be a little bit bigger." "Madam," he replied, "this is only the elevator. Your private suite of rooms is awaiting twenty-seven stories up!"

Christian, don't allow your little, limited understanding of God's wild, mysterious plan for your future rob you of the freedom and fun which can be yours in this uncertain moment. What screaming uncertainties are you facing today? Cancer? AIDS? Poverty? Bad job? No job? Confusion? Frustration? Lust? Anger? Hatred? Alcohol? Codependency? Being single? Being married? Being a parent? Being a child?

Don't think for a moment that where you are now is where you'll end up. The good, the bad, and the indifferent of today are mile-markers on the winding, wonderful road you're traveling to heaven. The rough, rocky terrain over which you are traveling today must not be confused with the sweet, sublime destination. As Paul the great Christian missionary said, "I consider that our present sufferings are not worth comparing with the glory that will be revealed in us." Paul wrote, "For in this hope we are saved. But hope that is seen is no hope at all. Who hopes for what he already has? But if we hope for what we do not yet have, we wait for it patiently" (Rom. 8:18, 24–25). No seeming certainty can override the mystery of God's love and the power His love sets in motion to save, heal, deliver, scare, thrill, devastate, and delight you right here and right now.

10

MASTERING THE ART OF ABUNDANCE

THE NEW MORE IS LESS AND THE NEW FAST IS SLOW

We are shipwrecked on God and stranded on omnipotence.

—Vance Havner

Lord, I crawled across the barrenness to You with my empty cup uncertain in asking any small drop of refreshment. If only I had known You better I'd have come running with a bucket.

—Nancy Spiegelberg

Over the last fifty years, the American standard of living has soared. What once was considered a luxury is today's necessity. Before World War II, a car was a rich man's toy. Today, we have more cars than licensed drivers to drive them. Two out of three Americans own their own homes. This year alone it is estimated over 13 percent of all homes sold will be second homes. We have so much stuff crammed in our homes, that according to the 2000 U.S. Census, the self-storage industry will exceed $17 billion this year, passing the motion picture business. Now that's abundance! Isn't it?

Here's my question. "Has this abundance of things made us happier?" It should, but survey after survey shows we're not satisfied with our lives at all. Polls continue to register the same fact that shows 80 percent of us over-achieving Americans are unhappy. Equating wealth with well-being isn't working out for us. Just more stuff is not the pathway to the good life, but we continue consuming in the hopes it might. Trends show that not even more money and more fringe benefits motivate us anymore.

Despite our unparalleled prosperity, we're no happier or fulfilled. Material things have made our lives more crowded, but of less value. The more we get, the more we want the next new thing. It's like living on a treadmill on which the speed dial just keeps getting turned to the right. Weird, but true. Could this be, in part, why we are so screwed up as a society? And to be honest, you might expect this from people with no claim to faith in God, but the brutal truth is Christians don't appear to be fairing much better.

For example, in 1955 the ratio of students to teachers was thirty to one. Today it is nineteen to one, but are kids learning more? Adjusting for inflation, real wages have tripled since 1947, while the cost of necessities has plummeted. In 1950, food represented one third of a family's total expenditures, today it's one seventh. The U.S. Gross Domestic Product alone is greater than the next five largest countries combined. Americans work fewer hours, and have more cars, cultural institutions, and more children in college than ever before.[1] And yet we live in a culture of complaint plagued by a growing and deepening attitude of entitlement. Experts bemoan the loss of our competitive edge in most every technical area simply because of our debilitating attitude of complacency. Thomas L. Friedman, in his sobering best-seller, *The World Is Flat*, says, "I do think Americans are oblivious to the huge changes. . . . Your average kid in the U.S. is growing up in a wealthy country with many opportunities, and many are the kids of advantaged educated people and have an attitude of entitlement. . . . The competition is coming and many of the kids are going to move into their twenties clueless about these rising forces."[2]

Nowhere is this lackadaisical attitude more acutely felt than in America's churches. If you don't believe me, ask the average American pastor who struggles week after week trying to please the unappeasable, to console the inconsolable, and to motivate the unmovable. Offerings are shrinking while waistlines are expanding. Pity the pastor who dares suggest God's blessing comes with obligations. The insanity of trying to comply with the demands of self-righteous, inward-focused church boards who expect their pastors to be omni-competent and omni-present, is driving the best and brightest out of the ministry. It's time to put the renegades back in charge of the revolution. It's time to call for the creation of a Renegade Nation in which the prevailing attitude is gratitude and the prevailing mindset is abundance.

As R4G's, we can change the world only by shifting our focus away from the material to the meaningful life—the life worth living and away from the selfish, "what's in it for me?" syndrome.

Abundance is not more for me. It's more for me, you, and everyone else. Where does this renegade mindset come from? None other than the original R4G—Jesus. He promised it when He said, "The thief comes only to steal and kill and destroy; I have come that they may have life, and have it to the full" (John 10:10). This same verse in The Message says, "I came so they can have real and eternal life, more and better life than they ever dreamed of."

LITTLE PIE PEOPLE

God gave us billion dollar bodies and trillion dollar brains, but what are we doing with them? We're using our mighty mountain moving capacities to stockpile our own survival stash for the apocalypse predicted by end time doom and gloomers. And as amazing as your brain is, in many respects, it's just like a computer—junk in, junk out. If you sow a thought and hold it over time you will reap a deed and ultimately a life. As a result of the cynical, small-minded, elitist worldview of many religions, we are prejudiced people who are convinced of the "little pie" theory of life.

If you adopt the belief there is only so much to go around, you are a "little pie" person. The scarcity syndrome dominates you. This morbid, tight-fisted philosophy says that since the pie we all eat from is finite, I've got to make sure I get my fair share before it's gone. This develops a getting, having, holding, and hoarding mentality. As a result, we have multiplied our possessions and lost our peace. We've learned how to get a job, but lost our joy. We've been all the way to the moon and back, but have trouble crossing the street to meet a new neighbor—no time, got to go to work. We've done big things, but not better things. We do more, but accomplish less. We work more, play harder, and have achieved the American dream, but we are sicker, sadder, and less satisfied with our accomplishments than our parents or our parent's parents.

These are the times of fast foods, small character, and surface relationships. These are the days of two incomes but more divorce, of bigger houses, but more broken homes. These are days of quick trips, disposable diapers, throwaway morality, one night stands, overweight bodies, and pills which do everything from cheer, to quiet, to kill. And as we go about chasing after God knows what, Jesus' warning is as relevant as today's headlines, "Beware! Don't always be wishing for what you don't have. For real life and real living are not related to how rich we are" (Luke 12:15, LB). But conventional wisdom has been trying to prove Him wrong for over 2,000 years without success.

Here's how it works. If you think small, you will be self-centered and self-absorbed. With a "limited pie" mentality it will be exceedingly hard to understand it's not all about me. As John Ruskin said, "The man who is wrapped up in himself makes for a very small package."

Religion plays a major role in creating and perpetuating the scarcity syndrome. If God created our world as a closed system and gave rules to regulate our greed, then our goal is to occupy the least amount of space possible and to want less, not more. In a static world without wonder and mystery, creativity is stifled and starved. And since resources are scarce, imagining a bigger, better world is futile. Think conservation not exploration. Don't dare expand your hope; just prune back your expectations. If your mind is programmed by a small, self-centered, resource-starved worldview, it is exceedingly difficult if not impossible to think abundance.

The kind of religious thinking that leaves me earthbound and self-focused can only produce a scarcity mentality.

Lest you think I'm being a little harsh, let's let Jesus give us His take. "Woe to you, teachers of the law and Pharisees, you hypocrites! You travel over land and sea to win a single convert, and when he becomes one, you make him twice as much a son of hell as you are" (Matt. 23:15). Religion by its very nature suffocates hope and therefore abundance.

He juxtaposed the "converted heart" idea to the rule-based religious approach when He said, "Good people bring good things out of the good stored up in their heart, and evil people bring evil things out of the evil stored up in their heart. For out of the overflow of the heart, the mouth speaks" (Luke 6:45).

He keeps bringing us back to the core issue. When the heart changes, everything changes. Until the heart changes, nothing changes.

The converted heart is free from the bondage of rules, regulations, threats, and prohibitions, for which there is no relationship attached. We are then free to fill our minds with possibilities. Nothing is too big or too hard for our God. He is the Creator and guarantor of our expanding abundance. He invites you to think, to aspire, and to dare to attempt great things. Embrace His expanding peaceable Kingdom and yours will be a journey into miracles and epic experiences. If you dare believe "nothing is impossible with God" (Luke 1:37), your mind will be flooded with possibilities and desires. Since you have a converted heart, a new heart with new desires and ambitions, you are free to imagine you can change the world in some meaningful way. The more you press into Jesus, the creator and sustainer of all life, the more you will begin to act out your most dominant thoughts. As Emerson said, "We become what we think about all day long." Jesus calls us to bigger things and better days as professional lovers, prophets of the possible, and agents of change. Armed with the Gospel, we are movement shapers and lifesavers. We lead movements, start industries, build companies, and create enormous wealth. Then we practice the divine-human agriculture of sowing and reaping, divine generosity, and sacred philanthropy.

Expanding your mind by focusing on God's promises frees you from fixating on the fear of scarcity. A vital, loving, trusting relationship with the giver of all good gifts will free you from confusing the gift with the giver. You will love God, not the things God gives. Fixed on Jesus and His provision in the now creates an overwhelming sense of gratitude. A thankful heart is the only antidote from F.U.D. (fear, uncertainty, and doubt). It is this freedom that creates the condition of which we are most in need, "No matter what happens, always be thankful, for this is God's will for you who belong to Christ Jesus" (1 Thess. 5:18, LB).

TWO POINTS OF VIEW

We seldom see things as they are, but as *we are*. That's why *how* we think and perceive the world determines how we occupy our space and time in it. Jesus taught us to perceive the world as a place of infinite abundance. That the insistent life has an infinite capacity to create and sustain abundance is a radical idea preached by Renegade Jesus. Why? Because everyone before and after Him embraces the theory of scarcity. Abundance is the birthright of every

R4G, but scarcity seems to rule the world, even the "Christian" world.

The scarcity mentality according to Jim Collins in his groundbreaking book, *Good to Great* creates a doom loop. You become a competitor, not a community builder. You can no longer enjoy the success of others because their success only diminishes yours. Outwardly you may say, "Good for you," but inwardly you think, "what about me?" Within a business, I see this disagreement as the source of all conflict. It fuels the conflict between companies, churches, team players, managers, and family members as well.

The scarcity mentality forces you to measure your life by what you lack. This constant assessment leads to fear and the sense God has somehow ripped you off. Demoralized and disappointed with God and the futility of gathering, we grow de-motivated. Why get up and try harder to get more of what I already have that doesn't satisfy? Why care about achievement at all if it is never enough or if for me to win, everyone else must lose? As Lily Tomlin said, "The problem with the rat race is even if you win you're still a rat."

If when you give, you have less, then why decrease your net worth? With a scarcity mentality, you can't envision quitting the rat race to start over at a saner more satisfying place or pace. Daring to imagine a life lived to serve the needs of others is not cost effective, so you stay chained to a job you don't like, suffocated by people you can't stand, behaving like a jerk you can't respect.

Scarcity is a lie that once believed and injected into the nervous system spreads like a virus. Left unchecked and unchallenged, it will become a self-fulfilling prophecy. If your dominant and prevailing belief is the pie is only so big, it won't be long before you self-destruct. The "gotta-get-mine" mentality creates a stagnant, stale, self-absorbed eco-system in which creative initiative, risk, and daring die. Therefore as we write the inner autobiographical scripts we live by, our story line reflects that there is never enough. We never earn enough, do enough, have enough, give enough, pray enough or love God enough. What's the answer? Get with it and speed things up, because you're already behind and as I overheard someone say in an airport the other day, "*The faster I go; the behinder I get.*"

The scarcity mentality is the culprit, which speeds everything up. Since the first embarrassing moment we experienced want or lack, our pace has quickened. Hurry is its firstborn, and burnout is its legacy. If you don't believe me, go out to any airport in a major city in America on a Monday morning. Sit down and watch the people running by to catch planes to destinations of someone else's choosing. Look into their eyes. See if you can detect any signs of joy, fun, freedom, or purpose etched on their faces. Airports are modern metaphors which beg the question, "Why are we moving so insanely fast?"

When I've asked people what they're after, the best I get usually is, "I'm just trying to close this deal so I can pay the bills." We end up chasing the big win. What "the win" is, we've not stopped to figure out. We're running after something we'll think we'll want once we lay hold of it. Solomon's warning against wasting our lives "chasing after the wind" falls on deaf ears and deflated souls. Driven by scarcity, we run until we break. And once we've hit the wall, we lay on our backs wondering what hit us. To answer that question requires thinking and thinking takes too much time. If I step aside to examine my life, you just might sneak past me in the night and pick all God's best gifts off the tree of scarcity, leaving me with nothing but leftovers. So we beg, "God patch me up and put me back in the race."

Mindless chasing leads to fanatical competition. The real prize here is not to get the "brass ring" for me, but to keep it from you. If the goal is winning against you, forget trying to create, invent, or produce anything. This kind of competition is consumption for envy's sake. It's like eating your seed corn in the winter because you're afraid your neighbor will steal it before spring. Eat today for tomorrow we die, but you'll die first!

The truly tragic thing about the having, holding, hoarding mentality is it keeps us divided, suspicious, and apart. Anyone who dares challenge my "having" is worth hating. This is sick and stupid. It's killing us. It is tearing us apart and in the Renegade Nation we will ban it forever. Hey, it's not a competition!

In the Renegade Nation, we have a worldwide family of which every Christ-follower is an automatic member. We are freed up, fun-loving innovators, and lovers of W.W.O.N.D.A. (win-win or no deal always!) We dare to be lavish lovers and liberal givers, because we believe better days and bigger things are up ahead. Our great and good God created everything for our enjoyment—sounds heretical from a religious point of view, doesn't it? (see 1 Tim. 6:17). He has promised there will always be enough. He will not abandon us or leave us fatherless. He is the creator, the author of abundance. Just look up at the vastness of His domain.

THE ABUNDANCE MINDSET

Let's play a game called "Pick a Number." In your mind right now, think of a number, any number. What number did you choose?

Was it more than a million? And if you didn't, why didn't you? It does reveal something about your mindset, because in reality there are few obstacles that exist beyond those of the mind. But thinking big and envisioning living a bigger life than you do now requires cultivating an abundance mindset, which is a bigger way of seeing the present and the future.

Let me give you an example of the power of big thinking. In 1998, Larry Page and Sergey Brin incorporated Google while still graduate students at Stanford University. According to *Fortune Small Business* magazine, Internet users perform over 150 million searches a day on the Google search engine. The Google search engine can access over 2 billion pages in seventy-four different languages. One study recently showed Google users used the search engine 13 million hours in one month. Compare that with Yahoo, which came in second with 5.4 million hours and you're talking explosive growth.

How did they get so big? I believe it began with their initial vision. The word "googol" is a mathematical term for the number 1 followed by 100 zeroes. While most people are likely to pick a number like 14 or 98 when doing the "pick-a-number" test, Brin and Page decided to pick a googol—1 with 100 zeroes.

Jim Reese, chief operations engineer of Google, says this about the company's founders: "It takes a lot of confidence and courage to go ahead and do that [be huge]. It's rare to find people who think on such a grand scale and are able to create a great product at the same time."[3]

Thinking big is a basic birthright of the J-life. We have a brand new heart, the very mind of Christ, and the indwelling power of the Holy Spirit. Jesus Himself said His purpose for coming to earth was to give us abundant life. So first of all, the abundance mindset is a new way of seeing things. One of the fundamental reasons I know I have a converted heart is I see the world differently than I ever could before.

Have you ever heard the old saying, "I'll believe it when I see it?" R4G's live in reverse to that axiom. We know once we believe it, we'll see. With time, faith, and action, we can see what we've imagined created in real time right in front of us. As a result, we look at life as an expanding set of possibilities. Abundance believes life is good, generous, and infinite. Look at all the amazing inventions we employ today as the fruit of an abundant mindset. As I'm typing this manuscript on a computer, the chip inside is made of silicon, which is sand. How generous of sand to reveal its secrets—that silicon can be made and a computer chip could power my computer, making possible the computation of billions and billions and billions of lines of codes so I could type on my computer and, in the blink of an eye, turn around and send it to your computer anywhere in the world. But as great as computers are, it took a brain in the body of a person who was operating out of an abundance mindset to believe it and then follow through to reality and viability. Thank God for the renegades among us who believe life has secrets it's willing to reveal to the curious, creative mind.

Thinking this way puts Paul's admonition to his friends in Ephesus in a modern context. He said, "I pray also that the eyes of your heart may be enlightened in order that you may know the hope to which he has called you, the riches of his glorious inheritance and the saints" (Eph. 1:18). What an astounding way to describe our God-given capacity to think, discover, and imagine. If the eyes of your heart can and should be enlightened, don't you think there's more to see and perceive? It's within our converted hearts that new visions stir and bigger, better futures first appear. That can't happen in a mentality of scarcity, but it happens all the time where the abundance mindset holds sway.

The abundance mindset is founded on a promise. Jesus guarantees a life that is generous. He promised, for example, if we would give we would receive. As a matter of fact, the more we give the more we receive. He promises you the more love you give, the more love you'll get back. The more you engage in acts of loving, serving, and helping other people, the more you'll find that people are motivated to love you and help you when you're in need. You get what you give and you get it in proportion to your giving. Sowing and reaping are the secrets and assurances of a divine, infinite abundance. You can change your life today by sowing better seed and more of it.

The abundance mindset is focused forward. Think of this amazing promise made so many millennia ago, "Forget the former things; do not dwell on the past. See, I am doing a new thing! Now it springs up; do you not perceive it? I am making a way in the desert and streams in the wasteland" (Isa. 42:18–10).

What a promise to live each and every day. Forget the former things. Don't dwell in the past, even a good one. What's God saying to us here? Look at all the things I've done in the past. Look how great they've been; look how generous I've been—how faithful. Look at how I've lavished my best gifts on so many. When you think about how great all this is forget it, release it, and let's you and me do it again. But what I've done in the past dwarfs what I'm willing to do for you right now and in the future. I'm doing new things through people who have an abundance mindset and are focused forward. It may be small now and it may be hard to perceive at first, but God is doing great things for and through ordinary people like you and me everyday. Why be left out of this wonderful world of abundance? Why would we trade a beggar's life for the abundance Jesus pours out on every R4G who is willing and able to receive?

I remember when we were building our first facility for Bellevue Community Church. We owned 280 acres of the roughest, most unforgiving land I'd ever seen. But it is nestled in the rolling hills of Tennessee and its potential was amazing. I knew we were in trouble the day our contractor came to me and gave me the figures on what it was going to cost to smooth out the hills to create roads and massive parking lots. I was overwhelmed by all the contractor jargon. Just to bring the sewer onto the property was going to cost a million dollars. When he saw the shock and horror on my face he gave me a big smile and said, "Don't worry. God has given me this verse on which I stand every day," and he quoted, "'I am making a way in the desert and streams in the wasteland.'" I took a little comfort, but as I focused forward I saw the promise become a reality, and so can you.

The abundance mindset is a daily discipline. I wish I could say once the eyes of your heart are open and you've experienced God's abundance you'd be set up for life, but I can't. No one gets up everyday automatically calibrated to abundance. But remember what the Scriptures say. "Because of the Lord's great love we are not consumed, for his compassions never fail. They are new every morning; great is his faithfulness" (Lam. 3:22–23). This means to keep and cultivate your abundance mindset is a daily discipline. It's not something you can do once and forget about it. It's kind of like getting married. Your marriage won't survive if all you do is pledge your undying love at an altar somewhere. That love needs to be restated and reaffirmed every day. I've been married a long time and I still need to hear my wife tell me every day she loves me. Love leaks and scarcity invades the undisciplined heart like weeds in an unkempt garden.

Every day God reasserts His commitment to provide us a joy-filled, freed up, abundant life. He is ruthlessly faithful and I've learned if you follow Him as an R4G, you'll find not only is He trustworthy, but He can do extraordinary things through ordinary people. Allow Him to cultivate an abundance mindset, which in turn feeds vision, imagination, and innovation, all of which fuel the future, a great future you and I can step into everyday.

CULTIVATING ABUNDANCE

It's one thing to confess abundance; it is another to walk in it 24/7, 365 days a year. To see it work, there are a few things we must do to make it so. One of the first things you must do is learn to slow down. Slowing down not only allows you to think, but it allows you to process life as it comes. It allows you to breathe easy and stay in this sacred never-to-be-repeated moment. Worrying about the future and whether there'll be enough out there for you merely stirs up the old stupid you. Aren't you glad that old idiot has been crucified with Christ? Yea God! He's dead and all he can do is stink up the place; so kick him out and take away his key. By God's grace live here and now where the abundance of God flows like a flood over your soul.

Are you well fed? Say, thank you, Father! Are you free to speak your mind? Say thank you, Jesus! Are you breathing fresh air, can you feel the warmth of the sun on your face, can you see the sky above you and feel terra firma beneath your feet? Say, Yea God! Have you ears to hear the sounds and vibrations of abundance? Then be grateful to be here at this pregnant-with-new-possibilities moment. Be still and know I am God, says God.

With all the promises of God's care, protection and all the evidences we R4Gs have for trusting His love, why is it we so easily give up waiting and start chasing after the wind? Maybe it's because we are unsure of His love or fear if we actually rest in Him, other people, particularly evil people who don't play by the rules, will elbow us out. If you feel this way, rest on this promise right now, "Rest in the Lord; wait patiently for Him to act. Don't be envious of men who prosper" (Ps. 37:7).

Maybe today's work is to wait for God. If He's not in a hurry, why should you be? And the emphasis here is not just waiting, but waiting patiently for Him to act. He is at work acting on your behalf right now, in this instant. And even though He may be silent, He is never still. Whispers and glimpses of the sacred surround you if you have eyes to see and ears to hear. Take a big, deep breath. Hold it! Now slowly let it out, saying; "God is on the job and all is well with my soul." This waiting, resting moment is God's gift to you. Take this opportunity to enjoy life, to have fun, to rest, to let God rule the world while you occupy this sacred space. What are we to do during this downtime? We do what David the great king did. "Be still, and know that I am God; I will be exalted among the nations, I will be exalted in the earth" (Ps. 46:10).

To cultivate abundance you must eliminate hurry. I don't mean you're never "in a hurry." We all fall behind due to circumstances beyond our control. I'm talking about hurry as a lifestyle—always rushing around in a huff is a symptom of scarcity. Why? Let's face it. Rushing around all the time—busy, constantly trying to bend the universe to our will—is just a cover-up. It's a cover-up for worry because we're afraid God's forgotten us, or maybe it's just the residual of our old religious insanity saying God only blesses those who deserve it. If you work really, really hard and stay in constant orbit around your religious duties, then maybe God might send a crumb or two your way. But remember this, Satan loves it when you're in a blur of activity, distracted, divided, and dissatisfied with what God has done for you. When you're tired and harried, you become an easy target.

Slow down. Lighten up. Live at a sane pace where you can hear God. Be free from worry of the future. Stop it now! What good has it ever done you? None! Be in this sacred moment focused on today's delights. Trust me, it will save you a lot of grief, regret, and heartache. If you're always in a hurry and stressed out, you'll make bad decisions and do things you wouldn't do if you had spiritual and emotional reserves. God's got your back. His promise of "daily bread" means He only finances the next steps. So remove tomorrow's worries from your brain's CPU. Use the extra room to savor this sacred here and now. Today is the only day in which you can come alive and truly enjoy this gift of life and all its wonders. Take time to think now. Start up the practice of journaling your thoughts. Make a list of the people to whom you're going to recommend this guidebook.

Cultivating abundance also requires living in a sacred rhythm. Think about it. God created the earth in six days and rested on the seventh. He didn't rest because He was tired. The Scriptures teach us He rested as an example to us. God's sacred rhythm is six and one. I work for six days and I rest one. This should be really good news for the workaholics among us. God's all for you working six full days. He says, for six days, lay your ears back and go for it. Make it happen! Plan, meet, dream, aspire, but on the seventh day, stop! Put it all down. Shut it off. Walk away. Put away your PDAs, your Blackberries and stay off the computer. Let the e-mails wait for one day. Detach. Come away with me and let's reconnect. Unplug yourself from all the things keeping you earthbound. Let God-thoughts fill this 24-hour space. Recharge, re-energize your spiritual, emotional, and physical batteries. You need a full 24-hour day for your soul to catch up.

The story is told of a South American tribe on a long march, day after day, when all of a sudden they would stop walking, sit down to rest for a while, and then make camp for a couple of days before going any farther. They explained they needed the time of rest so their souls could catch up with them. Take a lesson; live at a pace where you can hear from God and be free from the tyranny of trivial pursuits.

To live well, learn the rhythm of life as God created it. God worked six days and then rested on the seventh. The proper rhythm for living the best possible life is 6 and 1. Six days we work and the seventh we rest. If you break this rule, then you will eventually wreck your life. Violate this and sacrifice your vitality. Obey it and you can sustain your rhythm for a lifetime.

The call to live 6 and 1 is also a reminder to work with our hands and minds to earn our living. Work is a good thing, because it is God's thing. The rhythm of life is a period of sustained, intense engagement followed by a period of recovery. You need to rest, renew, and recharge your physical, emotional, and spiritual batteries.

To cultivate an abundance mindset you must learn to maintain your motivation. Passion is power and it creates an extra edge. Recently, a Dutch psychologist tried to figure out what separated chess masters and chess grand masters. He subjected groups of each to a battery of tests—IQ, memory, spatial reasoning. He found no testing difference between them. The only difference: Grand masters simply loved chess more. They had more passion and commitment to it. Passion may be the key to creativity.[4]

When I read that, my heart said, "Yes, that's it!" That's why God is so obsessed with love. Love is life. It created it and it sustains it. Love is the raw power which keeps this small blue marble we call home spinning in space.

Love for this moment creates energy. When I face the day with love in my heart, there is a spring in my step. I enter the room differently. I lean in to greet people, face to face. I smile knowing the love in my own heart will fill what might be lacking in the room. And if there are R4G's there, the love flows between us giving us the suspicion we're among fellow Renegades who are living free, having fun, and changing the world.

An abundance mindset crowds out weak wants and quiets half-hearted prayers. Religion and scarcity is the denial of desire. Real, authentic Christianity is the journey into desire. The Scriptures say, "Delight yourself in the Lord and he will give you the desires of your heart" (Psalm 37:4). It is not the denial of desire God seeks; it is the centering of desire, which is key.

What a promise. Find your fun in loving God. Love God with everything you are. Obsess on Him. Think about Him all the time.

See all of life through His lens of love. Stand in awe and wonder of His creative power. Marvel at God's abundant world bursting out all around you and to think He created all this for your enjoyment.

As Jesus was walking along a road one day, a couple of blind guys sitting on the side of the road screamed, "Lord, Son of David, have mercy on us." Jesus turned and asked a simple question, "What do you want me to do for you?" (Matt. 20:32). Jesus knew what they needed. But He still asked the question. He's asking it of you right now, right here. What great desire is burning down deep in your gut, so hot that you don't just *want* it, but you *must have* it? Remember, Jesus said that nothing is impossible with God. So ask big! So, do you know what you'd want if you could have anything? Ask big for there is nothing too hard for Jesus. A scarcity mindset keeps us from trusting God's love and His invitation to dream big and ask big. The Scriptures say, "You do not have, because you do not ask God. When you ask, you do not receive because you ask with wrong motives" (James 4:2–3).

Too often when people say the word "Christian" they think of people who have turned off or suppressed their desires and are living by rules and religious obligation. Nothing could be farther from the truth. Real Christianity invites us to let go of lesser, lower things and dare the most high and noble things. The Scriptures say, "Finally, brothers, whatever is true, whatever is noble, whatever is right, whatever is pure, whatever is lovely, whatever is admirable—if anything is excellent or praiseworthy—think about such things" (Phil. 4:8).

When Jesus confronted the woman at the well, she confessed she still had not found what she was looking for though she had four husbands and instead of making the same mistake a fifth time, she was opting for just living with the fifth guy. Instead of condemning her, he confronted her with the fact that only a vital, vibrant, fully passionate love relationship with God was going to ever fulfill her deep and abiding desire to love and be loved, to celebrate and be celebrated. It was true then and it is true today!

Embracing desire is recognizing that God wants more for us than we could ever want for ourselves! What is your heart to do right now that sounds insanely crazy and out of reach? Go ahead and dare to do it. Sixteen years ago, God put it in my heart and the heart of my wife Paula to start a church for people who didn't want to go to church. And when we told our "church" friends we wanted to build a great church for people who hated church, they thought we were crazy and they knew we were Renegades.

But sixteen years later, Bellevue Community Church attracts over 4,000 people to its four weekend services located on a beautiful 280-acre campus in a suburb of one of the greatest cities in the world. Starting with nine adults and a dream, we met in a public school for ten years. We never had any money to speak of, but every time we needed money to move ahead, God provided. When we needed millions of dollars to buy the land, develop the land, and build the buildings, God provided. Had we not set out with an abundance mindset, BCC would be today only a dream etched out on the back of a napkin in an Ezra's restaurant in Johnson City, Tennessee. But because we found a need and were willing to trust that God wanted to meet that need through us, we know that wherever God guides He provides. By experience, I have come to agree with Benjamin Franklin who said, "When a religion is good, I believe it will support itself; and when it does not support itself, and God does not take care to support it so that its professors are obliged to call for the help of the civil power, it is a sign, I am sure, of its being a bad one."

Keep dreaming big dreams, praying big prayers, and risking crazy for truth and beauty, love and honor. Never be afraid of looking crazy for the love of Jesus. What are you doing today that requires God to show up or you're gonna look crazy and maybe even go broke? Never be afraid to take the right risk for fear of what people might say or even for the fear you might fail, for the greatest tragedy is the risk not taken which could have created true wealth and abundance for you and thousands more.

Jesus lived, died, and lives today to make abundant life possible. How real and practical this abundant life becomes for you is up to you. What are you doing to create abundance in your life and the rest of the world? What risks of sowing and reaping do you have on the drawing board? What crazy ideas do you have that if acted upon could literally change the world? What are you doing today that will only make sense in hindsight?

God loved you and me enough to place us in this abundant place called earth. At just the right time, equipped with all the right gifts and talents, God placed you here. You are at a defining moment. Will you master the art of creative abundance for yourself and those around you, or will you live in a small, safe existence trying to scratch out a place to survive? Life is not a slow, sanguine, slog from the cradle to the grave with hopes of arriving in heaven with a well preserved, pretty, pampered body. It is a wild ride along the abundant road to real where we slide in sideways in a cloud of dust, thoroughly spent, totally used up, and with a shout loudly proclaiming—Wow!—What a ride! Let's do it again!

11

GROWING UP INTO GREATNESS

BEYOND THE BARNYARD, TURTLES LIVE ON FENCE POSTS

Waste no more time talking about great souls and how they should be. Become one yourself.

—*Marcus Aurelius*

Goodness does not consist in greatness, but greatness in goodness.

—*Athenaeus*

Like a lot of other kids my age, I grew up wanting to be a big leaguer. I had visions of becoming the next Whitey Ford, Roger Maris, or even Mickey Mantle. So as soon as I was old enough, I badgered my parents to let me play Little League baseball. Sign up day was on a Saturday morning. I was up and at the community center early. I wanted to arrive ahead of the other kids so I could be sure to get on a good team with a cool sounding name. When you're a kid, stuff like that is really important. When I got there, I was told they used a random drawing to choose the teams. This was supposed to prevent any one team from being overloaded with good players.

That next week I checked our mailbox everyday. I prayed and asked Jesus to get me on the Yankees. But I wouldn't be too hurt if I were on the Phillies, the Red Sox, or the Eagles. When the envelope finally arrived, I ripped it open to find I had been place on a team called—the Chicks. I thought, *Who in their right mind would name a Little League baseball team, full of young, impressionable kids, "The Chicks?"* But it was true. When I got my uniform, right across the front was emblazoned in big green block letters, "Chicks." And yes, you can imagine how ruthless the other kids were as they made fun of us, particularly as we came up to bat. They'd scream from the safety of their dugout humiliating things like, "Here come the chickens, the chicken feathers can't hit, chicken liver, chicken-lover" and my all-time favorite, "Hey Foster, don't lay an egg!" It's enough to scar a kid for life. As you grow up, there comes a moment of decision when we choose what team we're going to be on, and what name you'll emblazon across your heart.

Whatever you see when you look at yourself, especially if you are a Christ-follower, I hope it is not the word "chicken." During a pivotal scene in the 1969 movie *Easy Rider*, George (Jack Nicholson) said, "you know, this used to be a helluva good country. I can't understand what's gone wrong with it." Billy (Dennis Hopper) said, "man, everybody got chicken. That's what happened, man, everybody's got chicken."

BARNYARD BARRIERS

If I've learned anything for sure in this life, it's you cannot behave over time in a way different from how you truly see yourself. If you see yourself as a chicken, totally afraid and shame-bound, that's exactly how you'll behave. If you see yourself as a person marked out for greatness by God then you'll aspire to live up to that divine expectation. Too many people who claim to be "Christians" settle for a timid faith, a ticked-off God, and a tiny little sweet savior who fits on a chain, lives down at the church, and needs to be visited once a week.

I've spent my entire adult life around Christians and churches. And I'm convinced the greatest barrier keeping us from growing up into greatness is our constant, almost all-consuming obsession over our private sins and personal shortcomings. I'm talking about a self-loathing, not a healthy admission of real guilt. We confess our sins, but doggedly refuse to accept our acceptance in Jesus. We say inner peace is possible but seldom possess it for ourselves. We believe God can forgive anyone of anything except, of course, me and my unpardonable sins. We seem bent on seeing ourselves as sorry sinners whose souls serve as a breeding ground for shame. This toxic obsession over our unworthiness starves the spirit and shrivels the heart. Jesus can cure others, but not me. We must get down off our crosses, out of our chicken-little barnyards, and stop eating barbed wire for breakfast as penance.

Guilt is a good thing when it moves you to God for forgiveness, healing, and newness of life. It is God's gift to make you aware of how serious and destructive your sin is to you and potentially the rest of us. It warns us not to flaunt God's law and live in defiance and rebellion or we will lose our souls and forfeit our greatness. Guilt is God's alarm going off in your hearts saying stop, turn around, run to Me. Face your failures, confess your sins, and you will receive mercy, grace, freedom, and a new name (see Rev. 2:17). For guilt, God offers what we crave—the belief we are loved without regret, reserve, boundary, or breaking point. God knows we need love most when we deserve it least.

Real guilt is a good thing when it drives us into the loving arms of God. His free, full, and final forgiveness is the foundation of the J-life. The heart made new and set free by Jesus' resurrection power becomes the powerhouse of the R4G's passion for greatness. Yet too many of us, who claim to have been forgiven, allow guilt to grow into debilitating shame. And while guilt is the pain you'll feel for what you've done which God prohibits, shame is the pain you feel for the person you've become. What God says about your behavior will make you feel guilty, but what God says about you will never make you feel ashamed.

As a result we are slathered and saturated in self-doubt. Sure, we believe in Jesus, we believe He walked on the water; raised the dead and turned water into wine. We glibly profess to be Christians, but we fail to realize Jesus' life and power is born in us at the moment of conversion. As the Scriptures say, "I have been crucified with Christ and I no longer live, but Christ lives in me. The life I live in the body, I live by faith in the Son of God, who loved me and gave himself for me" (Gal. 2:20).

The life we live today we live by the power of Jesus—the one who loves me as I am, but refuses to leave me where He found me. By His power as prophet, priest, and king, I stand in a new relationship with God called to greatness and endowed with

God's power to be who He made me to be and do what He's called me to do.

I do sin to be sure, but Jesus has made me a saint capable of aspiring to and achieving true greatness. It was Jesus who had the audacity to predict we would do greater things than He (see John 14:12). So why are we so scared of our sin shadow and why, in Jesus' name, would we ever settle for acting like beggars who've lost their birthright? I don't know the full answer, but I am positive dead-as-a-door nail, performance-driven, shame-based religion is the primary culprit.

Week after week we're warned about becoming too prideful and cocky, when truthfully most of the Christians I've met are nowhere near either. Get honest with the typical believer and they'll tell you they feel more like chickens scratching for the next random morsel. Wake up! You are an eagle, not a chicken. You are destined for greatness and you do not honor Jesus with your false humility, fake sincerity, or small-minded faith.

Shame-bound and crippled by self-doubt, we're left to fixate on our sins and when we tire of that, we nit-pick each other to death. We beg God to morph us into sinless, flawless super saints without a clue we might be the way we are for some greater, nobler purpose. We're convinced it's God's will we have a fashion model figure and a leading man's physique; if only we could stop sinning so much and put away the Ho Hos. And when we do manage a meager change or two and nothing falls from heaven we get hacked off at God; wondering if this Jesus stuff works for a lowlife like me. But do we ever stop and think, maybe our weaknesses are God's strengths and our limitations are God's perfect design for greatness?

This idea was illustrated brilliantly in one of my favorite movies of all time, the 1998 Mark Johnson movie *Simon Birch.* Based on the popular novel, *A Prayer for Owen Meany* by John Irving, it is the story of a twelve-year-old boy named Simon Birch who, despite his physical handicaps, believes God has a plan for his life. Simon was born with an abnormally small heart. Failing to die within the first twenty-four hours as expected, Simon defies the odds and survives to adolescence.

Simon is a disappointment to his parents and the target of cruel childhood pranks. He had every reason to question his self-worth and purpose for living, but he never does. Simon embraces his condition; resolute in his conviction God made him for some great, heroic, yet to be revealed, assignment.

Joe, Simon's best friend, doesn't believe Simon. He doubts there is a God after the accidental death of his mom. Simon's classmates mock him relentlessly, regarding his divine resolve as an indication of his strangeness. On one occasion his Sunday school teacher hurriedly tries to hush him so he won't "frighten" the other children with his crazy notion that God actually has a plan for his life.

Simon's own pastor can only see his liabilities. In a poignant conversation between the two, Simon asks, "Does God have a plan for us?" The minister hesitates then says, "I like to think He does." Simon says, "Me, too. I think God made me the way I am for a reason." The minister says, "I'm glad that, um, that your faith, uh, helps you deal with your, um, you know, your condition." "That's not what I mean," Simon states. "I think I'm God's instrument. He's going to use me to carry out his plan." Agitated by Simon's unshakable confidence, the pastor cautions, "It's wonderful to have faith, son, but let's not overdo it." With that he waves for

Simon to leave, shakes his head, and whispers with an air of cynicism, "God's instrument?"[1]

Do you believe God has destined you for greatness? The great Creator created you. He loved you when you were His avowed enemy (see Rom. 5). So do you really think He's gone to the trouble of loving you back to life just to leave you a slightly sweeter sinner than you were before? No, no, no! You have a new heart, a new name, new family, a new destiny, and a bright expanding future. Yea God! Say it, Yea God!

Another deterrent to greatness is the rise of the new therapeutic society. For every condition we have a disease, a name, and more reasons to medicate, justify, and excuse. We seem more than willing to define ourselves by our defects. I know I am walking on thin ice here, but it's worth risking being misunderstood to make this point—in Christ we are new creations. Yet in the recovery movement at large, the concept of defining ourselves by our defects is sacrosanct. People introduce themselves, "Hi, my name is Dave and I'm an alcoholic." I understand this is an important device for a period of time, but is this the way it always is? I just can't imagine the great men and women of the Bible standing up and defining themselves by their most notorious past sins.

The Scriptures tell us we are more than conquerors through Jesus, the one who loves us back to life (see Rom. 8:37). We are not our deficits and past sins. We are a redeemed people; a holy nation of priests, prophetesses, and professional lovers. Our very names are written down in the Lamb's Book of Life (see Rev. 21:27). When God looks at you and me He sees a favored son or daughter He cherishes. I love Paul's point of view, "There has never been the slightest doubt in my mind that the God who started this great work in you would keep at it and bring it to a flourishing finish on the very day Christ Jesus appears" (Phil. 1:6, The Message). God has begun a great work in you. Yes, you! You're far more than a "saved" sinner. To God, you are worth loving, worth indwelling, and someone through whom He plans to build His kingdom on earth; i.e. The Renegade Nation. Is this what you see when you look in the mirror? If not, why not? You are free to see yourself as God sees you. You are His plan for changing the world. Yes you! Not some Arnold Schwarzenegger machine-gun-toting super saint, but you and me, His super sheep!

THE CALL TO GREATNESS

As I write this chapter, today's *USA Today* headline reads, "Act of Defiance made Parks 'Mother' of a Movement." It is hard to believe Rosa Parks' simple act of refusing to give up a seat on a city bus would be viewed today, fifty years later, as a world-changing act of courage. Yet it was her small, right place, right time, renegade act of defiance, which sparked a revolution. None of us are the same because of it. For Rosa, it didn't matter what people called her; it only matter what she answered to. Living in a southern culture, they labeled her "inferior." She answered, "child of God" and changed the world sitting down.

She was a forty-two-year-old seamstress whose gutsy act galvanized a generation of R4G's, including the likes of Rev. Martin Luther King Jr. This unlikely "mother of the civil rights movement" was fined fourteen dollars for her defiance. It seems like a small price to pay to kick-start a revolution. She refused to settle for second-class citizenship. She believed she was made for greatness.

As a child of God, she had every right to any seat on any bus anywhere at anytime. Sometimes greatness says stand up, stand up here and now. When conventional wisdom says move back, you're just a black, insignificant woman in the Deep South, greatness shouts I shall not be moved! Greatness is the call to be renegade real when the crowd is morally, socially, politically, and religiously wrong.

One of the most outrageous predictions Jesus ever made was: "I tell you the truth, anyone who has faith in me will do what I have been doing. HE WILL DO EVEN GREATER THINGS THAN THESE, because I am going to the Father. I will do whatever you ask in my name, so that the Son may bring glory to the Father. You may ask me for anything in my name, and I will do it" (John 14:12–14, emphasis mine).

What a mind-blowing, ego-altering, soul-expanding, charge the gates of hell prophecy and promise! As a follower of Jesus, I'm going to do greater things than He did. To fulfill this prophecy all I've got to do is to ask. Question: How much big asking am I going to do if I see myself as a chicken nobody, a dry drunk, or just a sinner barely saved by grace? Not much! That's why most Christians settle for pecking at worms in the barnyard when they should be spreading their wings to fly. Stop sifting through scraps and start soaring through stars. And don't tell me to calm down. That's been our problem—we're too calm when we should be "all shook up." We're fiddling while Rome is burning. We are playing a sonata on the deck of the Titanic when we should be manning the lifeboats. We're rearranging furniture and straightening pictures in a burning building. It's time we stop doing things better and start doing better things. God is among us and better days are within our grasp. Welcome to the revolution!

Join the mass movement of renegades for God who dare embrace greatness as their destiny. I wholeheartedly agree with Marianne Williamson who said:

> *Our deepest fear is not that we are inadequate, our deepest fear is that we are powerful beyond measure. It is our light, not our darkness, that most frightens us. We ask ourselves: who am I to be brilliant, gorgeous, talented and fabulous? Actually, who are you not to be? You are a child of God. Your playing small doesn't serve the world. There is nothing enlightening about shrinking, so that other people won't feel insecure around you. We are born to manifest the full glory of God and the true magnificence of the Spirit of Man that is within us—it's not just in some of us; it is in us all. As we let our light shine, we unconsciously give other people permission to do the same. And as we are liberated from our own fear, our presence automatically liberates others.*[2]

I remember as a kid watching my dad's black and white Zenith TV. Their slogan was, "the quality goes in, before the name goes on." That describes you to a "T". You have greatness ahead of you, because you have it on you. Jesus put it there when He kept His promise to place a new heart in you. That is exactly why religion never satisfies long term, in part because it leaves you unchanged and therefore unchallenged.

You are destined for greatness. Royal blood now runs in your veins. You are a child of the King and you come from a long line of brave hearts. And the day Jesus converted your heart was the hour you became a full participant in the worldwide revolution called the Kingdom of God. You have joined a gunless, bombless army of great godly men and women. Within our chests beat a warrior's heart. It is a new heart fueled by love, guided by truth, and driven by desire. Our fight is not with flesh and blood for political power, but with principalities and powers for the hearts and souls of men and women (see Eph. 6:12). You and I are the promise born of Jesus' prayer, "Thy will be done, thy kingdom come on earth as it is in heaven." As Brother Lawrence said, "We ought not to be weary of doing little things for the love of God, who regards not the greatness of the work, but the love with which it is performed."

STUCK IN MEDIOCREVILLE

Pop singer Jimmy Buffet's signature song bemoans his "wasting away in Margaritaville." I know a lot of "Christians" who are wasting their lives in a place called "Mediocreville." It is way past time we leave the old ghetto of gutless religion and run to the revolution for which we are destined. Let's leave the negative neighborhoods of nervous stomachs, bent backs, and furrowed brows. Get up, stand up, and stand tall with your face toward the Son. This is our God's war for the world and we need to be smack dab in the middle of it with our hearts undaunted and our flags unfurled (see Exod. 17).

Rocky is a movie about a mediocre boxer who dares to aspire to greatness. Heavyweight champion Apollo Creed's original opponent canceled three weeks prior to the fight. No legitimate contender could be found. As a promotional stunt, Creed chooses a local fighter to give him a chance at the American dream. As fate would have it, he chooses Rocky.

One of my favorite scenes is when Rocky (Sylvester Stallone) visits the office of boxing promoter George Jergens. Jergens says, "Rocky, I've got a proposition I'd like to make to you." Rocky guesses, "I know you're looking for sparring partners, and I just wanna say I'm very available, you know." "I'm sure you are," said Jergens. "Absolutely," said Rocky. "Sparring with the champ would be an honor. And you know what, Mr. Jergens? I wouldn't take no cheap shots, either. I'd really be a good sparring partner, you know."

"You don't understand me, Rocky. My proposition is you fighting Apollo Creed for the world heavyweight championship."

Rocky pauses for a moment, thinking, then says, "No."

"Listen, Rocky. Apollo's seen you fight. He likes you. He wants to fight you."

"Well, it's just that, you see, aahh, I fight in clubs, you know. I'm a real ham-and-egger. This guy, he's the best. It wouldn't be such a good fight. Thank you very much, you know. I appreciate it and all that."

"Rocky, do you believe that America is the land of opportunity?"

"Yeah."

"Apollo Creed does. And he's going to prove it to the whole world by giving an unknown a shot at the title. And that unknown is you. He picked you, Rocky. Rocky, it's the chance of a lifetime. You can't pass it by!"[3]

What Apollo offered Rocky, Jesus offers you only on a much grander scale. Jesus bids you leave the old life behind and grow up into the champion you are destined to become. Think of it, the capacity for greatness is within you right now, right here. Not average, not even good, but great. It is not enough to be good when greatest lies just before you. So why do so many of us Christians settle for a small, feeble, secondhand, second-string life? Could it be we've settled for religion's highest ideal—be good? Every night I left the house as a teenager, my dad said, "Be good." I've even caught myself saying it to my kids, "Be good." And that's our problem isn't it? We've settled for being good when we could be great. Jim Collins said, "Good is the enemy of great. And that is one of the key reasons why we have so little that becomes great. We don't have great schools, principally we have good schools. We don't have great government, principally because we have good government. Few people attain great lives in larger part because it is just so easy to settle for a good life."[4]

William Faulkner said, "Always dream and shoot higher than you know you can do. Don't bother just to be better than your contemporaries or predecessors. Try to be better than yourself." There is nothing more maddening than to have a glimpse of the person you were supposed to be, but never became. Where have all the dreamers gone? You can't run a revolution armed with Robert's Rules of Order. Pew warmers and petty personalities do not attract legions of men with hearts of lions or swarms of strong, smart, and fully engaged women. I believe we are at crossroads where the future hinges on the creation of a Renegade nation. We need R4G's who dare to live free, have fun and change the world. As John Wesley, the founder of the Methodist church, said, "Give me a hundred men who fear nothing but sin, and desire nothing but God, and I will shake the world. I care not a straw whether they be clergymen or laymen; and such alone will overthrow the kingdom of Satan and build up the kingdom of God on earth."

As freed up, joy-filled R4G's, let's be the change we want to see in the world. Let's bring energy and excitement back to Monday morning. Armed with the knowledge that good is the enemy of great, we'll dare to be great in our families, our marriages, our businesses, and our love for people. We will be great lovers as we live for an audience of One-Jesus.

We will identify what we're great at and we'll do it in a great way. And because we love God, we will do everything with excellence. We will not tolerate mediocrity in ourselves or let it slide by in our mates. We believe if it bears His name it deserves our best. We do not fear death because Jesus died so we need never fear it. We are not bad men made good but we are dead men made alive. We follow the One who walked into Jerusalem knowing full well He would be stripped, beaten, and crucified. But He knew death could not hold Him, denial could not distract Him, and all the threats of men could not dissuade Him. His love and the love He instills in those who follow Him is the greatest force for change the world has ever seen. We do not fear the future for we have lost our lives when we took His up.

In the movie *Harry Potter and the Sorcerer's Stone* when Harry first arrives at Hogwarts, he goes through a brief orientation during which the headmaster Professor Dumbledore makes this statement, "The east corridor is off limits to everyone who doesn't want to die a horrible death." I want to be the one who goes to the east corridor, to the place of greatest need. I want to be the one who helps steer our movement back to the heady days when we believed anything was possible. Let's be innovators and instigators who follow Jesus into the hard places. Let's pull people out of the jaws of death and despair. I don't want to be stuck in a safe place. I don't want to be found going to church, I want to be the church and follow Jesus bravely and boldly to wherever bars and barnyards keep God's elect in bondage and burn down the coops and plow under the fences.

@ THE CORE OF GREATNESS

In C. S. Lewis's children's series, *The Chronicles of Narnia*, young heroine Lucy meets a majestic lion named Aslan. He is ruler over the enchanted land of Narnia. Making a return visit a year later, the children discover everything has changed and they get lost. After a series of dreadful events, Lucy finally spots Aslan in a forest clearing. She runs over and throws her arms around his neck. She buries her face in his mane. The great beast rolls over on his side. Lucy falls, half sitting and half lying between his front paws. "Welcome, child," he says.

"Aslan," says Lucy, "you're bigger."

"That's because you're older, little one," answers he.

"Not because you are?"

"I'm not. But each year you grow, you'll find me bigger." How true. How wonderful. The bigger you get, the bigger Jesus will seem, though He always has been big even when you thought Him small. The bolder you pray, the bigger will be the answer. But if you stay small, Jesus will still be huge, but only seem tame and temperamental to you. Believe me, an underfunded savior who writes spiritual checks that God won't cash is worse than no savior at all.

At the core of true greatness is the heart of a lion, not a chicken. When we talk about someone being lion-hearted we are describing qualities like honor, truth, courage, goodness, bravery, sacrifice, and strength. One of Jesus' titles is the lion of the tribe of

Judah. The fuel of this greatness is love. My greatest human achievement is to love Jesus, to love what He loves, and love whom He loves. In the Renegade Nation we are a sea of professional lovers. Love is an abundant and renewable source of power and with it at the core of my life I will, "Never be lacking in zeal, but keep your spiritual fervor, serving the Lord" (Rom. 12:11). With love I defeat fear for Jesus tells me, "There is no fear in love. But perfect love drives out fear" (1 John 4:18).

The foundation of greatness is identity. I came across this story told about Alexander the Great. A young soldier in his army fled in the heat of a battle. He was brought before Alexander who asked, "What's your name?" The boy hung his head and whispered, "Alexander." The courageous leader yelled, "What is your name?" The boy shamefully said, "Alexander." To which Alexander the Great whispered, "Change your conduct or change your name."

Someone took the time to analyze the faces of ninety famous people who were photographed by Yousoff Karsh and included in his book, *The Faces of Greatness*. According to the study, seventy of the men who posed for Karsh were physically unattractive. Thirty-five had moles, cysts, and warts. Thirteen had noticeable freckles or liver spots. Twenty had obvious traces of acne or other pimples, and two had highly visible scars.

These blemishes did not deter them. Picasso, the renowned painter; Thornton Wilder, the great playwright; Richard Rodgers, the composer of many popular musicals; Christian Dior, the honored designer—all had imperfections which were obvious to the world. What might have embarrassed lesser men just added character when they posed before the ever-truthful lens of the portraitist.

We need a different orientation in how we see ourselves. Learning to see yourself accurately starts with looking from the inside out. This is a unique feature of the J-life. Because of who I am and whose I am, I then determine how I must live. It is an inside out approach. No need to check current trends or popular opinion to determine what kind of man I will be today. As the apostle Peter put it, "you have been chosen by God himself—you are priests of the King, you are holy and pure, you are God's very own" (1 Pet. 2:9–10, LB). Jesus is my leader and His love leads the way.

The work of greatness is to serve. Jesus made it clear, "whoever wants to become great among you must be your servant" (Mark 10:43). Mother Teresa is a woman synonymous with greatness. This correlation may have resulted from her philosophy of greatness. She believed, "We can do no great things; only small things with great love."

Jesus defined greatness in God's kingdom as servanthood. Out of this spirit, hospitals, universities, mission movements, and orphanages have been founded by R4G's who poured their lives and fortunes into helping relieve suffering and ignorance. George W. Truitt, the great Texas Baptist leader said, "It is not the talents one has that make him great, however many and brilliant they may be; it is not the large accumulation of wealth that secures peace and honor. In none of these measured by God's standards does greatness reside. The true greatness consists in the use of all the talents one has in unselfish ministry to others."

If the work of greatness is service to others, then surely the attitude of greatness is humility. Humility is not denying the power you have, rather it is acknowledging it flows through you and not from you. The Scriptures are clear and practical at this point:

> *Do nothing out of selfish ambition or vain conceit, but in humility consider others better than yourselves. Each of you should look not only to your own interests, but also to the interests of others.* YOUR ATTITUDE SHOULD BE THE SAME AS THAT OF CHRIST JESUS: *Who, being in very nature God, did not consider equality with God something to be grasped, but made himself nothing, taking the very nature of a servant, being made in human likeness he humbled himself and became obedient to death—even death on a cross!*
>
> —Phil. 2:3–8, emphasis mine

As I said earlier, humility is the God-given self-assurance which eliminates the need to prove to others the worth of who you are, and the rightness of what you do.

The seeds of greatness grow in the imagination. Of all the wonderful abilities God instills in us, great is the ability to dream and imagine in our minds a preferred future and then see it through to reality. A great example of this is the church Paula and I founded in Nashville, Tennessee. Today, if you visit "The Music City" and drive out to what we call Hope Park, you'll see a beautiful drive which leads back to a scenic setting with a beautiful, attractive, modern building, all dedicated to the gathering and growing of a Jesus community. On your drive back you'll see rolling hills, trees, turkeys, and roaming herds of deer. It's a beautiful place. It gives you a sense of arrival. It's a place where, week after week, thousands of people gather not just to worship Jesus Christ, but to learn how to celebrate Him, thank Him, and also to learn how to worship Him everywhere else—at home and in the marketplace.

As beautiful as this church campus is, you should have seen it before the imagination and the providence of God got a hold of it. There were two huge sections of land, basically abandoned and deemed impossible to build upon. Many developers had tried to make it work and no one could. There was no sewer and the land would not percolate for the use of septic tanks. It was, basically, several miles of washed out gullies, exposed rocks, and dead and decaying trees. It was property no one wanted because it was so unforgiving and expensive to develop.

And yet when I walked out on those 280 acres in the mid-'90s, I could see in my mind and imagination what could be created there over time. As I asked our leaders to walk on the property, I invited them to use their God-given imaginations to see what could be, not what was. I said, "just imagine the seas of people who will be turned on to Jesus here." We asked God for a modern day miracle. We exercised our faith and inspired others to do the same. We trusted God to create on this holy ground a rally point for Renegades and He did. Today, in one of the greatest cities of our land there stands a testament to what a group of R4G's can do when they dare to imagine great possibilities and then dedicate themselves to getting it done.

There were many who believed and others who didn't. One local pastor took me aside and told me God told him "in his spirit" we would never build on the property. And yet, today, there she stands, a beautiful monument to the goodness of Jesus Christ and His relevance in the real world and also a testament to the abundance created by the imagination as fueled by the will of God.

Imagination is amazing when you think about what it can do with very little. For example there are only twelve musical notes, yet there is an endless variety of music. For the painter, there are only three basic colors to work with, but look at the breathtaking beauty expressed in the great works of art. Museums and private collectors vie for possession of great treasures all created by ordinary people who applied their imagination using only three colors. Poor architects are really in a pickle for they have only lines, curves, and angles. And yet look at the varieties and styles from the leaning tower of Pisa, to the London tower, to the pyramids, to the Empire State Building, to the Aztec Temples. Mathematicians have only nine numbers, but consider the infinite number of computations possible. Look at the digital revolution, all based on nine numbers and zero. Wow. What a God! What a world of endless possibilities.

The genius of greatness is the creative tension between my part and God's part. If God is great and I am called to be like Jesus, then I must act. Faith demands I move from trusting God in the abstract to showing my love in practical ways. Steven Spielberg said, "Good ideas are only given to you for a limited amount of time. If you don't act on them, they belong to someone else." Growing up into greatness requires seizing the opportunity of a lifetime during the lifetime of the opportunity.

Greatness requires not just knowing what to do, but doing it. The courage to leap into the unknown is trust. Not just any kind of mild, milquetoast trust, but the kind that leaps into an unknown future at the prompting of a known, trustworthy God. I'm not advocating childishness or self-aggrandizing foolishness; these only lead to greater pain and disappointment. But I do agree with Aldous Huxley who said, "A child-like man is not a man whose development has been arrested; on the contrary, he is a man who has given himself a chance of continuing to develop long after most adults have muffled themselves in the cocoon of middle-aged habit and convention." Greatness requires child-like trust in God to break in and come through. If mustard seed faith will move mountains, then let's get on our climbing boots and start walking up hill.

GENERATING GROWTH

Henri Nouwen said, "I can only fly freely when I know there is a catcher to catch me. If we are to take risks, to be free, in the air, in life, we have to know when we come down from it all, we're going to be caught; we're going to be safe. The great hero is the least visible. Trust the catcher."[5] That's how we grow up into greatness by trusting our catcher—Jesus the Christ. Because we know His heart, we dare to trust His love and follow His lead. We gain confidence and courage as God interrupts our plans with new marching orders. Because we can trust His love, we have faith to follow His lead knowing He will never lead us to a place He has not already gone Himself. Day by day, out here on this non-religious road to real, God meets us, walks with us, and grows us up into greatness. How? Let's look at a few ways.

God uses the indwelling Holy Spirit to grow us up. At the moment of conversion, we were all given a new nature in which we experience God through His Spirit at work in our heart, mind, and conscience. It is the Holy Spirit within us who is guiding and giving us a sense of peace about the rightness of our present path. As David said, "The steps of good men are directed by the Lord" (Ps. 37:23, LB).

Jesus promised just before He ascended back to the Father that

He would send a comforter, not only someone to calm us but to lead us (see John 14:6). This indwelling is God's sensing device assuring us we're headed toward God's blessing. For example, Toyota is developing a safe technology to keep the driver's eye on the road. An image-processing computer system developed by Toyota uses a camera near the steering wheel to detect when the driver stops looking straight ahead. The system flashes a light on the dashboard display and emits a beeping noise when the eye starts to wander. If the driver still doesn't respond, the brakes automatically begin to kick in. Sound like fantasy? At this writing, Toyota promises it will be available very soon. If Toyota can provide this kind of technology, surely God can lead us through the power of His indwelling Holy Spirit.

God also uses daily discipline to grow us up over time. Disciplines like daily prayer and savoring the wisdom of sacred Scriptures renew our minds and inform our thinking. God uses the everyday disciplines of getting up and getting to work on time to teach us the importance of responsibility. He uses messy, unruly, rough-edged people to develop the discipline of extending love and help to people who make it difficult to do either. God uses the mundane and the routine. He uses ruts, routines, and tedious tasks to build character into us self-starting revolutionaries. The Scriptures predict, if you're faithful in little things, you'll be faithful over big things (see Matt. 25:23). As an old preacher told me years ago, "David, if you're too big to preach in a small place, you're too small to preach in a big one." This bit of overlooked wisdom is huge and I know terribly gifted people who have yet to learn its life-changing reality. There are tons of good people with talents which can take them places their character cannot keep them.

God uses wise counselors to increase our thinking-power. Benjamin Franklin said, "He who cannot be counseled cannot be helped." Surely by now you know life is not a solo sport. God's very first "not good" was that it's not good for man to be alone. In the Old Testament we're introduced to the principle of "iron sharpening iron." We need our band of brothers or band of sisters who can call us on our actions when they see us adrift.

Trusted friends serve as sounding boards and safety checks. They can tell us the things we might not want but need to hear. Growth in the J-life requires trusting, honest relationships with other people who are both *with it* and *with us* on this journey to life outside conventional Christianity. Thank God for the people He sends to watch your back and give you a sense of perspective and direction. When the going gets rough, you'll need the camaraderie of other R4G's who aspire to greatness too. Around the edge of an English pound is engraved the words, "Standing on the shoulders of giants." Growing upward into greatness is impossible alone. We must stand on the shoulders of those who have walked this way before us and have left a legacy worth imitating. Read the biographies of great men and women of God and learn from their amazing lives.

God uses defining experiences to move us from good to great. Adversity is one of life's most potent teachers. It's during dark downtimes we see God's faithfulness most dramatically. If we'll trust Him, He will turn the adversity to our advantage and make us better, not bitter. The great missionary, Paul, asked for a recurring problem to be removed so he could be more effective. And yet the response was, "My grace is sufficient for you. My power is made perfect in weakness. Therefore I will boast all the more gladly about my weakness so Christ's power may rest upon me" (2 Cor. 12:9). Some of your greatest breakthroughs will come in the midst of silence and suffering. This is how God grows us up into true and genuine greatness. God's grace is not merely unmerited favor, but it is His direct personal power enabling you and me to be who He created us to be and to do what He has called us to do.

Maybe you're saying to yourself, right now, I'm at the most horrible place I could ever be. It could be the death of a child after a prolonged illness, the end of a career, a prolonged period of unemployment, or an ugly divorce that's left you shredded and victimized. Maybe you're in the middle of a season where God seems silent. Maybe you've just moved to a new town with no connections, no friends, and all you could think to do was to wander through a bookstore—where you and I have found each other in the pages of this book; Yea God! The pain and loneliness you now feel, God will translate into a new future bigger and better than anything you could have imagined if you dare trust His love and follow His lead. Remember, there is no rut so deep you cannot leave it; there is no sin so bad God can't forgive it, and there is no dream so dead God can't resurrect it.

God uses outrageous, bodacious claims to grow us up. Jesus promised nothing is impossible to those who believe. He said mustard seed faith could move mountains and prayer could actually move God to perform miracles. Jeremiah dares you to, "Call to me and I will answer you and tell you great and unsearchable things you do not know" (Jer. 33:3). Sounds too fantastic to be true, doesn't it? And you know what they say, "if it sounds too good to be true, then it probably is." So the more religious we become, the easier it is to explain away God's outrageous claims as cute stories about a God in another place and time. Bible stories of burning bushes, promised lands, and little boys slaying giants with slings shots are good for Sunday morning but hardly germane for Monday morning.

Trusting God and taking Him at His word is a risky business because it might make me appear foolish or fanatical. The last thing we want is to be accused of religious fanaticism. So over time, I prune back my expectations and settle in for the safety of the Christian ghetto; that walled-in garden exempted from the vulgarity and vice of the real world. I lay aside my shield of faith, helmet of salvation, and sword of the Spirit and take my place alongside other cynical saints who dismiss freedom as dangerous, fun as childish, and dreamers of great deeds as shallow and vain. "I too was once giddy over Jesus," they say, "but now I'm a scholar whose tastes turn toward the deep profundity of the desert fathers." Impressed with our "spiritual depth" we've become fulltime students of dead men's thoughts on the Bible. We don't do what it says, we just talk about the meanings of Greek words as we inhabit a world of leather-bound Bibles, highlighters, study guides, and endless lectures of self-appointed experts who assure us miracles have ceased. Doesn't this sound like fun? What we need are not the *deeper truths* of Scripture, but a deeper commitment to the simple truths of Scripture.

I have a great example of this from my childhood. Though I was raised in the city, I spent my summers on my uncle Henry's farm. After hauling hay all day on a sweltering August afternoon, I went wading in a nearby creek to cool off. As I made my way along the creek bed back to the house, I came upon a strange sight—a turtle sitting atop a fence post. I thought, "man o man how does a lowly little ole turtle get up on top of a fence post?" The only conclusion I could come to is somebody had to put him there; my uncle Henry had set the turtle up there as a joke. I have never forgotten that strange image burned in my memory. And from that day to this I have been finding turtles on fence posts everywhere I go and in the most unlikely places.

God specializes in putting turtles on fence posts. He loves taking otherwise common, ordinary people, placing a servant's heart in them and then accomplishing great extraordinary things through them. As you travel down this non-religious road to real life, be on the lookout for God's turtle on fence posts. And while I can't speak for the entire turtle population, I do know that every R4G longs to be a turtle on a fence post of God's choosing. We want to live a life explained only by the direct intervention of God. We want to live like Jesus lived, love like Jesus loved, and leave behind the fruits of a godly life. And as I told my brother many years ago, "you gotta waste your life doing something; it might as well be something big." And it might as well be you who God raises up and sits on the fence post of true and lasting greatness.

The Bible is full of the exploits of otherwise ordinary people who God choose for greatness. Think about it, Abraham was an idol worshipper, who God called to be the Father of his chosen people. Moses was a fugitive from justice living in exile as a hermit on the backside of the desert who God choose to deliver his people from bondage. King David was an adulterer, a miserable father, and a duplicitous leader, yet God sent the Messiah through his lineage. Rahab was a prostitute, Peter was a loud-mouthed malcontent, Thomas was a doubter, John Mark was a deserter, and the apostle Paul was a co-conspirator to murder. And yet all these men and women were turtles on God's fence post of destiny. If He can use such renegades, surely He has something great in store for you.

Though you may have been called a chicken or hidden in your shell like a turtle, I challenge you to be great for God. As an R4G, never settle for a lukewarm love or a mediocre life. Never settle, sour, or sit long in the critic's chair or the cynic's corner. God is good and He has predestined you be a turtle on a fence post. Never stop believing God has great things for you to do. Believe He has you exactly where He wants you so lean in and look up. As the nineteenth century French philosopher Ernest Renan said, "To act well in the world, one must die within oneself. Man is not on this earth only to be happy, he is not there to be simply honest, he is here to realize great things for humanity, to attain nobility and to surpass the vulgarity in which the existence of almost all individuals drags on." And as the great missionary Paul said, "Let us not become weary in doing good, for at the proper time we will reap a harvest if we do not give up" (Gal. 6:9).

12

WELCOME TO THE REVOLUTION

CALLING FOR THE CREATION OF A RENEGADE NATION

Oh God, raise up in this nation a new breed of ministers, men and women who are willing to love Jesus and save the Church from its worst enemy—itself.

—*Mike Yaconelli*

The Church must be forever building, and always decaying, and always being restored.

—*T. S. Eliot*

I came across an interesting article, which listed the names given to groupings of animals. For example, a group of bats is called a colony; a group of buffalo is called a gang; and a group of tigers is called a streak. Some of the names were as funny as they were descriptive. A group of giraffes is called a tower, a group of hippopotamuses is called a bloat; and of course a group of female lions is called a pride. But I think the most descriptive name is what they call a group of rhinoceroses. Believe it or not, a three-ton rhino can run up to thirty miles an hour, but they can only see about thirty feet in front of them. Maybe that's why they call them a "crash!"

If I were given the task of assigning a name to the present state of American Christianity it would be—a fragment. I would call a group of churches—a stagnate. I would call a group of Christians—a divide. I would call a group of pastors—the unappreciated. And before you dismiss these names as just my own cynicism, consider the sad state of the American church.

Today, most people in America see little connection between God's business and church business. That shouldn't be surprising when you pick up *USA Today* and read that the Boston Catholic Diocese had to sell 90 million dollars worth of real estate to cover legal fees for settling sex abuse scandals which continue to proliferate. Can this be the revolution Jesus envisioned? Christianity has become big business. I'm not opposed to doing things orderly or businesslike, but we seem to be more concerned with redeeming the church as an institution than advancing the Church Jesus promised would storm the gates of hell.

I believe the greatest danger facing the church in America today is irrelevance and invisibility. The results of the 2001 American Religious Identification Survey (ARIS) revealed the number of Americans in 1990 who said they have no religion was 14.3 million; by 2001, the number grew to 29.4 million. According to a recent article in *U.S. News & World Report,* the total number of Americans who attend weekly worship services has declined from a high 40 percent in the 1960s to a new low of 25 percent in 2004.[1]

If these trends continue, the church as a cultural force for good will, for all practical purposes, will be kicked to the curb. Christianity, as a force for positive change, is being marginalized. This drift is not the result of a governmental conspiracy, but the fruit of the "siege mentality" spreading across much of America's Christian landscape. A retreat mentality has us holed up in our walled Christian gardens. The result is that Christ and the Gospel message are slipping off people's radar. Our current culture is not hostile toward the Gospel. They're just indifferent and if we're honest, who can blame them.

North America accounts for 15 percent of the worldwide Christian population. We think we're the leaders of the revolution, when in truth we've been passed over while we try to get our act together. So how is our 15 percent doing? Not too well, when you consider 85 percent of the churches in America are somewhere between flat-lined and free-falling in attendance. Our society is in a post-Christian era where most people are cynical about religion as an institution; even those raised in church. Only a return to the Jesus-led, renegade revolution where people take priority over programs will allow us to turn the tide. So, welcome to the revolution, my renegade friend, where we will go beyond just *going to church* and start *being the church* everywhere we go.

We have had glimpses of this new revolution in the past ten to twenty years. I remember my first trip to Saddleback Church just south of LA. They were meeting in a public school building, playing loud instruments, and not wearing suits and ties. I even saw women wearing halter tops and short shorts to church—what a scandal. But it all seems pretty tame by today's standards. But lest we forget, long before Rick Warren became famous for writing *The Purpose Driven Life,* he was considered a renegade and his group didn't take too kindly his leaving the denominational label out of his church's name. When I wanted to plant BCC within my own denomination, leaving the name out was a deal breaker. I am glad to say that has changed, but we need to go much further now.

I appreciate the efforts of Willow Creek Community Church in Chicago. Today they are the benchmark of church efficiency and effectiveness. But there was a day when just going to one of their conferences could get you fired. I have found Robert Schuller, pastor of the Crystal Cathedral in LA, to be of tremendous benefit. I remember giving his great book *Your Church Has a Fantastic Future* to a pastor friend of mine in Atlanta. He took the dust jacket off so people wouldn't know he was reading a book by renegade Robert. Other players have come on the scene such as Andy Stanley in Atlanta and Ed Young in Dallas. All of these have taken the *go to church* model to new heights and for that I say, Yea God. But we are nearing the end of the *go to church* movement while seeing the birth of a new *go be the church* revolution.

The seeker movements have helped revitalize thousands of churches. As a result hundreds of thousands of people now *go to church.* But this new kind of Christian is a far cry from the compliant church members who occupied America's churches in the fifties and sixties. Full devotion to Jesus and His redemptive agenda is now becoming the new norm. This is a good thing, but it is producing a generation of renegades who are no longer content with and can't be contained by the old clergy-laity distinctions and I for one say it's about time.

The renewal movements of the mid-eighties and nineties have created a hunger for a real spiritual revolution where we want to go be the church rather than go sit in a church and be entertained. Big box church buildings and big room Bible studies with expert lectures do and I believe will continue to have their place, but it will take more, much more to move the Renegade Nation back into the mainstream. Men and women who are turned on to Jesus are no longer content with doing "church work"; we want to do the *work of the church* out in the real world among our friends and in the daily flow of life—too cool; right? Yes, but trust me, not everyone is praising the Lord for what's coming.

ONE TEAM; MANY PLAYERS

Years ago, General Dwight D. Eisenhower sat at a conference table staring into some of the most intense faces he'd ever seen. He'd just unfolded plans for D-Day. If successful, the Allies would win the war. But if they failed, Hitler would, for all practical purposes, rule the world and darkness would descend on the entire earth. Eisenhower looked out at this diverse group, so many strong leaders, different opinions, large egos and said, "Men, it's one team, or we lose." That's the open door before us right now. Will we who are many rise above the pettiness and become one, finally fulfilling Jesus' prayer in John 17 that we would be one united in heart, mind, and soul?

As R4G's we want to change world. We are on a quest to create a climate in which the radical love of Jesus Christ can call, capture, and radically alter otherwise independent, self-reliant, self-willed men, and women, and convert them into fully devoted R4G's whose life goal is to love well and live well. We are a nation of freeborn, fun-loving, world-changers who will not abide living in a walled-in religious garden surrounded by a sea of people starving for what we have more than enough of—hope. The aim of our revolution is to set people free and fill them up with joy. We are an army of professional lovers who are bound and determined to set other people free in Christ.

The movie *Gettysburg*, based on Michael Shaara's *The Killer Angels* brings to life the three bloodiest days of American history. The first scenes take place a couple days before Gettysburg. Colonel Joshua L. Chamberlain (played by Jeff Daniels) of the 20th Maine Regiment receives 120 Union soldiers who have mutinied. Chamberlain is told to shoot any who won't cooperate. He says, "I've been ordered to take you men with me. I'm told if you don't come, I can shoot you. Well, you know I won't do that. Maybe somebody else will, but I won't. So, that's that.

"Here's the situation," he continues. "The whole Reb army is up that road a ways, waiting for us. This is no time for an argument. I tell you, we could surely use you fellows. We're now well below half strength. Whether you fight or not, that's up to you. Whether you come along is . . ." He pauses and then continues, "Well, you're coming. You know who we are. But if you fight alongside of us, there's a few things you must know."

Matter-of-factly, he states, "This regiment was formed last summer in Maine. There were 1,000 of us then. There are less than 300 of us now. All of us volunteered to fight for the Union, just as you did. Some came mainly because we were bored at home . . . thought this looked like it might be fun. Some came because we were ashamed not to. Many of us came because it was the right thing to do. This is a different kind of army. If you look back through history, you'll see men fighting for pay, for women, for some other kind of loot. They fight for land, power, because a king leads them, or just because they like killing. But we are here for something new. This has not happened much in the history of the world. We are an army out to set other men free."[2]

This is the essence of what "the Church" of Jesus is about; setting all people free and every person free. This is our passion, our privilege, and our divine obsession. But we too have mutineers among us, but rather than run away, they slither and slink among us aiming their cynicism and unbelief at the heart of our zeal. They are out to civilize Jesus and hijack the revolution. So far, all they have won are a sea of empty church buildings, aging congregations, and shrinking treasures. But what we have lost, we are about to take back. Let them appoint committees and commissions to study the problem of the shrinking church in America. While they do that we are running to recast the revolution as the vision of our founder and CEO—"go out and train everyone you meet, far and near, in this way of life" (Matt. 28:19, The Message).

RE-CASTING THE REVOLUTION

Carly Fiorina, the CEO of Hewlett Packard and engineer of the infamous merger with Compaq, said to the graduating class of MIT, "A leader's greatest obligation is to make possible an environment where people can aspire to change the world." In the Renegade Nation, we aspire to change the world by the fueling and funding of a global revolution aimed at the radical reclamation of the human heart. We are unapologetically driven by a passionate pursuit of the divine scandal that every life matters to God.

As followers of Jesus, we will be the Church, not just go to church. Like the early church, we may meet in homes, offices, schools, or Starbucks. Our gatherings will be populated with hungry, happy people who ache for a conversation and dialogue about the life and claims of our founder—Jesus. In the Renegade Nation (the Kingdom of God, see Matt. 6:33), we will be less concerned with events and more focused on process. We welcome the wonderful new wireless, wall-less, flat world. Thanks to the death of distance, the new church world is flat; more like the first century milieu in which our revolution was born.

R4G's refuse to shout at the wind, preach to the choir, or bemoan the present conditions. We're through arguing and complaining. We are instigators of change and anxious to join other Jesus followers to create a Renegade Nation dedicated to recasting the Gospel as a revolution of non-religious love. We seek to join Jesus wherever He is moving, understanding that some of us plant the seed of the gospel, while others of us water, but it is only Jesus who makes it grow to bear the fruit of conversion (see 1 Cor. 3:6). Here are a few of the practical ways we can reboot our thinking to welcome the new world.

From religion to relationship. I hope I've convinced you by now that the J-Life is a relationship, not a religion. It's hard to believe that, of all of the people in the world to love, God loves you. He loves you as though you were the only person on the planet to love and He loves all of us as He loved each of us—too cool. Of all the people in the world to know, He longs to know you and me. Jesus died for the privilege of loving us back to life. His aliveness makes a close, intimate relationship with sinners like us possible. This is nothing short of revolutionary.

Religion cannot confine God's wild, bloodstained, grave splitting love inside its dogmas and doctrinal statements. Walls can't contain the bigness of Jesus. Pedigrees and protocols can never civilize and modernize it. Now is the time to turn every house into a chapel, every heart into a temple, and every conversation into an opportunity to bear witness to His love. Think of it, of all the places in the universe God could choose to live, He chooses to live in your heart and mine. As Revelation 3:20 says, "I stand at the door and knock. If anyone hears my voice and opens the door, I will come in . . ."

From accepting Jesus to following Jesus. We need to recast the message from "Accept Jesus," to "Follow Jesus." Where did we get this idea that Jesus needs our vote of confidence? Jesus calls me to come to Him, adopt His agenda, and follow His lead. He is Lord and I owe Him everything. I am a glad and willing servant of the one who emptied Himself and crawled up on a cross to remember me to God. We are participators, not glib, detached commentators. And while the J-life is a deeply personal one, it is never private. I refuse to "go to church" to practice a private, prosaic faith. When I do gather with other R4G's to worship God in a building, I'm also learning how to worship God everywhere else too. What other world religion invites you and me so personally into the revolutionary activities of its founder? And yet that's exactly what we do as we follow Jesus.

From good to great. I drove by a church building the other day that looked like a good gust of wind would blow it over. There was cardboard in some of the windows, the grass was knee high, and the tin roof was rust-laden. Yet painted on a big sign in big block letters was the name, "The Holiness Jesus Only Tabernacle of Prosperity." On the sign was an advertisement for a healing service, which is held every Friday night. I thought the building could use some major healing. This would be funny if it were an isolated case, but it's not. Mediocrity and Christianity have become synonymous to the vast majority of Americans. This too will change in the Renegade Nation.

Excellence in every area of our everyday lives is how we prove Jesus is important in the real world. We take Saint Paul's prayer seriously, "And we pray this in order that you may live a life worthy of the Lord and may please him in every way: bearing fruit in every good work, growing in the knowledge of God" (Col. 1:10).

Steven Covey said, "Because the church is a formal organization made up of policies, programs, practices, and people, it cannot by itself give a person any deep, permanent security, or sense of intrinsic worth. Living the principles taught by the church can do this, but the organization alone cannot." I know God is not the author of confusion and that organization does have a place, but I also know that over time policies and procedures are elevated to the level of doctrine, which then squeeze the life out of the very organism they were created to serve.

Aspiring to greatness, not just average or mediocre, is a way to create influence and get people to take us seriously. I'm not just talking about the state of our sanctuaries, but the beauty and maturity in our souls. The way we express this commitment to excellence at BCC is in our four core values. They are: we value the potential of people, the priority of service, the persuasiveness of quality, and the power of hope. Quality is the new apologetic in our culture. If you do things with quality and excellence, people take what you say seriously. If you don't, they won't—period.

From fail safe to safe to fail. Jesus was the ultimate risk-taker. He was bold and audacious. He dared to love us when we were hostile toward Him and had no use for Him. He left the majesty of Heaven to be born in a barn to a teenage, out-of-wedlock, peasant girl. How then could we, who love Him most, be any less renegade than He? We are audacious people because we love, serve, and follow an audacious God.

The heart and soul of a R4G is the desire to make a difference. To do that requires having the courage to take risks to do what's never been done. For example, as I'm writing this, Apple just introduced their new video iPod. To make room for this new untested gadget, they stopped selling the iPod mini. What's crazy about this is that the mini is by far their best-selling model. When asked why they stopped selling the mini, Steve Jobs said, "You have to change when you're on top." How right he is, but how hard it is to do.

The great thing about our relationship with God is that success is not guaranteed up front nor does it need to be. As a matter of fact, the Scriptures assure us when we're weak, He is strong through us, and if we fall seven times we will rise eight. When we're broken, God is able to pick us up and make us stronger than ever before. We need more risk-taking renegades in the revolution creating systems, and environments where the real needs of people can be met in practical frontline ministries where the love of Jesus takes on flesh and blood.

From boring to intriguing. As a kid, my biggest beef against going to church was how unbelievably boring it was. How could sitting in church for sixty minutes on Sunday morning seem like an eternity? I've found, as I've gotten older, that most people, both children and adults, who opt out attending any church or religious service do so because it is, indeed, deadly boring, not because they don't feel the need for worship. This is tragic and it must change.

Typically, in church-going America, we get up and go to the same building, sit in the same seat, sing the same songs, stand by the same people, hear basically the same message, offer the same response, and go out and live the same old way. Nothing ever changes—much. The result is we've made worship boring and Jesus irrelevant. About this dilemma Annie Dillard said, "It is madness to wear ladies' straw hats and velvet hats to church; we should all be wearing crash helmets. Ushers should issue life preservers and signal flares; they should lash us to our pews. For the sleeping God may wake someday and take offense, or the waking God may draw us out to where we can never return."[3]

People in the Old Testament who trivialized worship died for it. Aren't we glad we're under grace?

Is there a greater sin among men than taking the greatest news the world has ever known and boring people to sleep with it? But we're doing it and churches are sitting empty as a result. But let's be honest too; who wants to endure the rants and raves of a religious know-it-all who gives simplistic answers to really complicated questions? We want mystery, intrigue, and inspiration when we gather in the presence of a Holy God. No, we don't need all the answers, but we should leave amazed with God's grace and incredibly intrigued with His plans for our futures. The prospects of better days and bigger things calls us to press into Jesus and get in on what He is doing in the world.

From critic to contributor. Way too much of what goes on in the name of Christian activity is name-calling, moralizing, and political posturing. It appears at times that there's no difference between sitting in a church or a political rally. Sunday after Sunday scathing sermons assign blame to the Democrats or the Republicans, to Washington or the White House, to Disney or Hollywood, or whoever happens to be the biggest most impersonal entity we can galvanize our constituency against. Rather than put down other people, R4G's want to raise up Jesus. We love Jesus, worship Jesus, and believe Jesus is the sole answer for what's gone wrong with the world. That doesn't make us simplistic or shallow, but it does fire us up to be true agents of change with a real message of hope to a world swimming in pain and despair. We must stop "telling" people about Jesus and start showing them with our words, actions, deeds, kindness, and generosity. We are not reluctant lovers trying to meet only the minimum requirements for entrance into Heaven. We are joy-filled, freed up R4G's who love Jesus, love life, and love people.

Each one of us has been given a set of gifts and abilities. We all have a certain measure of faith to aspire and inspire greatness as we use what we've been given to serve the good. I may write and I may speak, but you may sing and play. One guy in my B.O.B. (Band of Brothers) is a research scientist at Vanderbilt. He speaks the language of a scientist with an R4G heart. Jesus is everywhere using the most amazing people to stir us up and love us back to God. He can and will use anyone. You don't have to ask God for permission or spend years locked up in a seminary. If you are a follower of renegade Jesus, you are a player. You need to get on the playing field and add your verse, tell your story, and help fuel the revolution.

From worship "here" to worship "everywhere." In the Renegade Nation worship is wall-less, wireless, and flat. By this I mean, for Renegades, worship isn't something we huddle in cathedrals to do one day a week. Worship is what we do everywhere we go, in everything we do, and with every breath we take. Our worship is walless (any place will do), wireless (we can connect with each other and to all the resources we need via the Internet), and flat (The top down is now bottoms up). This is new and it is radical, but its viral and tipping point potential for the spread of the gospel is off the charts.

Traditionally, we Christians gather to worship on Sunday mornings. The buildings we gather in are called churches. The largest, most expensive space in our church buildings is called the worship center. In the church of my childhood we called it the sanctuary. Worship was done one day a week (Sunday) in specific locations (churches) in dedicated spaces (sanctuaries). The message: Worship is something you go to church to do on Sunday morning in a sanctuary where you rotate between sitting, standing, and singing while staring at the back of other people's heads. When it's over you reenter the real world where none of this seems relevant or useful. And while we are "at church" we sing songs we don't understand, carry Bibles we don't read, and listen to preachers who bore us numb. When we bow our heads to pray, our minds wander all over the place and when we extend our hands in fellowship we plaster smiles on our faces to hide the pain, loneliness, and feelings of disconnection.

To be sure this kind of weird behavior will continue, but it's already showing signs of a siege mentality, which is a shame; for there's a revolution coming that will flood some churches organically, spiritually, and numerically. This isn't my hypothesis; it is happening right now all around us. Let me be quick to say I think gathering to worship Jesus is not only important, our Lord mandates it. Going to church is a good thing, but it is not a God thing unless we "go be the Church" once we leave. Being the Church in the real world is where Jesus is moving. God's forceful, unstoppable kingdom cannot be walled in or franchised out to professional Christians (like me). Worship in the Renegade Nation is a way of life, not a building or place to visit once a week. Worship is done anywhere, anytime, by anyone, even notorious sinners. King David shouted, "Let everything alive give praises to the Lord!" (Ps. 150:6, LB).

From join a church to join the revolution. I was raised in a religious tradition where not even death could remove you from the membership rolls once you joined a church. Not only is that wrong; it's corrupting. Joining a church is not like joining a country club, Kiwanis, or some other civic organization. As a matter of fact, the church as an organization in our culture has become a stiff, staid idea. We should have seen it coming and changed on our own. But the wonderful new wireless, wall-less, flat world is forcing us to change or die.

In his book *Revolution,* George Barna says all recent statistical data points to the fact that the church, as an organization, has zero impact on culture. In other words, a serious breakage exists between going to church on Sunday and being the church on Monday. Attending church is a good thing, and hopefully most of the time, a God thing, but never an end in itself.

Let's return to our revolutionary status. Following Jesus means we move out of our churches to live the J-life in the real world.

Every R4G is a missionary. Every brother is a preacher. Every sister is an evangelist. Loving Jesus in the real world is far more dynamic than just parking our membership in a church. Praise God for the diversity and variety in His Church. From preaching, singing, worshipping to evangelism, the church is blessed with a mosaic of methods God chooses to bless.

A gathering called a church is not a clubhouse; it's a lighthouse. Church buildings are not hotels for the holy, but hospitals for the hurting. Our gatherings should be more like an emergency room than a luxury hotel where only the self-righteous gather to polish their halos. Our reputations should not be centered on our awesome worship music, our killer kids program, or happening youth group. Our churches should be the first place people run to when they've screwed up big time. Every local Jesus outlet should include believers, but also the broken, the bruised, the battered, and the bored. Wherever, whenever, or however we worship, it must be a gathering of both notorious sinners and scandalous lovers who with the guts and gusto form one choir and sing Terry Taylor's revolutionary love song called "Breathe Deep."

Politicians, morticians, Philistines, homophobes
Skinheads, Dead heads, tax evaders, street kids
Alcoholics, workaholics, wise guys, dim wits
Blue collars, white collars, warmongers, peace nicks

Breathe deep
Breathe deep the Breath of God

Evolutionists, creationists, perverts, slumlords
Deadbeats, athletes, Protestants and Catholics

Housewives, neophytes, pro-choice, pro-life
Misogynists, monogamists, philanthropists, blacks and whites

Breathe deep
Breathe deep the Breath of God

Police, obese, lawyers, and government
Sex offenders, tax collectors, war vets, rejects
Atheists, Scientists, racists, sadists
Photographers, biographers, artists, pornographers

Breathe deep
Breathe deep the Breath of God

Gays and lesbians, demagogues and thespians
The disabled, preachers, doctors and teachers
Meat eaters, wife beaters, judges and juries
Long hair, no hair, everybody everywhere!
Breathe deep the Breath of God

—Terry Taylor; The Lost Dogs

THE 4C COVENANT

While visiting an insane asylum, a man noticed all the insane people were on the field outside, but there was only one guard. He asked the lone guard, "Aren't you afraid?"

The guard said, "Absolutely not."

He said, "Don't you believe since you are the only one here, these people could over-run you and break out of the asylum?"

The guard said, "That's impossible."

The man asked, "Why is that impossible?"

The guard replied, "Because lunatics don't unite."

This being true, Christians lean toward lunacy, because we fear uniting more than death itself. And yet our Lord and leader prayed we'd be together. He said so when He prayed that we would be one as He and the Father are one. It is the one thing we, His children, have denied Him.

To make the Renegade Nation a possibility, I propose a simple 4C Covenant. This would give us a framework for how we could relate in unity without the need for uniformity. May I suggest that our covenant life could be expressed using these four words; consensus, connection, calling, and compassion.

- Our consensus is Christ
- Our connections are organic
- Our calling is to engage culture in conversation and dialogue
- Our compassion is practical and frontline.

1. In the RN Our Consensus is Christ. It is hard to imagine, but there are people who call themselves Christians who do not believe Jesus is the Son of God who lived, died, and was resurrected. So let's just get this straight; in the Renegade Nation there is no doubt about who is our founder, president, and CEO. Jesus is our lover and our Lord. He is the One upon whom we all agree. Jesus asked the Pharisees this pointed question, "What do you think about the Christ? Whose son is he?" (Matt. 22:42). We think Jesus is the best thing to ever have happened to the human race. He is the Prince of Peace, Wonderful Counselor, and our Mighty God. He is the head of the Church, the Lord of the world, and the coming King who will usher in a new Heaven and a new Earth. But while He tarries, we will be about His business—the building of His peaceable kingdom across the face of the earth.

Under the Lordship of Jesus, there is plenty of room for diversity. In the Renegade Nation we welcome the Calvinist and the Armenians, the Charismatics and the Presbyterians, the Baptist and the Methodists. We love High Church, Low Church, and no-church music. We love the contemplatives and the activists. The preaching of the evangelist and the scholar lift our hearts, feed our souls, and deepen our minds for God. Hymns, choruses, chants, and groanings take us into the spiritual where we experience God the Holy Sprit moving among His people. Whether you wear a robe, a suit and tie, or a pair of jeans and a Hawaiian shirt, the name of Jesus sounds just as sweet to us. However it is you love Jesus, praise Jesus, know Jesus more and make Him known, we like it. If you are helping people on down the road to real Jesus—we like the way you do it.

The Apostles' Creed puts it very well, "I believe in Jesus Christ, God's only Son, our Lord, who was conceived by the Holy Spirit, born of the Virgin Mary, suffered under Pontius Pilate, was crucified, died, and was buried; he descended to the dead. On the third day he rose again; he ascended into Heaven, he is seated at the right hand of the Father, and he will come again to judge the living and the dead."

Even if you're still considering the claims of Christ, we want you here with us; for we love to share what we know and to hear what you care about for we both help each other on this journey to life outside conventional Christianity. But just understand, to us, Jesus is the beauty out of which the rest of the world's glory flows. He is life, our life, all of life, for every life.

2. *In the RN Our Connections are Organic.* How I long to be around real people who love to talk about Renegade Jesus. I've been thinking about, studying, and talking about Jesus all my life and I find Him more fascinating and intellectually stimulating than ever. What I am bored with is talking about religion and which church is the "best" church. Reading books or attending conferences on how to build a bigger, cooler more hi-tech church building or small group program has no appeal for me. But I love doing life with other R4G's who want to grow in the J-life or ask questions about Jesus, or life, or love, or relationships, or a thousand other cool things we can learn from each other. I do love hanging out with people who know how to bring Jesus back into the cultural conversation without sounding preachy.

R4G's who feel called to be mainstreamers inspire me. Since I live in Music City USA, I love hanging around artists who believe their art must be awesome or their Jesus has no voice. Talking with businessmen about how to bring the love and compassion of Jesus into the workplace is too cool and something I can get lost in for hours and hours. It is fun, being with people you like, talking about stuff you love. That's all we do in the Renegade Nation!

Bottom line; we need each other. God made us to thrive in relationships. Life goes best when we have meaningful connections with other people we like and are attracted to. In the Renegade Nation, we don't care what church you attend, or what denominational label you wear. If we sense God putting us together, if we like each other and if we feel an attraction or an affinity, we are going to hang together regardless of where we go to church or don't go to church. As R4G's, we look for organic alliances based on friendship and compatibility.

We loathe forced fellowship. I can't tell you the number of times, as a pastor, I've tried to pair people up based on zip code, age, marital status, and some other arbitrary way of forcing people on each other. Just because people have kids and live on the south side of town doesn't mean they'll make a spiritual connection leading to deep, rich, intimate friendships. How dumb was I to try it and man how done I am with ever trying to do it again.

In the Renegade Nation we connect for reasons of the Spirit. We ask God to lead us to the right people. Who are the right people for you? The people who you like, want to be like, and want to be around. We can't wait to be with people we respect and feel will challenge and help us grow up into greatness. People who are accepting, encouraging, and inspiring are the people with whom we will forge life long friendships and long-term alliances.

3. *In the RN Our Calling is to Engage Culture in Conversation and Dialogue.* Anne Rice is known as "the Queen of the Occult." After selling millions of novels about vampires and witches, she announced, "I promised from now on that I will only write for the Lord." Rice has become a Jesus person. Her first novel since her conversion, *Christ the Lord: Out of Egypt*, portrays Jesus as a seven-year-old. When asked why she wrote the book she said, "I wrote this book to make Christ real to people who had never thought about Him as real. I wrote this book to make the readers care so much about Him that they see him perhaps as never before. I wrote it for all my readers and for all readers. *Re-telling the Christian story is the essence of my vocation.* And we re-tell that story so that it can be heard anew. That has been going on since the Evangelists in one form or another. I am no Evangelist, but I

am an artist who wants to make the most significant art I can make"[4] (emphasis mine).

Anne Rice is right on. Retelling the good news to our generation is the core occupation of every R4G. Past religious methods of reselling the gospel were primarily confrontational; such as preaching, revivals, door-to-door evangelism, or witnessing. Witnessing usually means giving a canned presentation of "the plan of salvation" to a total stranger in under five minutes. The pay off is having them bow their heads to repeat a prayer to seal the deal. Does this work? Not much, if at all. And even if it does, there are very few people who have the personality it takes to confront total strangers about deep spiritual decisions. So what are the rest of us to do?

In the Renegade Nation, we've stopped trying to win people to Jesus or get them to church so the preacher can get them down the isle at the invitation. We've started loving people just because they are worthy. We've started opening up conversations and dialoguing with anyone who's willing. We've given up preaching for listening. Instead of handing people tracts and running off to hide like roaches in a kitchen when the light is turned on, we're giving them our time and attention. Instead of telling people what we've been taught, we're sharing with them what we've learned. Rather than make them sit still while we instill, we're the ones sitting still as they pour out their hearts.

This is such an exciting time to be out on the road to real. There are so many honest seekers and questioners these days. Like Jesus did, we're engaging people in conversation and dialogue. We are glad to tell what we know, as well as admit to what we don't. All this is possible because we trust the Gospel. We know God's heart

(He is not willing that any should perish but all come to repentance) and we trust His love to give us good words to express His great love. We are not arrogant, self-righteous, know-it-alls. We are happy, humble know enoughs; glad for the privilege of telling others where we've found bread. We have an unshakable conviction that Jesus doesn't need defending, just let loose. And with confidence we can say, "I am not ashamed of the gospel, because it is the power of God for the salvation of everyone who believes" (Rom. 1:16).

4. *In the RN Our Compassion is Practical and Frontline.* Talk is cheap and in the Renegade Nation, we will back it up with showing our compassion for people in practical ways. I remember hearing Millard Fuller, the founder of Habitat for Humanity, tell of the first house President Jimmy Carter helped build in Atlanta. After several years passed, President Carter asked Fuller to take him over to the neighborhood. He wanted to see how it looked after a decade. When they turned into the subdivision and onto the street where President Carter's house was located, they were impressed with the well manicured lawns and the well maintained houses. Every house and every lawn were impeccable. Fuller stopped in front of the house President Carter built. The two men got out to take a better look and noticed a young boy standing in the yard. Fuller walked up to the boy and asked, "son, do you know who built this house?" The boy said, "Yes sir, I do." Thinking the boy would acknowledge President Carter's contribution, Fuller asked, "Who built your house son?" The boy answered, "Jesus built my house." A little dumfounded and tongue-tied, the two men agreed. The point is we make Jesus real when we do practical works of kindness.

In the wonderful new wall-less, wireless, and flat world, our faith must be expressed in practical, frontline social action. The Bible is clear, "But if someone who is supposed to be a Christian has money enough to live well, and sees a brother in need, and won't help him—how can God's love be within him? Little children, let us stop just saying we love people; let us really love them, and show it by our actions" (1 John 3:17–18, LB). Jesus said something as small as a cup of cold water given in His name is a great thing with God.

Today's R4G's will not be corralled in their church buildings. We are not content with spectator spirituality. We want to do something tangible to change the world. Maybe it's building habitat homes, or feeding the homeless, or going to the gulf coast to help with hurricane relief. It may mean moving across the country, across the city, or just walking across the street but the distance or the location isn't the point. There are as many creative ways to show the love of Jesus as there are people themselves. The point of this part of our 4C covenant is we are no longer waiting for someone else to move. We will not wait for our overworked, underpaid pastors to think up something for us to do. We will be the change we want to see in the world. We will take the lead and the responsibility to rally the troops to action. Our new aliveness will lead us to be Jesus to a hurting world. We will turn our churches into need meeting centers. Our congregations will not have to beg us to get off the sideline and out of the pew. Because we are lovers, we are doers too.

Wherever and whenever we can join with a good group of people to help relieve suffering, whether they be Christian or not, we will lend our hands and our hearts. We will join the millions of other good souls who believe "being good" leads to "doing good." And side-by-side we will figure out what makes each other tick and who knows, we just might find a bunch of Renegades out in the highways and hedges just where Jesus said we'd find them, just waiting for someone like you to show them the on-ramp to the road to real.

RENEGADENATION.NET

In 1980, Roberto C. Goizueta became the president and CEO of Coca Cola International. He was the president until his death in 1997, when he died of cancer. In late 1996, while speaking to the Chicago Business Club in downtown Chicago, he stated these interesting facts some research had discovered: "A billion hours ago, life began on earth. A billion minutes ago, Christianity emerged. A billion seconds ago, the Beatles appeared on the *Ed Sullivan Show*. A billion Coca Colas ago was yesterday morning. Right now, the consuming vision of my life is how to make a billion Coca Colas ago be this morning." Now that's the spectacular power of a vision for, of all things, sugar water. Imagine what we can do in the Renegade nation as we network together to live free, have fun, and change the world. I hope this book has been insightful and helpful, as we've gone a little farther along this journey to life outside conventional Christianity. I pray you will be an R4G without apology!

If you are new to the family, then welcome to the ride of your life. If you've renewed your faith after taking an off ramp for a while, we're glad you're back and we missed you. Or maybe you're still in the "kicking the tires" mode of your spiritual journey.

Wherever you find yourself, I am glad to be on the journey with you. I can see better days and bigger things ahead for us all.

We need big thinking, visionaries like you among us again. We need visionary leaders, risky lovers, and movement shapers to get this boat afloat. Are you the next Billy Graham, Mother Teresa, Rick Warren, or Martin Luther King? Of King's visionary prowess, James Wallis noted, "The vision of the beloved community was the foundation for the agenda of the Civil Rights Movement. It was and is both powerful and compelling. But visions don't mean much if they're not tied to concrete agendas and campaigns to advance them. Without the practical agendas of civil rights and voting rights King would have remained only a visionary dreamer, not 'a drum major for justice,' the epitaph he chose for himself."[5]

Today's need is for Renegades with visions of practical ways to restart the revolution. I heard Ravi Zacharias say once, "There are no movements moving ahead without someone at the head moving them." Welcome to the Revolution, my renegade brother and sister. We need you now more than ever. This is a breakout moment, but to seize it we've got to believe what we do matters. We need giants of faith who are out to change the world. But we need new bold *agendaless* agendas and great, articulate teachers. We need authentic lovers living integrated lives with God's vision for the future.

If we accept this new assignment, together we can launch new movements, feed the hungry, fight AIDS, heal the brokenhearted, and influence the world. Will you dare to "be" the change we've been waiting for? Will we be the generation who goes beyond going to church and starts "being" the church everywhere we go? As the great world-shaker Paul said, "I consider my life worth nothing to me, if only I may finish the race and complete the task the

Lord Jesus has given me—the task of testifying to the gospel of God's grace" (Acts 20:24).

I want to leave you with a poem that a fellow renegade wrote to me. While in the hospital, God laid me on her heart. And during a time of great pain and questioning, she reached out from her hospital bed and touched me during a particularly dark time in my own life.

I'm Why You're Here

I'm the father of a prodigal son
Praying that one day my child will come home

I'm the mother whose baby girl just couldn't stay
And I wonder why God had to take her away

I'm the teenager struggling to find my voice
I'm the businessman faced with a dishonest choice

And I'm why you're here
I'm why you're here

I'm the single mom working three jobs to survive
I'm the husband in love with an unfaithful wife

I'm the seeker who wonders if faith is the answer
I'm the patient who's faced with inoperable cancer

Whatever my lot, He has caused me to stay
Where you foster my hope, and His love lights my way

And I'm why you're here
I'm why you're here

Your words give me power and strength to prevail
In this battle we witness 'tween heaven and hell

And when I fight demons of pain and regret
You gently remind me, "We are not home yet!"

I cling to your message of grace and redemption
That blots out transgressions without exception

So remember it's me you speak to on Sunday
Giving me hope and visions of one day

When Christ will return and dry every tear
But until that day . . . I'm why you're here.

NOTES

CHAPTER 1

1. Michka Assayas, *Bono* (Riverhead Books, 2005), p. 201.
2. David Murrow, *Why Men Hate Going to Church* (Thomas Nelson, 2005), p. 1.
3. Roy Hattersley, "Faith Does Breed Charity," Guardian.co.uk; last accessed 4/19/06.

CHAPTER 2

1. Gary Wills, *Saint Augustine* (Viking Adult, June 1, 1999), p. 139.
2. George Barna, *The State of the Church 2005* (The Barna Group, 2005).
3. Public domain.
4. Julie Foster, "Anti-Public School Movement Grows," www.worldnetdaily.com, last accessed 4/19/06.
5. Barna, ibid.
6. C. S. Lewis, *Mere Christianity* (Harper San Francisco, 2001), p.52.
7. Lyle Schaller, conversation with author on 2/23/2005.
8. C. S. Lewis, *The Four Loves* (Harvest Books, 1971).
9. Michka Assayas, *Bono* (Riverhead Books, 2005), p.204.

CHAPTER 3

1. Kenneth Scott Latourette, *The First Five Centuries* (Harper Brothers, 1937), p. 112.
2. Rodney Stark, *One True God* (Princeton University Press, 2003), p.61.
3. Darren Philip, "Moby: Faith, Salvation, and Everything in Between," *Relevant*, May/June 2005, p. 64.

CHAPTER 4

1. Quoted in Henry Parry Liddon, *Liddon's Bampton Lectures*, 1866 (London: Rivingtons, 1869), p. 148.

2. C. S. Lewis, ed., *Letters of C. S. Lewis*, p. 248; cited in: Fr. Thomas Dubay, S.M., *Fire Within* (San Francisco: Ignatius Press, 1989), p. 286.

3. "There's No Solving the Mystery of Christ," *Chicago Sun-Times*, 1-16-04.

CHAPTER 5

1. Edyth Draper, *Draper's Book of Quotations for the Christian World* (Wheaton: Tyndale House, 1992). Entries 11488–11490.

2. Brennan Manning, *Ruthless Trust* (HarperCollins, 2000), p. 2.

CHAPTER 6

1. David W. Leebron, *The Call to Conversion* (Harper San Francisico, 2005), pp. 19, 32.

2. J. I. Packer, *Knowing God* (Intervarsity, 1993).

3. *The Journal of Communication and Religion*, March 2005.

4. J. C. Ryle, *Holiness* (Nolan Publishing, 2001).

5. James Frey, *A Million Little Pieces* (Anchor Books, 2004), p. 42.

6. http://www.usatoday.com/tech/news/2006-03-14-postsecrets_x.htm?POE=TECISVA, last accessed 6/22/06.

7. C. S. Lewis, *The Great Divorce* (Macmillian, 1974), pp. 96–98.

8. *The Call to Conversion* (Harper San Francisco, 2005), pp. 1, 3, 4.

9. Dallas Willard, *The Spirit of Disciplines* (Harper, 1991), p. 31.

10. Author unknown.

CHAPTER 7

1. "Couple Guilty of Keeping Boys in Cages for Years," *Chicago Sun Times*, 1-16-04, p. 40.

2. Penny Brown Roberts, "Scalia: Faithful Live for Christ," www.2thead vocate.com, 2005. Last accessed 6/21/06.

3. "The Lostness of Humankind," *Preaching Today*, Tape No. 118.

4. Henri Nouwen, "Beyond the Mirror," *Christianity Today* 35, no. 5.

CHAPTER 8

1. *Cat on a Hot Tin Roof,* MGM, 1958.
2. "Taking God's Keys," *Leadership*. Fall 1998, p. 57.

CHAPTER 9

1. Bill Bryson, *A Short History of Nearly Everything* (Broadway Books, 2003), p. 10.
2. Brennan Manning, *The Ragamuffin Gospel* (Multnomah, 2000), p. 162.
3. Brennan Manning, *Ruthless Trust* (HarperCollins, 2000), p. 57.

CHAPTER 10

1. James K. Glassman, "Whine, the Beloved Country!" http://www.taemag.com last accessed 4/19/06.
2. Thomas L. Friedman, *The World Is Flat* (Farrar, Straus, and Giroux, 2005), p. 264.
3. FreshMinistry.org; 11-05-02.
4. *USA Weekend,* Jan 1-3, "Get Inside Your Head," p. 11.

CHAPTER 11

1. *Simon Birch,* directed by Mark Johnson, Hollywood Pictures 1998.
2. Marianne Williamson, *Return to Love* (Harper Paperbacks, 1996), p. 191.
3. *Rocky,* directed by John G. Avildsen, United Artists 1976.
4. Jim Collins, *Good to Great* (HarperBusiness, 2001), p. 1.
5. Henri Nouwen, quoted in *Raw Faith* by John Kirvan.

CHAPTER 12

1. *U.S. News & World Report,* 4-19-04, p. 72.
2. *Gettysburg,* directed by Ronald F. Maxwell, New Line Cinema 1993.

3. Annie Dillard, "Teaching a Stone to Talk," *Christianity Today* 40, no. 9.

4. www.randomhouse.com/features/annerice/christQA.html, last accessed 4/16/06.

5. Jim Wallis, *Faith Works* (Random House, 2000), p. 281.

R4G

ABOUT THE AUTHOR

David Foster is one of the nation's leading voices in the newly emerging wireless, walless church revolution. His passion is to be *"an agent of change with a message of hope to a world in pain."*

He is founding and senior pastor of Bellevue Community Church in Nashville, Tennessee. In 1989, without connections or denominational backing, David and his wife Paula launched Nashville's first seeker-targeted church. Today, over 4,000 attend one of the four weekend services held at Hope Park, the church's 280-acre wooded campus.

Foster is known as a street-smart communicator who uses humor, real life stories, and practical application to inspire everyday excellence. His unique motivational insights help people see the invisible, feel the intangible, and achieve the impossible.

He is the President of Foster Media Group (a consulting marketing company) and the CIO of Renegade Nation.net; an Internet gathering for the emerging church conversation.

He received his training from Free Will Baptist College in Nashville, Mid-America Theological Seminary in Memphis, Tennessee, and he has an earned doctorate from the Reformed Theological Seminary in Jackson, Mississippi.

How to get in touch with David Foster?
For more information on Dr. Foster's books, consulting, and speaking services visit his Web site:
www.fosteringhope.com